PSALM
Matthew ~ ...
I John 8:20

Joy of the Lord

Simple Answers to Big Questions

Ron Johnson

2nd Edition

ISBN 1494813653

EAN978-1494813659

Contents

Simple Answers to Big Questions

Each story in this book is God's way of answering a big question that that I encountered in life. Use this index to know when one might be right for you.

Would like to know the difference between...

Would you like to know...

Jenny's Prayer

I often hear people say that they are seeking truth. To me, seeking truth is very dangerous. The only way to know truth is to judge what we are hearing by what we know. Jesus said to seek Him with all your heart! I believe Jesus is the truth so if we have Jesus then we have truth! Pretty simple isn't it? We simply seek Jesus and truth is the result. Joy enters in our life through the peace of having our focus on Jesus!!!

I pray that everyone who reads this book will be inspired to have a deeper and real relationship with Jesus Christ. Life is full of Joy knowing that Jesus can be your Brother and Best Friend! So I invite you to asked Jesus Christ into your heart. Go and spend time with your Best Friend; the one you can trust and believe in! You know He is waiting for you. Life has no meaning without Jesus. He is the Way, the Truth and the Life. God loves you!!!

People say Jenny is lucky to have me. I say I am blessed to have Jenny. Actually, our relationship is not an accident. It is the answer to Jenny's prayers. You see, I found a prayer book in Jenny's purse and it was opened to this prayer. If you try to shut the prayer book, the binding would crack. I believe this prayer is the answer to why Jenny and I are so blessed. I believe in the power of prayer and if you think Jenny and I have a special relationship, and then read this prayer and you will know why.

The prayer was titled: *FOR A HAPPY MARRIED LIFE*

"Lord, bless and preserve my cherished husband whom you have given me. Let his life be long and blessed, comfortable and holy; let me forever be a blessing and a comfort to him, a sharer in all his sorrows, a consolation in all the accidents and trials of life. Make me forever loveable in his eyes, and forever dear to him. Unite his heart to mine in the fondest love and holiness, and mine to him in sweetness and charity. Keep me from all ungentleness; make

me humble, yet strong and helpful that we may delight in each other according to your blessed word. May both of us rejoice in you Father God, having our portion in the love and service of God forever. In the name of Jesus I pray."

Now you know why Jenny and I are so blessed! Our relationship to each other has always been and will continue to be blessed by our Father because of Jenny's request and because Jesus said He gives you the desire of your heart. So I have Jesus' Word on it!

If the message of this book impacted your life or you need to reach out to someone you love, I invite you to call me at (513)377-1727.

Loving you all now and forever from Ron, Jenny and Jesus!

www.CoffeeTimeWithJesus.com
(513) 377-1727

Abortion, Are You Forgiven?

About a year ago while camping next to a young couple, Paul and Alice, the question of abortion came up. They had three children ranging from ages 5 to 10. These children were very happy and very spontaneous. Their laughter was so contagious and Jenny and I enjoyed being around them. One morning while having coffee with my best friend and brother, Jesus, I heard a knock on my door. Alice had stopped over to ask if I would turn my car around. My car has a bumper sticker that says: *A child or a choice.* Alice explained to me how hard it was for her to look at that bumper sticker and said, "You see, I had one when I was quite young."

I ask her if she knew that God had forgiven her for the abortion. Alice got a little disturbed and asked me how I could possibly know God's will, about her relationship with her boyfriend, and then about 6 months later she ran forgiving her? I told her I know for sure God had forgiven her. She ignored what I said, but she proceeded to talk about the abortion. He had a broken into her again and he wanted to have some fun for old time's sake. She said no, but he forced himself on her. The result was an unwanted baby. The old boyfriend wanted nothing to do with her or the baby and told her how to fix the situation. So Alice went to check out the clinic. The cost was $415.00 and might as well been $4,000.00 because Alice was still in high school. On her way home from the clinic, in her dad's car, while sitting at a red light crying out to the Lord, "*What should I do?*" a car bumped into her bumper. The driver of the other car told her he was an auto body mechanic and a new bumper and paint would cost $415.00. He offered her the cash and said I never want to hear from you again.

Alice took the money as a sign that God wanted her to terminate the baby. It means to her that it looked like God provided the money. As they started the procedure, Alice started crying and asked them to stop but they said it was too late. She has never forgiven herself or the boyfriend. We talked about forgiveness and how I knew she was forgiven. To convince her, I told her this story:

Let's say you're married about a year when your first precious baby girl comes along. You and your husband love her and you are so happy that you are even a stay-at-home mom. You take care of your little girl with such loving care and devotion. Everyone says what a good mother you are. Then your neighbor, an old man living next door has become like a grandpa to you because he is so helpful. One day, a family emergency came up and you call grandpa next door and ask him to watch your little girl who just went down for a nap. You tell him to call you if the baby wakes up and that you'll only be gone 15 minutes.

Upon arriving at home, you found the kitchen a bloody mess! Then you see the grandpa covered in blood. He has killed and mutilated your baby girl. You immediately call 911 and they arrested grandpa. Grandpa says he doesn't remember anything. Your baby is dead and you want justice, so you prosecute him and grandpa gets life in prison.

Fast-forward 15 years, and you now have three wonderful children and you are getting along in life. Then one day, you see the grandpa out of prison and living next door to you again. A flood of emotion comes all over you, and you start to relive the death all over again. Then to add insult, grandpa walks into your yard and apologizes to you. He says, "I see you have three more children. I want you to know I have learned my lesson, so if you ever need a babysitter you can call on me."

You know Alice, according to society today your reaction is justifiably correct when you tell him to get off your property and never talk to you again. You feel your loss is unforgivable and you don't understand how the court can turn him loose on society again. In your mind he is still a killer and should be locked up.

I know God loves you! I know God forgave you totally. In my story, if you said I forgive you grandpa and let grandpa baby sit your three children, people would say you are crazy. I know God is not crazy! God must have forgiven you because He gave you three more of his children. These are his precious children and he gave them to you. It is very obvious that you and your husband are loving parents. God made the right choice, in forgiving you and trusting you with three more children. In my story it would be very hard to forgive grandpa, but I think you can forgive him if you do not have to trust him again.

Proverbs 3:5 Trust in the Lord with all your heart, and lean not on your own understanding

I have been thinking about this a lot, you see God knows the intentions of our hearts so He can forgive us and trust us. We have been commanded to forgive everyone but our trust is in the Lord not mankind. So forgive all who trespass against us, not only because we are commanded to, but also because love is forgiveness and forgiveness removes guilt, and shame, and condemnation, but put your trust in the Lord says the Lord!

2 Corinthians 5:18-19 Now all things are of God, who has reconciled us to Himself through Jesus Christ, and has given us the ministry of reconciliation, that is, that God was in Christ reconciling the world to Himself, not imputing their trespasses to them, and has committed to us the word of reconciliation.

You see in these verses that our mission or our ministry is to reconcile ourselves and our neighbor back to God through forgiveness, not holding our sins or their sins against them. I mean, who are we to hold trespasses against someone or ourselves if God Himself tells us not to and that Jesus does not hold them against us.

Also the fact that you cried dunning the abortion tells me you were already sorry and repenting. Alice, please forgive yourself, we are commanded to love our neighbor as ourselves.

Mark 12:30-31 And you shall love the Lord your God with all your heart, with all your soul, with all your mind, and with all your strength.' This is the first commandment. And the second, like it, is this: 'You shall love your neighbor as yourself.' There is no other commandment greater than these."

You see there is no other commandment greater than these. It must really be important to God to call these the two greatest commandments. To love God you must first trust Him. Jesus said you can keep all the commandments but if you have not done them without charity you have done nothing.

1 Corinthians 13:1-3 Though I speak with the tongues of men and of angels, but have not love, I have become sounding brass or a clanging cymbal. And though I have the gift of prophecy, and understand all mysteries and all knowledge, and though I have all faith, so that I could remove mountains, but have not love, I am nothing. And though I bestow all my goods to feed the poor, and though I give my body to be burned, but have not love, it profits me nothing.

We are not complete in life until we love ourselves. God created us to be in His image and likeness, (loving all, kindness to all and forgiving all) the difference between sounding brass of a tinkling cymbal and true forgiveness is love. To love yourself you must forgive yourself. To love others you must deny yourself pick up your cross and follow Jesus. These are impossible if you do not know the love of Jesus and Father God!!!

1 John 4:7 Beloved, let us love one another, for love is of God; and everyone who loves is born of God and knows God.

You see we cannot be born of God without love, and loving others as ourselves is how we prove we are of God.

1 John 4:8 He who does not love does not know God, for God is love.

Again God is love and we are to be the love of God on the earth, if we don't love others and our self then we are not of God.

1 John 4:9 In this the love of God was manifested toward us, that God has sent His only begotten Son into the world, that we might live through Him.

We are to live through God and to do that we are to manifest the love of God in the world. We manifest the love of God by letting God's love flow through us to the people of the world through forgiveness. Yes, forgiveness and love go hand in hand! You cannot have one without the other.

1 John 4:10 In this is love, not that we loved God, but that He loved us and sent His Son to be the propitiation for our sins.

Here God is saying He loved us first. He proved he loved us first because He sent His only Son to be the propitiation for our sins. So what better way to show love than to lay down His Son's life for us? Just accept God's love and forgiveness and then become love and forgiveness. Jesus is our example for life! Jesus trusted His Father and we can trust our Father in heaven just as Jesus did. We have the same Father as Jesus.

1 John 4:11 Beloved, if God so loved us, we also ought to love one another.

Notice God did not put conditions on His love. Whether you love Him back or not, that will never stop Him from loving you. So to be loved on earth is to love others and to expect nothing in return. The moment you expect love in return you are setting yourself up for hurt. You can expect love from God always but not from man. When someone hurts you, check your spirit, and ask yourself, "Why do I need them to love me?" It could be you are not rooted in love of the Father!

So anything that is not of God, like unforgiveness toward us, it needs to be dealt with. I know God will very gently bring up sin issues and ask us to repent. God only asks us to repent one time for a sin issues, and you already repented during the procedure. So if the issue comes up again and again you know that it is from the devil trying to bring on guilt and shame and condemnation. Don't listen to the devil. Instead listen to God's Word that says you are forgiven.

Acts 3:19 Repent therefore and be converted, that your sins may be blotted out, so that times of refreshing may come from the presence of the Lord,

To me, this Scripture says repent that your sins (plural) may be blotted out, (removed, cast down, or ultimately forgiven) and times of refreshing shall come from the presents of the Lord. Isn't that cool to think of God's forgiveness as refreshing and I can tell you there is absolutely nothing on earth that will satisfy your craving for love like the presence of God in your life.

Life is so special and so rewarding that when we are in Jesus Christ and allow Him to dwell in us. Jesus said to bring heaven to earth and I believe your three children are part of that heaven. So know you are loved by God and forgiven by God. Life is so short to let a mistake rob us of the Father's love. So when you see a bumper sticker like mine, don't go into guilt. Use the sticker as a reminder to tell yourself how much God loves you and has forgiven you! Praise God for His love for you and that He sent Jesus to show us His love. Jesus is the ultimate forgiver, lover, and the one whom we can put our trust in!

John 8:10-12 When Jesus had raised Himself up and saw no one but the woman, He said to her, "Woman, where are those accusers of yours? Has no one condemned you?" She said, "No one, Lord." And Jesus said to her, "Neither do I condemn you; go and sin no more." Then Jesus spoke to them again, saying, "I am the light of the world. He who follows Me shall not walk in darkness, but have the light of life

Let him without sin cast the first stone, and when they left one by one Jesus ask where are your accusers? She said they all left and

Jesus said neither do I accuse you, now go and sin no more. Alice, that is how you make the devil and sin (unforgiveness) flee. You turn a negative into a positive and quote a scripture at the devil. Alice, I believe you are courageous and can love yourself. I believe God's Son, our brother Jesus paid the price for our mistakes so we don't have to pay again and again. Guilt is from the devil. Don't listen to him! Be free to enjoy your blessings and know that God is in love with you and who He created you to be – a Christ-like forgiving Christian and light of the world. Don't hang your head but instead hold it up high and be a light to the world and tell everyone of God's great forgiveness.

> **John 8:12** Then Jesus spoke to them again, saying, "I am the light of the world. He who follows Me shall not walk in darkness, but have the light of life."

Alice, I want to talk to you about forgiving the boy that took advantage of you. Again, the devil says you have the right to hate him. After all he forced himself on you. I know he was listening to the devil. When the devil said, "Go have your way with her you need this, it will make you happy and you will feel like a man," he listened to the devil. Then, when the result of his action should have been to take responsibility and be a man, the devil said tell her to kill it and be done with it, and he listened again!

We have all listened to the devil. When the man bumped into your bumper and gave you the $415.00 you thought it must be a sign from God to go ahead with the abortion. Yet we know in our hearts that God would never pay for an abortion! It is so easy for the devil to tell us to look back and see our sins as monumental mountains that cannot be forgiven. Our past is one of his best weapons so if the past comes in your mind and it is condemning you just remember that reminder of the past is not from God! When that happens, remember to focus on Jesus and that devil will run and take his guilt, condemnation and shame with him. I believe to our loving Father the sin comes down to a moment of time where we made a decision to hear Father's voice or the voice of the devil. Jesus said in John 10:27:

John 10:27 My sheep hear My voice, and I know them, and they follow Me.

I believe we must seek to hear the Father's voice and to know it, or we will be lost and listening to the voice of the devil condemning us forever. Just thank God for forgiveness, then walk in His forgiveness and love as the Father loves us unconditionally. When Jesus told the woman to go and sin no more, Jesus was saying you are forgiven. We must receive the forgiveness of God for our sins or the forgiveness is of no effect. To go through life not knowing God's forgiveness is more tragic then the sin itself! Jesus said we are made in His image and likeness! God is love and so are we! Forgiveness is allowing God to love us again!

We also have to discern signs.

Matthew 16:4 says *A wicked and adulterous generation seeks after a sign, and no sign shall be given to it except the sign of the prophet Jonah." And He left them and departed.*

Jesus said walk by faith not by sight! The decision to have the abortion was partly made because of what Alice thought was a sign from God, yet Jesus said signs and wonders follow a believer not lead a believer. If Alice just knew this verse of Scripture she would not have accepted the money as a sign. We as a people are so blessed to live and have our being from a God that will forgive us and continue to teach us until we understand we are forgiven.

Mark 16:17 says and these signs shall follow them that believe.

Notice signs follow the believer! So we all have to discern who we are listening to and whether signs are from God or from the devil! Alice, I do not know if you prayed for the money to have an abortion or for a sign from God about abortion. I do know you received a sign and acted on that sign thinking it was from God. Jesus said my people die for lack of knowledge. Do not let a lack of knowledge keep you from knowing the true forgiveness of Jesus Christ.

Alice, in your case people might say you chose to abort the baby. So you are no different than the grandpa in the story. People can be so cruel. They are letting the devil talk right through them. Jesus talks a lot about discerning our thoughts in the Bible. My sheep know my voice and obey. You know God tells us to forgive and put this whole situation behind us. Are we listening to God when we say I cannot forgive myself? The devil will bring this up over and over. So don't listen to him! Resist the devil and he will flee. We resist the devil by having a relationship with Jesus, knowing Jesus and being like Jesus! Jesus sees us the way He created us to be, we should be able to look into the mirror and see Jesus looking back at us. Our past is the past but the future is looking to our relationship with the Father and Jesus and Holy Spirit. When we dwell in Him we cannot get mired down in self-pity. The joy of the Lord is our strength! Yes we have Joy in the Lord, when we forgive our self's, like we are commanded to!

Back to the boy for a moment, the devil says that sin is too big to forgive. You have the right to hate the boy, after all you wouldn't need an abortion if it was not for him, and the devil will bring plenty of people to support us in our unforgiveness. The real sin is not discerning our thoughts and the signs. The real sin is not seeking God and not making the knowledge of God our first priority in life! If knowing God is not our first priority in life, then we are like wave of the sea, tossed by the wind in any direction.

James 1:6 But let him ask in faith, with no doubting, for he who doubts is like a wave of the sea driven and tossed by the wind.

We ask in faith that God will forgive and He does! Put your faith in God and His forgiveness and forgiveness is a done deal. Forgiveness is so real, so full of light and edifying you will cast that mountain into the sea forever and watch the devil flee.

Let us take one more look at the work of the devil so we can discern his handy work from God's work! When we sin we feel weak and out of control and in that weakness (self-condemnation) we look for a quick fix of momentary happiness instead of letting the joy of the Lord being our strength.

Then when we see the far-reaching effects of our weakness, like an unwanted baby on the way and the devil brings in a momentary quick fix, which is another sin (abortion). The problem seems to be fixed but then the devil comes in with guilt, shame and you to cover it up with lies. Then he tells us this sin is too big for God to forgive (another lie). The quick solution is always the work of the devil but if it doesn't appear to be working. He rushes us into the quick fix by loading us with what if questions, like *what will your parents say? Who will take care of the baby? Where will the money come from?* Lies, lies, and more lies! This is truly bondage to the devil. Let us get to the truth that sets us free. Jesus said honor our parents and don't lie to them. Jesus said not to worry about tomorrow for Jesus is with us and Jesus said He is our Provider, so the money will come from somewhere! Take every thought captive! GOD FORGAVE US AND WE ARE FORGIVEN!!! Seek God with all your heart, mind and life, not momentary happiness! BE FREE IN THE KNOWLEDGE AND LOVE AND FORGIVENESS OF CHRIST JESUS!!!

The truth is, I know we have all listened to the devil sometime in our life. We have all looked for a sign of some kind to guide us, and if the truth was known that God did not forgive us we would all be in hell for sin. Thank God for forgiveness! The sooner we forgive, the sooner we live! The word forgiven is found in 38 verses in the Bible and 20 verses in the New Testament, so it must be important. I believe Jesus stressed the importance of forgiveness because He knew we all need forgiveness.

Luke 6:37 "Judge not, and you shall not be judged. Condemn not, and you shall not be condemned. Forgive, and you will be forgiven.

So judge not, condemn not but forgive everyone and you shall be forgiven. I thank God for sending His Son, Jesus to show us how to live and how to forgive! Jesus forgave us all. No words of judgment or condemnation came out of the mouth of Jesus and it would sound horrible if they had. Why doesn't it sound just as horrible from our mouth? We are to be sons of the Most High God and the bride of Jesus. All God asks us is to forgive ourselves and others. Yes, forgive the boy and ourselves, for when we forgive we are truly set free. Jesus said He is the light and the truth will sets us free. So undo those burdens and be free to love and be loved by Jesus!

18

Jesus became man to take on the sins of the world and while he is still a man, Jesus forgave us all. We should take on His nature and forgive all the people that have wronged us. Jesus is our example of perfect love, perfect forgiveness and the perfect example of what one life lived for God the Father can do! Catch the loving forgiveness of God and the devil run. When you know you are a son or daughter of the Most High Father God and that Jesus is your brother, this world will be a better place because you are in it! Start forgiving yourself for it is a very good place to start, and reach out from there and start today.

Jesus is not, will not and will never be a fool. Jesus paid the ultimate price for us so we must be worth the ultimate price that He paid. Don't be a fool! Rejoice in the fact that God sent His own Son to redeem us! Receive the forgiveness and the joy it brings! Forgiveness is our gift from God and our gift to everyone that has wronged us. Love flows from love not from hate. Jesus is our example of how to live and how to rise above the trials and sins of life.

I have heard people say that if I forgive them, I'll look weak and they will harm me again. Some say forgiveness is a sign of weakness. These are lies from the devil! Does forgiveness kill? Does forgiveness steal? Does forgiveness destroy? No! Absolutely not, but unforgiveness does all three!

In this situation I said I believe God blessed Alice with three children after her abortion and used the gifts of three more children to prove He had forgiven her. Jesus showed me I was wrong. What if you had an abortion and could never have children because the procedure went wrong? Does the fact you cannot have children mean you are not forgiven? I believe God's Word that says He forgives all, and the life of Jesus proved it and that is all the proof we need! I believe all means all. Jesus never made a distinction for any special kind of sin. So we must forgive all including ourselves. When we make any kind of distinction for a sin, we are actually giving more power to the devil by saying this is too big even for God to forgive. You see how stupid that is! Jesus said in His word all things are possible. So forgiveness is possible. Alice, forgive all and be set free knowing Jesus loves thee!

I praise you Father and Jesus and the Holy Spirit for your love for Alice and her husband and I praise you for their three wonderful children. I praise you for making them in the image and likeness of you. I praise you Jesus that they will never be ashamed of anything in their past, because your forgiveness is that complete! I pray that the young boy who forced his desire on Alice will find your truth Jesus, and be set free to become who God created him to be.

I praise you Father and Jesus that because of Your love for us we are forgiven, and in that forgiveness we can also forgive! I praise you Jesus that even the people that perform the abortions can be forgiven if they seek You first in their life and set their hearts on believing in Jesus that came and died for us all! For I know it is Your truth, Your love and Your goodness you put in us that leads a man to repentance. With no exceptions forgiveness of God has no boundaries, except we grieve the Holy Spirit by not forgiving others!!! Live in truth and be free, knowing the God of the universe loves us and wants us free. Free to love and be His sons and daughters that serve Him without any guilt or shame from the past!

Jesus said "My truth will set you free" and it does! The truth is you are forgiven so get out there and be a child of God, living, breathing, out speaking the word of God boldly! The Joy of the Lord is yours just because you ask God for it!

YES WE ARE FORGIVEN!!! EVEN FOR ABORTION!!!

I think it was in June of 2012 while having coffee with Jesus that Jesus told me to change my bumper sticker. It reads: *A CHOICE OR A CHILD.* Jesus gave me a picture in my mind of a new bumper sticker that said *abortion* in bold black letters on white paper like the white paper of the Bible, and then in red letters it read *you are forgiven* like the red letters of the words of Jesus in the Bible:

ABORTION
YOU ARE FORGIVEN

Jesus told me to talk to my friends Joe and Erin about the bumper sticker and I did! Guess what? They knew someone that could print the stickers for me and he did them for free. When I went to his office, he liked the bumper sticker so much that he was going to print some for himself, only his were going to say: *Abortion, Jesus forgives*. When he showed me his I said I like that better and do mine that way. On the way back to the camper, I felt a thump on the back of my head and heard a voice that said "that is not what I said" to which I replied "Okay, Lord!" Immediately, I called and asked to had mine changed to *You Are Forgiven*, the next morning Jesus said His wording would lead people into conversation with me and then Jesus could flow through me or anyone that had one of these bumper stickers and we, Jesus helpers could tell them about the love and forgiveness of my Jesus.

I have gotten requests for these bumper stickers and God has gotten them free for everyone! So don't be ashamed and spread the good news!

One more word about bumper stickers, I had one that said: *A choice or a child*. In my heart, my intention was to bring an awareness of life being killed. In doing so, I brought guilt and shame and condemnation to others. I am so joyful that my Jesus showed me a better way. I know it is the goodness of God that will lead a man to repentance; where guilt, shame, condemnation will lead you into despair, depression and maybe suicide.

Please ask God if your message is the right message and listen for His voice and obey.

I love my Jesus and He loves me enough to turn me around when I have the wrong message. I love my Jesus simply because He simply loves me!!!

Simply in love with my Jesus!!!

Jenny, Ron and Jesus love you all!

Adam and Woman

In Genesis, God created man and saw that he was lonely. There was no suitable help meet for him. So God created woman for Adam. God called her his wife. Adam did not call her Eve until after the fall or sin of man. The word *wife* means my lady. And Eve means mother of my child. So before the fall she was named for who she was and after the fall she was named for her function. Notice that God named us for who he created us to be not for our function in life. I know God has a special name each one of us because we are special.

As I grew up, I thought a wife will made you whole. I couldn't wait to have a wife so I could be whole. In Genesis, I now realize that Adam was whole because of his relationship to God. They walked and talked in the cool of the evening, every night. They had a great relationship. God saw Adam was lonely so He created a help mate, for him. You see, I misunderstood I thought a wife would make you whole. So in reality I was making my wife God. Anything you are filling up your life with is an idol unless it is God! I fully expected Jenny to make me whole. We all have something we think is going to make us whole. For some it is material things, others it can be drugs, whatever path you choose to make you whole, if it is not God you are on the wrong path. I put unreal expectations on my wife and then expected her to live up to those expectations. I now know that was a recipe for disaster.

Back to Genesis for a moment, God told Adam if you eat the tree of good and evil you will surely die. But Adam ate of the tree of good and evil and lived. So what died? His relationship with God died. God no longer walked in the cool of the evening with Adam. As you read the Old Testament you see God talked to only a select few. He created a place called the Holy of Holy's and only after great preparation could anyone enters to talk to God. Losing the personal relationship with God is the biggest loss to mankind that is possible! For us not to be able to talk to God is not comparable to any other sin. The human race was cut off from relationship with God except through profits!!!

Now fast forward to the coming of Jesus. Jesus came to show us the Father. Jesus came to be our example in life. Jesus came to be the atonement and the forgiver of our sins. Jesus is the perfect sacrifice and He is the Lamb of God. I believe the most important reason that God sent His Son was to restore our relationship with Him. Yes now because of Jesus, we can all talk to God any time we want. Remember the veil was ripped from top to bottom. Jesus opened the door of communion with Him so we have access 24/7. This is just as big if not bigger than the forgiveness of sins. Our relationship to our Lord and Savior is the most important relationship you can have. I will try to explain the importance of this relationship in this letter.

If you think that you have to get cleaned up to come to God, you're in the Old Testament. Come over to the new where God cleans you up and makes you new (born again). The apostles were all sinners when Jesus called them. Jesus said come follow me, He did not say clean yourself up and then follow me. Jesus did not ask the apostles to repent and follow Him because He knew it is His truth, His goodness And His love that leads man to repentance. It is knowledge of God that sets us free. Jesus in His Word said to ask for revelation and wisdom to be set free. What God wants more than anything is for us to know His voice and to follow Him. Jesus said my truth will set you free. Believe in Jesus and be set free.

What does Jesus want us to believe? Please believe the one who gives life. The name God means source of life. Please believe the one that never stole anything. Jesus even told us to pay taxes. Please believe the one who forgives the past as if it never happened. Jesus forgives sins and said they were removed as far as the east is from the west. Remember this: it is so important because if a sin of the past comes up again and again, you know it is the devil because God removed the sin as far as the east is from the west. God is for forgiveness while the devil is guilt condemnation and shame. We all hear from the devil every day – it is temptation. We have to learn discernment! Jesus said my sheep know my voice and follow me. Please pray for discernment to hear the voice of Jesus and know who is talking to you. Quick note, Jesus is love so to discern whom you are listening to, see if the message comes from love or hate. Remember that forgiveness is love and unforgiveness is from hate. Please don't believe in the devil, who says I am here to kill, steal, and destroy your life here on earth, and for eternity.

I think everyone knows that Jesus died on the cross to forgive our sins. That is love! Jesus took the beating on the whipping post so we don't pay for our sins. That is love! Jesus is our atonement for sin. That is love! Why did Jesus rise from the dead? *To restore our relationship with Him and the Father.* Jesus restored our relationship to what it was before Adam sinned. That is love! With one act of love, Jesus forgave all mankind all the way back to Adam! With the same act of love Jesus forgave all the future sins of the mankind forever! Do you realize the forgiveness of sins through Jesus destroyed the works of the devil forever if we only believe!

Jesus came not only to forgive our sins but also to show how to live a truly perfect life of loving others. Because of Jesus, we see how the love of God in us manifests in a life of loving others and dying to our selfish ways. Jesus said follow Him. In other words look to His example to know how to live. We now can talk to Him any time we want. What a blessing this is! The more we use this blessing the better our relationship becomes. Jesus, before he died said IT IS FINISHED. I believe Jesus was talking to the Father saying I have showed them your perfect Love and have been the perfect example of the Father's love for all mankind. YES JESUS IS LOVE AND HE PROVES IT EVERYDAY!!!

So how does IT IS FINISHED affect us? When you know for a fact the God of the universe sent His Son to show us how to live, how to love and ask nothing in return except for us to believe, you are in the truth that sets us free. Hearing God's voice every day is more nourishing than the greatest meal. That is why I say man can no longer hurt me. I don't need people to change to please me. I don't need the approval of others to give me self-worth. I have a relationship with God. God gives me my self-worth and makes me a pearl of great price that Jesus paid for. I love everyone because I see them as God sees them.

God is my source of life and joy, not my status and job. Circumstances in life do not determine my joy; my joy comes from knowing the truth of God's word. I know for a fact the Holy Spirit dwells in me. The same Holy Spirit that raised Jesus from the dead now lives inside of me. I have to be worth everything to God because He gave His everything for me. Do you get that? Jesus gives me His Holy Spirit!!! I'm in the kingdom, why would I let what someone said or didn't say hurt me? Why would I let the past hurt me? Jesus said that I am a pearl of great price and He paid the price so we can take every thought captive and if it is not of God cast it down. I don't mean war against the devil for putting bad thoughts in your head. I mean focus on Godly thoughts and watch the devil thoughts flee. It really is that simple! Where your heart is so will your thoughts be. Focus on God and ask Him, "*What are we going to do today?*"

I look forward every day because I never know what God has in store for me. I love to wake up early and have coffee with Jesus! We talk about everything. I live to manifest Jesus everywhere I go. I tell everyone I meet that I am blessed. They see me pushing Jenny in the wheelchair and wonder how can I be so joyful? One person asks why I call myself blessed. I told them that I have Jesus living in me. I cannot be defeated, because the only thing that comes against you in this world is the devil and Jesus defeated him and made an open show of his defeat. This same Jesus lives inside me and I love Him and He loves me! Invite Jesus into your heart and Jesus will show up with all you will ever need to succeed!

So what does God want from us now? Simply to believe His Son paid the price, and is our example of how to live. For example, if I sin I know God is there to cleanse me of all unrighteousness. I don't believe I need to beg God for forgiveness because Jesus said I'm forgiven. Saying please forgive me to the Father is almost like saying I don't believe you when you said I'm forgiven. Instead I thank God for forgiving me and say I want to stay in the right relationship with you Father and I praise you for letting me see these faults of mine and showing me how to resist them and make them flee. To make all your faults flee do as Jesus did, talk to the

25

Father 24/7. Never let the cares of this world take your mind off Jesus and your relationship with Him.

Jesus said not to worry, so a worry-free life is possible. Focus on Jesus! Jesus said take life one day at a time and don't worry about tomorrow so that must be possible also. Keep your Focus on Jesus! Jesus said to heal the sick, raise the dead and cast out demons with the words He said. So it must be possible too! You might say, I can't cast out devils or heal the sick or raise the dead. Oh yes you can! Jesus told us to, all it takes is faith in the Name of Jesus. You see Jesus wants you to be so in love with Him that the two of you become one, like man and wife. Jesus and you can be so intimate that your thoughts are his thoughts and when you reach out and to touch someone it is actually Jesus touching them. Jesus said we will be his brides. We have the same power and authority in this world, which Father gave Jesus when he was here. Jesus said so in His Word.

My wife Jenny could tell someone, Ron will do that for you and fully expect me to do it. She knew me so well that she did not have to ask me, she knew my will was to help others and I would just do it! Jesus wants us to know His will so well that we can speak for Him. Jesus is love so if you ever have doubt about the will of God, think, or ask yourself, would love do this? If love would do this then you are in the will of God and God will flow through you and into the person you are praying for. Jesus said that His will be done on earth as it is in Heaven. So bring heaven to earth and give Jesus to someone hurting. The love of Jesus or I should say Jesus' love for us is so pure, that sin will flee in the presents of God's love. Focus on Jesus! Sin is of the devil and the devil will flee in the presents of God so invite God into your life and watch things change!

Whatever vice or addiction you are dealing with in life, Jesus can handle it. Notice I did not say you could conquer it with Jesus. I said Jesus will conquer it with you! Talk to Jesus like the problem is fixed already. Thank Him for restoring your life, your marriage, your health, or whatever your affliction has been. Faith is the substance of things hoped for and the evidence of things not seen. You by yourself cannot change your marriage or your addiction or whatever is your vice. But with God all things are possible. ALL THINGS NOT SOME THINGS ALL THINGS!!!

When you start focusing on Jesus you will find that nothing can hurt you. Maybe you had a terrible childhood and you share that with others and you find someone else that had an even worse childhood. It is good to share life experiences but don't make that your focus, instead focus on what Jesus did for you. The relationship you had with your dad has no bearing on your relationship with your real Father. Jesus said we are made in the image and likeness of God, not our dad and mom. We cannot let the shortcoming of our earthly mom and dad become the distorted way we see our relationship with God. You see we think in terms of our body but God is talking Spirit. Our image and likeness is in the spirit of God. God is love – love is forgiving and patient, etc. We are to manifest God's love here on earth to everyone. Jesus said to love your neighbor as yourself.

To love yourself you have to know Jesus and who He created you to be. Not what you think you are, but who He created you to be. Because I know Jesus loves me, you cannot hurt me. If I need you to be a certain way to make me happy then I am deceived. If I put expectations on any one I am setting them up to fail and for me to be hurt and disappointed. You can see this problem everywhere. Look at preachers on television that get so popular and then maybe do something stupid and all the good things they did goes down the drain. Everyone condemns them and is disappointed in them. Put your faith in God and never be disappointed. Jesus said to seek the approval of others is putting yourself in bondage to that person. Everyone on earth that has a problem can trace it back to someone that let him or her down, father or mother or church etc. That someone is human, and in all of mankind there is only one human that did not disappoint anyone. Jesus is our example of how to live! Do as He did, love others and expect nothing in return. You might even get crucified for it but don't stop loving others or yourself. Jesus forgave them as they crucified him.

Do you have the love of Jesus flowing through you, get up every day and dedicate your life to doing the work of the kingdom? Read how Jesus lived and walked on earth, read how Jesus brought

Heaven to earth and loved everyone unconditionally. Ask for wisdom revelation and knowledge of Him. Jesus is looking for someone to flow thought every minute of every day. Yes you can watch Jesus transform your life right in front of the mirror. If you ask, He will give you all you need to be loved or to be a light in the world. You can radiate the love of Jesus to everyone you meet. As my new friend Jeff put it, drip Jesus juice everywhere you go!

The truth of God's Word should be our source of life. Life all comes down to this, we are all in a struggle. We can trust in God and believe in God and live with God in us or we can kick out the truth and live with the devil. Jesus made the path very clear, He gave us a manual called the Bible. He gives us the Holy Spirit and showed us how to win freedom from the devil. Moses asks God how this is possible and Jesus answered saying (I will be with you), the question has never changed and the answer is the same, today, tomorrow and forever! ALL THINGS ARE POSSIBLE FOR I AM WITH YOU!!! I know Jesus is with me and this is the most awesome revelation any man can have. So go proclaim the word fearlessly and know Jesus is with you! There really is no gray area for Jesus said 'you are either for me or against me'!

Jesus dwells in me so I can love you the way Jesus loved us unconditionally. You can no longer hurt me; the past can no longer hurt me, life can no longer hurt me because I know the love of Jesus gives me power over life and death. I will never die! Jesus said he who loses his life for my sake will surely live and he who loves life will die. I lay down my life to the only one who can give life – JESUS! And JESUS loves you also so welcome into your heart!

We love you Jenny and Ron and Jesus.

Church Love

Last night Jenny and I attended a little church not far from the campground. It was a nice friendly church with mostly older people. The second we walked in people were welcoming us. Everyone smiled and we were able to talk a little because we were early. After the service the pastor greeted us and I started getting Jenny ready to go.

An older couple came over to talk to us again. The woman had what I would call a very stern face. She looked like the type that had opinions and would let you know she had them. I am not judging or criticizing her looks just stating the facts because they are important to this story. Her husband wanted to know how long we were married. I told him 40 years last November 11. He proudly stated they been married 58 years. I said, "Congratulations! That is quite an accomplishment."

His wife said, "I heard you talking before church when you mentioned that you two live in a camper and are full time campers for four years now." I said, "That's right."

"You have gone to a lot of different churches haven't you?"

"Yes. We have been in a lot of churches in the last four years."

"My husband and I used to travel a lot also, and we went to a lot of different churches. We found a lot of churches out there that did not have any love in them at all. As you travel do you find a lot of churches without love also?"

I said, "Actually, I don't."

She was surprised and said, "We know other people that travel and they found there weren't many loving churches also." She continued, "I find that hard to believe that every church you go into is a loving church? It was almost a rhetorical question! Almost like, I was lying." She went on to say, "We found so many churches that had no love. I find it hard to believe that every church you went to was a loving church."

I replied, "You know, when Father God sent His Son, Jesus came to show us the love of the Father. Jesus came to be the love of the Father. I believe Jesus is our example of how to live and how to love! Jesus gave love freely to everyone everywhere and we are to give love freely to everyone everywhere. So when Jenny and I go into a church we don't walk in testy; we go in to give love freely to everyone. We are to be love as Jesus is love; we find love in every church we go in to because Jesus lives is inside us and so we bring Jesus everywhere we go. It is pretty simple! You see we have the love of Jesus in us and the Joy of Jesus in us, and we just let the love of Jesus flow through us."

They just stood there for a moment looking like they were in deep thought. Then her husband looked at me and said, "It was nice meeting you." He looked at his wife and said, "I'll bring the car around front for you."

The wife continued to look at the floor for about another 45 seconds or so and then she lifted her head toward me and with a beautiful smile on her face. She told me, "Is there any way we can help you?" It was like God transformed her right in front of my eyes and it only took Him 45 seconds. I believe she had the love of Jesus in her heart all her life and was just waiting to bloom! The love of Jesus is so powerful and when you witness Him transforms someone you want to share His marvelous deed with everyone so they too can enjoy Him and Glorify Him.

Jesus in His Word said some sow, some water and some reap. I believe most of the time we sow and sometimes we water but when you reap, you witness the transformation and your heart will jump out of your chest with the Joy of watching someone set free. As I drove back to the camper, I started thinking about all the people that sowed into her and how many people watered. I wondered how many of them thought nothing happened when they sowed or when they watered. I pray they all see the transformation in her now that it happened. I do know you will never experience the Joy of transformation unless you start sowing and watering. Then relax and let God be God. Rejoice and be glad for someone is set free.

30

The love of God is the transforming power of grace and love!!!

Thank You Jesus for your transforming grace and love! Jenny and I love having you in us and we love knowing You are with us every second of our life.

I just want to think out loud for a minute. Think how many people judge the church they go into within the first few minutes of being there. Within a minute or so they form a judgment, and that judgment will probably make the difference between them hearing and receiving the message for that day. We can actually block our receiving by judging our circumstances.

When Jesus talks about love in His Word, He calls love as charity. Today we think of charity as giving and sacrifice and we are right. If we think of love as giving instead of a two-way street, which is like the Barney Song – *I love you do you love me etc...*, our whole life will change. I believe the two-way street of love came from and was birthed out of the need for love from people that do not know Jesus.

So much of our culture today is built on wrong principles.

Happiness of the world versus Joyfulness of the love of Jesus.

Sympathy of the world versus compassion of the love of Jesus.

Love of the world versus the charity of Jesus.

Don't let the devil steal your joy by what others say or don't say. Just be the love of Jesus and Jesus will flow through you and you will see Him transform people and in return you will receive the Joy of the Lord that is totally unexplainable!

Thank you Jesus for loving us!!!

Jenny and Jesus and I love you all and wish you transforming Joy.

Coffee Time with Jesus

I am extremely blessed to have coffee with Jesus every day! Let me tell you how this came about. Forty-one years ago, I was working for Jenny's foster father Don. He ran a plumbing business out of his house.

Every day we started and ended the day in Don's kitchen having coffee. In the morning, Don would give us our jobs for the day, and at the end of the day we filled out our timesheets in Don's kitchen while having coffee. Jenny was Don's foster daughter; she was only 17 years old but enjoyed having coffee with us every evening. I loved this time because I thought Jenny was quite cute. I loved the way she would enter into our conversations. She was going steady with some guy or I would have asked her out on a date. I found myself looking so forward to our coffee time at Don's house.

One night I came in from work and Jenny was doing dishes. She told me Don and his wife had gone out for the evening. Jenny asked, "Do you still want to have coffee while filling out your timesheet?" I told her that I would love to have coffee and she made some fresh coffee. Jenny had developed a very hard personality, from being raised in foster homes all her life. She never let this protection down. That night was no different except we were alone in the kitchen. She poured our coffee and went on doing the dishes, she had her back to me when I said, "Jenny, you act so hard, but I believe there is a sweet little Jenny inside of you, just aching to come out." Jenny turned around with a cigarette in her mouth, a dish in one hand and flipped me the bird with her other hand. You see why coffee is so special to me.

Sometime later Jenny and I started dating and always enjoyed coffee together. When we had our children, they grew up knowing that when Jenny poured coffee that was our time. The children and

I could be in the middle of a board game on Sunday afternoon, and when Jenny made coffee, our kids knew that Jenny and I would have some quiet time. Even our grandchildren learned that Jenny and I shared coffee time every day. One time while on a short road trip with friends and our grandchild, we stopped to gas up the van. Our friend said he was going into the convenience store to get coffee. Taylor, our grandchild went in with him. While in the store our friend asks Taylor, "How does your papa drink his coffee? Taylor said, "Real slow!"

In 1997, Jenny started doing some odd behaviors. Odd words came into in her vocabulary. Just some scuttle changes in her personality. Eventually after a few years of testing, we were told that Jenny had Picks disease. In 2001 as the picks disease progressed Jenny stopped drinking coffee. Coffee time became a very lonely time for me.

So how did coffee and my relationship with Jesus get started? In early 2009, I was really struggling with Jenny not being healed. You see, I had gone through the *Be In Health* teachings about 8 times. I had repented of everything possible. I thought I was having a good relationship with Jesus except that He would not tell me what the spiritual block to Jenny's healing was. I had gone into depression and some anger towards God. I felt dejected and rejected and alone. My prayer life consisted pretty much just asking God: *"Where are You?"*

Then one day I saw Peggy, a teacher at the Be In Health church and she asked me what was wrong. I told her, "I was giving up on God." She asked me, "How's your prayer life with Jesus?" I said, "Fine!" She then asked, "How is your relationship with Jesus." I answered, "I don't know Him anymore." Then Peggy said, "That is your problem!" So I went back to the camper and sat outside with Jenny. I asked God, *"What does a relationship with You look like?"*

"What was it like to date Jenny?" Jesus asked. I started telling God what dating Jenny was like. I said I could not wait to see her, to hold her, to know everything about her. It was exciting to be with her, to hear her voice, to watch her and most of all to spend time with her. Then Jesus said the coolest thing! He said, "That is what a relationship with me looks like and it is 4 o'clock let's have coffee together."

I started to cry as I asked God, "Do you really want coffee with me? You see, about 8 or 9 years ago Jenny had lost her love of coffee, I really believe it was because she couldn't talk anymore so she seemed to just forget about our coffee time. I would still have coffee twice a day but Jenny didn't even want to sit down, therefore coffee time for me had become a very, very lonely time. Jesus said, "Yes! I want to have coffee with you every day. Actually, *we* need to talk every day."

Immediately, I made coffee and poured Jesus a cup. We started talking and talking – and here it is three and half years later and we are still talking! Jesus has revealed so much during our coffee time that to miss a day would be terrible. Jesus has become my very best friend. I live to be like Him, I live to talk to Him but most of all I live to hear Him. His voice is so soft and gentle yet firm. Jesus has the coolest personality. One morning I made coffee that I had bought on sale, it was horrible and when Jesus tasted it, He said, "Why did you buy this coffee? Don't you trust me to be your provider?" I went and bought better coffee for us.

My time with Jesus has been so fruitful for Jenny and me. I go to bed at night and pray for Jesus to wake me up early so we can enjoy more time together. What does fruitful mean? It means Jesus and I are on the same page, in the story of life. For example, I used to think I had to be a better person to come to Jesus. Now I know Jesus calls us first to follow him and in our quest to seek Jesus we actually are called by Him first. Jesus called each apostle usually while they were working and said, *"Come, follow me."* Jesus never told the apostles to go to a deliverance ministry and clean yourself up first. He said follow me because Jesus knew it is His goodness that will lead a man to repentance.

If you set some time aside for Jesus every day and talk to Him like you are talking to your best friend, He will talk, laugh, and cry with you. The word says we are to be the bride of Jesus. Your bride knows everything about you. He knows your most personal thoughts, ones you would not trust anyone else with. Jesus is that personal with you if you let Him. So turn off the television and the radio and sit down with Jesus and hear His voice. The best part of this relationship is Jesus will never leave you or forsake you!

Dear Jesus, today in our quiet time my thoughts went to another question: "In an emergency, who are we to trust?" Let's say Jenny suddenly took a turn for the worst. I have two options, first is to call 911 and turn Jenny's care over to the hands of doctors – doctors I probably do not even know. If Jenny died my friends would say I did everything I could do, and everyone I know would console me saying the same thing. What if I found out Jenny was mistreated while under the doctor's care? I could say those stupid doctors messed her up and I'm suing them. I'm sure almost everyone would agree with me that I'm doing the right thing. They would even agree with me suing the doctors if I felt they did something wrong.

Option two would be to call on Jesus and let His Word be true! To walk by faith and not by sight is not a suggestion in the Bible. It is a stand of faith. I'm calling on the Ruler of the universe. Jesus the one that formed us from dust and then breathed life into us, He is all I need. God will never let you down or forsake you, plus He has given us his Word. Jesus in his Word said not to worry so I will not worry about the outcome because I know that Jenny's life is in the best hands.

Now if it was the will of Jesus to take Jenny home with Him and give her life eternal, He has that right. Yes I would miss her just as much as if I had sent her to the doctors and she died under their care. The difference for me is I know it was not a mistake from human hands that took her away. It was the right timing from my Lord and Savior to give Jenny her special reward of being with Jesus and Father forever. I love Jesus with all my heart and respect Him and the decisions He makes. There is nothing on this earth that could ever fill the void of not having Jenny with me, except the love of Jesus and knowing that I made the right choice in trusting Jenny's life, and my life to the one who created them!

I know some people will say I should have called 911 and in their minds I did not make the right choice. The doctors are human and subject to the circumstances of life, just like we are. They can make mistakes. Let's play the *What if* game: What if the doctor had a hangover, or what if the doctor had a headache, or what if the doctor was thinking about a personal problem? It would be easy for him to miss something in his diagnoses.

You know we are human too but if we lost a loved one we hold the doctor to a higher standard and sue him. If we win the lawsuit and are awarded a large amount of money, we spend the money on ourselves trying to please our flesh. That route never brings satisfaction to us. I have actually heard people say, "At least they can buy a little happiness with the money." That is so sad because we are trying to please our flesh with flesh and it never works.

You see by trusting Jesus I don't have to worry about any of that. I have a totally clear mind and I am free of worry knowing that Jenny has the absolute best care, actually a divine doctor who never makes a mistake. Jesus sees the whole picture and His timing is always right. You see I trust in God! Not man and I do not worry about what man says. When you trust in God and believe God and have surrendered your life to God worry is a thing of the past. Jesus said he who dies to self will surely live but he who lives for self will surely die. I died to my selfish desires and live to trust, and believe, and have all my faith in God my Father! In my old selfish desire I would like Jenny and I to die at the exact same time so neither of us suffer any loss. Now by trusting God and dying to myself I can truly say Jesus I love you and respect your decisions and trust you with Jenny's and my life.

I love my coffee time with Jesus! My life is so full of the joy of knowing Jesus that a day without Jesus is impossible to think about! So spend some time with your best friend, the one you can trust and believe in. You know He is waiting for YOU!

Jenny and I are so blessed to have this wonderful relationship with Jesus and we live to be like Him in word and deed! We live to have the eyes of Jesus and the heart of Jesus so Jesus can flow through us to others. Jesus came to be our example of how to live and I will follow Him all my days. I praise Him for having coffee with me and giving me understanding that provides comfort and Joy which is strength to carry on. I see His strength in Jenny and I know He continues to bless us every day. All praise and Glory are yours Heavenly Father through Your Son Jesus my Best Friend I pray!

36

Dear Vietnam Vets

Jesus said He is the light and the truth that sets us free. We all want to be set free of this Vietnam War. Light makes the darkness go! So instead of putting the Vietnam War in a box and trying to keep the lid closed, let's open the box to the light of day. We want people to know the truth. We want to be set free! We are not helpless. We have our minds and we can ask God in our life and with Him we can be set free.

How???

We all meet on Monday every week. Why can't we meet at the V.F.W. once a week? There, we could start writing down the truth about what happened in Vietnam. One by one until we each have a chapter in the book. That's right! We can write a book of truth that if we ask God for guidance. We will be a true witness to people around the world of what Vietnam was to us. We can explain how pure our motives were for going. We can explain to everyone how complicated the war became and how our hands were tied not only in our desire to do good in Vietnam but also in our own defense.

I know we really don't want to relive the war over, but in reality we are reliving the war over in our sleepless nights. I believe we can put a stop to these night terrors. This book can be sent to our government officials and even if only one or two of them read it then those two more people will know the truth. They cannot hide from the truth. It will bring light into their hearts and how they vote. God said all things are possible to those who believe! I believe in God and I believe there is something wonderful about getting your experience on paper. Jesus knew the importance of writing down His life story. He wrote the Bible for us all. There is real comfort in writing down our story. That is when someone says to you, "Were you in Vietnam?" You can just hand them the book and say, "My story is chapter five" and go on your way, knowing they have the truth and you don't have to relieve it again. Don't try to keep a lid on the box, BLOW IT OFF!

It is way past time for the American people to know the truth. I remember when Ronald Reagan died. There was such an outpouring of love for America. It was truly great to witness it. I remember watching Nancy on television, with tears in her eyes, saying, "I thought they forgot about my Ronnie." Just because people don't seem to pay attention doesn't mean they don't care. Open up a new awareness of the truth about Vietnam. People do care and they want the truth!

We all know how it was the lies that John Kerry told congress about us being baby killers that broke the spirit of America to fight. With one big lie, John Kerry changed the outcome of the whole war. It silenced the guns and planes and brought the great efforts of thousands of young men to a terrible conclusion. If one lie can do all that, how much more powerful is the truth going to be when finally told by the men in this room. Please ask God to be your witness! Ask God to guide you into truth and then thank God for doing it! GOD WROTE US A BOOK, CHAPTER AFTER CHAPTER ON HOW TO LIVE A GOD PLEASING LIFE! If you read the Bible and take one chapter at a time there doesn't seem to be much power there, but put all the chapters together and you have real life changing power! We need to get the truth out about Vietnam also! You may be hearing in your head right now that *'one more book will not make a difference'*. I guarantee you the voice you are hearing is not from God! God wants the truth out there and it is up to you in this room to get it out.

In a way, Jesus is like the marines – He is looking for a few good men. You can make a difference! In fact, you are the difference! You are the few good men!!! Set your goal and start running! The victory is in your story. Please start each meeting with these simple words: *"Dear Heavenly Father leads us to and let us write THE VIETNAM TRUTH!"*

I would like to add one more thing to think about. At the end of every chapter ask for forgiveness and give forgiveness to all. Forgive the North Vietnamese, your captain, even John Kerry and all you can think of. Most of all forgive yourself! Be specific. Name the names of the ones you forgive and maybe that person will read it and know they are forgiven and through that forgiveness he will be set free! That is the goal to be set free, to reach the goal set others free.

The real story in your book will not be '*is my story worse than theirs*' but it will be how God transformed your life in writing your story. I believe you will meet God, find forgiveness, and have a new outlook on life. Life really is about loving others like how Jesus loves us. You actually went to Vietnam to love others, to help others, and to give freedom to others. Tell your story people! The world is waiting. GOD IS WAITING! Go love someone! Give the beggar on the corner 5 dollars and watch him smile, then look in the mirror and I bet you are smiling too! Doing something that small can put a smile on your face and a little joy in your heart. Think how life changing this truthful book about Vietnam will be. Just love unconditionally and you will be loved unconditionally! Face it, you would have laid down your life for Vietnamese freedom, and that is love. You wanted more than life itself to give the gift of freedom. Now you can. You have a second chance to give freedom to the world and this time to yourselves!

Discernment

Am I a sinner saved by grace? I was taught by man that I was! Am I a son of God learning to walk like a son? Jesus says so and I believe Jesus! Is being humble calling me a sinner saved by grace to other people? No. Is being humble washing the feet of my fellow men? Yes. I am not a servant hoping God notices me being humble, I am a son of God who humbly serves! I serve because I am a son of God not to be a son of God! Jesus served us because He is a Son of God. I don't serve to be a son of God, I am a son of God and I am made in His image and likeness. I don't grow weary in my well doing because I am just letting the love of Jesus flow through me. You too are a son of God! Being humble is not what we say; it is what we do! Loving others is not telling others I love you. Love is what we do! Believe me, others will recognize and believe in our love and our being humble by our actions way faster than if we just humbly say I love you I really do! I am a son of God who was bought and paid for by Jesus himself and if I miss the mark and sin I can repent and have the Grace of God to save me! Now, that is some good discernment, thank you Jesus! Jesus loves me and I know it. That is some good identity!

Jesus let me know right from the start of our journey together how important discernment is! Some people I know will not even admit there is a devil let alone admit the devil can talk to you and they will never admit they listen to him. We have all heard the voice of the devil and we all listened but not all have discernment to know who they are listening to. Jesus talks a lot about hearing his voice. The Bible has 456 verses with the word voice in it and in everyone Jesus is talking about discernment. I would think it is very important to God and yet, I don't seem to hear much about discernment from the pulpit. You do not need to read too long in the Bible to find it.

Genesis 2:20-25 So Adam gave names to all cattle, to the birds of the air, and to every beast of the field. But for Adam there was not found a helper comparable to him. And the Lord God caused a deep sleep to fall on Adam, and he slept; and He took one of his ribs, and closed up the flesh in its place. Then the rib which the Lord God had taken from man He made into a woman, and He brought her to the man. And Adam said: "This is now bone of my bones and flesh of my flesh; She shall be called Woman, because she was taken out of Man." Therefore a man shall leave his father and mother and be joined to his wife, and they shall become one flesh. And they were both naked, the man and his wife, and were not ashamed.

Notice after Adam named everything on the earth, Jesus discerned there was no helpmate for Adam. Jesus discerned Adam needed a help mate and Jesus created one for him!

Why do you think Adam and the Woman had no shame about being naked? Why is the fact they are naked so important that it had to be mentioned in the Bible at all? The day before you married your spouse, if you were with her or saw her naked, you would have great shame and yet after you marry her there is no shame of being in her presence naked. The shame has been removed by commitment to each other. I believe that is why the first Scripture after creating woman Genesis 2:24 talks about commitment and the two shall become as one and they had no shame being naked in front of each other. Notice when the apostles made the commitment to be born again and asked Jesus into their heart the two – Jesus and you – also became as one and had no shame about following and living as one with Jesus Christ. Like the apostles, we can discern too whether or not to accept Jesus as our personal Savior. In doing so we receive boldness to tell the world about this new relationship we have with my Jesus! Just as Adam could communicate with the woman immediately upon her birth, we can communicate with Jesus immediately when we are born again. How do we communicate with Jesus, we simply need to discern his voice!

There are 45 verses in the Bible that talk about being naked. Some of these verses talk about the shame of sin and how sin will bring on shame while standing naked before God while some verses talk about the innocence of not sinning and the innocent beauty of standing naked before God. I am making a point, something as simple as being naked needs to be discerned as to whether it is innocent, good and of God or of the devil and evil! Commitment to your spouse Jesus can change your discernment and open your eyes or make you want to hide your heart from your bride Jesus or come boldly and in purity and innocently before your bride Jesus. Adam and the woman at this point were without sin and therefore without shame talking to God in the cool of the evening. We too can come to Jesus and experience the love of God by the cleansing power of forgiveness! Jesus gave us power and discernment and we must be able to discern Jesus is real, Jesus is love and use the heavenly power of forgiveness!

> **Genesis 3:1-7** Now the serpent was more cunning than any beast of the field which the Lord God had made. And he said to the woman, "Has God indeed said, 'You shall not eat of every tree of the garden'?" And the woman said to the serpent, "We may eat the fruit of the trees of the garden; 3 but of the fruit of the tree which is in the midst of the garden, God has said, 'You shall not eat it, nor shall you touch it, lest you die.'" Then the serpent said to the woman, "You will not surely die. For God knows that in the day you eat of it your eyes will be opened, and you will be like God, knowing good and evil." So when the woman saw that the tree was good for food, that it was pleasant to the eyes, and a tree desirable to make one wise, she took of its fruit and ate. She also gave to her husband with her, and he ate. Then the eyes of both of them were opened, and they knew that they were naked; and they sewed fig leaves together and made themselves coverings.

Why would having your eyes opened even be an issue to Adam and the woman? They could see just fine. Do you see the need for discernment even in the Garden of Eden? Do you see the devil is real? Do you see in Genesis 3:1 that the Word said that the devil talked in words that Woman could understand and Adam was right with her, so I think they both heard and did not discern!

Where did the thought of being like gods come from? All they knew was good and pure so where would a desire to know about evil come from? The devil in the form of the serpent was able to talk to them and put so many ideas in their heads so fast they were not able to discern good from evil! The devil is the source of sin and just as he brought sin into the Garden of Eden he will bring sin into your house if your guard is down. And your guard is down when you will not even admit the devil is real.

You will not let a snake in your house but you will let television in your house. And just as the devil talked so fast to the Woman he will talk through the television, radio, computer and phones so fast you will not be able to discern his thoughts. Actually the devil is so cunning that he will cause you to sin and then let you blame God for it. I truly believe discernment of voices or thoughts is the most important skill we can learn. I believe discernment is a skill that we should learn and that is more important than reading, writing and math. Without discernment, we are truly lost and we are an easy target for the enemy!

No one has walked the earth and not heard these voices. I hear people talk about movies and television programs that only have a little bit of sin in them. I myself have watched movies and said I wish they would leave that one part out and it would be a good movie. I bet you have too! You see we have discernment but we chose to ignore our discernment and somehow let the desire to be entertained override our discernment. The problem for me is I have read Genesis and I know what my Lord thinks about even taking one bite of forbidden fruit can do to my life and to the lives of my children. I thank God for Grace and forgiveness. I thank God for discernment!

Where does discernment come from? How do we learn right from wrong? What are some good effects of discernment? Knowing good from evil or right from wrong! Discernment will bring great Joy. For example, say you teach your children not to touch the stove because it may be hot, and the heat will burn you! In doing so you are teaching them to respect the heat of the stove. As your child grows and learns to respect the heat of the stove you can teach them to use the heat to warm and cook food with this heat. You will teach them which end of the pan to hold while cooking. They will learn the good side effects of heating food and how heating food will remove germs and change thing like cookie dough into cookies. Then you teach them to discern how long it takes to cook the food, etc. They will also learn that too much heat can start a fire and fire can be deadly. Discernment in cooking can make a big difference in taste, odor, safety, and enjoyment.

I believe we all have some basic ideas about discernment! I believe we have all heard that little voice in our head say check your gas gauge as you are driving down the road. I know I ran out of gas one time and thought, *"God why didn't you remind me?"* only to think back on the day and realize Jesus had reminded me to check the gas gauge three times today and I ignored Him three times. Isn't it amazing the first thought I had was to question God or in a way blame God for letting me run out of gas? If you have ever blamed God for anything in your life, you have heard the voice of the devil.

Now because of discernment, I have a new very Best friend. My new Best friend not only tells me things like check your gas gauge, but tells me how to discern good from evil. This discernment can lead me to heaven and hell decisions! Has anyone committed a sin against you that was so bad or monumental that you thought you can never forgive them? I know you heard the voice of the devil. In fact, now you know you heard the voice of the devil! Jesus said forgive them Father for they know not what they do, after being beaten beyond us recognizing Him and then being nailed to the cross. When you have thoughts about forgiving others you are listening to the voice of Jesus and any thoughts about not forgiving is the voice of the devil. My Jesus said:

John 10:27 My sheep hear My voice, and I know them, and they follow Me.

I know we have all heard the voice of Jesus and I believe listening to His voice and knowing His voice is so important because it will determine where we will spend eternity! Yes, discernment is important. It is fundamental and I believe it to be the most important tool we have against the devil. Truly, if we can't discern who we are listening to, we are lost, we are double minded, and we are looking through a glass darkly. Depression, double minded, and multiple personalities will all start in your brain and I believe came from never been taught how to discern. Jesus said being double minded makes you unstable in all your ways.

James 1:8 He is a double-minded man, unstable in all his ways

So being double minded can be dangerous and will make you unstable. So what is the answer? How do I get better? How does one become single minded?

James 1:5 If any of you lacks wisdom, let him ask of God, who gives to all liberally and without reproach, and it will be given to him.

Notice that in James 1:5 it says *'if any of lack wisdom'*. Who is our source of wisdom? *'Let him ask of God'*. When you need wisdom we are to go to God! We are to look for each other for direction, edification, compassion, fellowship, and a desire to know our true source of wisdom is "GOD!" No man can give you wisdom! God gives us wisdom liberally and upbraids not; remember knowledge puffs up our ego but wisdom will make you humble.

1 Corinthians 8:1 Now concerning things offered to idols: We know that we all have knowledge. Knowledge puffs up, but love edifies.

Have you ever heard teenagers talking about their parents like their parents are dumb? When that same teenager gets to be say 25 years old he starts to realize how smart his parents are. Humble parents will let their lad boast and be puffed up for a time because they know the wisdom seeds they planted in their son will spring up and the love of Jesus Christ will bring him away from false idols like diplomas that puff up and he will turn to the author of what truly matters "charity that edifies"

For me, wisdom is being humble and wisdom is knowing my self-worth comes from the love God has for each one of us. You see why your source of wisdom is God the author of Charity! We cannot love without God in our heart and we cannot love ourselves without the wisdom of God in our hearts! Yes I believe it is impossible to love from your brain, people try to define love from their brain but you cannot love without God in your heart. Knowing God is not enough. Adolf Hitler knew God but Hitler did not let God into his heart. Hitler had no discernment! Please ask God into your heart right now!

You see wisdom will overcome being double minded! You can overcome being double minded by simply asking God for wisdom. Pretty simple isn't it? Think of all the people who are suffering and taking all those drugs. I pray for them to have an awareness of how much God loves them and for them to see God as their source of Joy which is our strength. I think today we tend to go to man for knowledge and man's knowledge is so limited. Man has medicine, man has recovery systems, man has sympathy, and I believe sympathy is one of the worst and most used tools the devil has today.

What a shame when we have the word of God to take us above the problems and give us peace from being double-minded and unstable! By looking to man, we are asking man to fight the systems but the real problem is not knowing who we are in Jesus and knowing who Jesus says we are. I am not a sinner saved by grace. I am a son of God learning to walk like a son. Being humble is not calling myself a sinner to other people, being humble is washing the feet of my fellow men. I am not a servant hoping God notices me being humble, I am a son of God who serves! I don't grow weary because I am just letting the love of Jesus flow through me. Whatever you asks God, ask in faith and you shall receive!

James 1:6 But let him ask in faith, with no doubting, for he who doubts is like a wave of the sea driven and tossed by the wind.

If you feel like you have no direction in life and if you are unstable or double minded, then comes a doctor who says I think this medicine will help. After a while the doctor's medicine doesn't help and he sends you to a different doctor and you begin a quest for the right doctor. Then someone else says God can help but you have no faith and no hope in God because you have prayed for years and never received any relief. You think at least the doctors have studied for years on how to help others and so you put your faith in him. I believe the doctors and their medicine may have helped others and certainly are to be commended for their efforts and for their heart's desire to help others. Even though from time to time their medicine has helped others, we know they are limited to their earthly knowledge.

Sympathy will let you ask God, "Why does this happen to me." Sympathy will only bring you down and keep you down. Sympathy gives you the right to stay broken. Sympathy says, "It's okay they should never have treated you that way." Sympathy puts the blame on the other person which allows you not to forgive! Sympathy is permission from others to point the blame on them and label them as the problem. You know 'if it was not for them I would not have done what I did, so it is their fault!' I believe giving sympathy to others is letting the devil talk through you!

If you have read the life of Jesus Christ and looked at what He commanded us to do, God gave us power over sickness, death and the devil! How can we ask God questions when God gave us everything that we need to rise above our problems? It's like telling your son that the stove is hot and after he burns his hand 100 times, he looks at you and says, "Why you not told me the stove was hot again?" Compassion is telling the boy before he burns his hand "you go near that stove and there will be bad consequences." Compassion is showing him the dangers of a hot stove. Compassion is laying down your life long enough to teach him to stay away from the stove and as he gets older showing him how to use the heat of a stove for good.

Sympathy would say "oh honey you burnt your hand again, I wish you would learn, let me bandage it for you and I will get you some ice cream to comfort you, you poor thing you just do not understand the stove is hot, do you?" Jesus said sin is death! The consequences of sin is death, I don't hear any sympathy there. Jesus does not have sympathy but through the compassion of Jesus we have forgiveness. Compassion is forgiveness and forgiveness is freeing, uplifting, edifying and loving each other, not sympathy like, here let me make it better, have some fatting comfort food like ice cream!

Jesus is our example of how to live and how to forgive. Jesus also said He will forgive sin and the consequences of sin if we believe in Jesus enough to repent. Repenting is not feeling sorry for ourselves because we sinned a 100 times, repenting is turning away from the wicked ways of the devil and turning to God and saying help me seek You Lord. Repenting is not being saved by grace. It is recognizing we have the gift of Godly grace to allow us to seek Him and turn away from the things of the world.

Sympathy allows you to stay in sin, but grace says, "Get up and follow me again!" Grace and compassion will lead you to discern where your heart is. If you truly yearn for a heart to follow Jesus you will use the grace of God to start out new today. You will ask God for His compassion to give others the love of Jesus. You will have a desire to read the life of Jesus and to be the life of Jesus. Compassion will bring the life of Jesus into your heart. Compassion will change your reading of the Bible from trying to learn about Jesus to reading to become Jesus. Compassion is becoming Jesus on the earth. We are His ambassadors. We are to represent Jesus, we are the continuation of the love of Jesus and we are here to build His kingdom and not some man-made denotation of His kingdom!

When you minister to others about life in Jesus, I hope you realize life in Jesus will turn them away from sin. I have seen how God cleans people without ever telling them they are in sin and without telling them they need to forgive. Jesus leads us to forgiveness by changing our hearts. Jesus will walk them into forgiveness by showing that He forgave them, not just telling them He forgives them. Telling someone to forgive is putting the burden on them and in reality they are trying to forgive because they know it is a sin but their heart did not change. If they see what a pure heart looks like when they look at you, your job of giving them the love of God unconditionally – that is even before they forgive, repent, and change their ways – will be so easy and you will not grow weary in your well doing. They see the love of God in you and they will know that His love is real. They will know, see and long for the love of God! You will not need to try to make something happen. You will rest in the love of Jesus yourself and watch him bring the increase. Forgiveness has to come from the heart! Forgiveness is a position of the heart. forgiveness is allowing Jesus into your heart. Jesus said it is His goodness that will lead a man to repentance!

> **Romans 2:4** Or do you despise the riches of His goodness, forbearance, and longsuffering, not *knowing that the goodness of God leads you to repentance?*

Please read and see that we are to teach the goodness of God by living the goodness of God and God will lead thee to repentance. We live the love of God, we live the goodness of God, and we are to be as Christ-like ambassadors until Jesus comes again. I used to envy Adam and the fact Jesus would come and talk to him in the cool of the evening, until I heard the good news. I can communicate with my Jesus 24/7. Jesus came and made my time with Him so personal that I don't even need an appointment and I don't need a telephone! In fact the only requirement is I need the desire to communicate with God. Isn't Jesus so great and His plan has unlimited minutes and no roaming charges, no monthly bills, it is the only one plan you don't sign up for! You simply desire to communicate and Jesus is already listening and by the way, listening is what we are compelled to do also.

Listening is a big skill we need to learn. Discerning our thoughts or voices will be impossible if we do not listen. The best marriage in the world will fall apart if we don't listen to our spouse. We will drift apart and backslide if we turn off our hearing. Please ask God for good listening and then prepare to hear His voice by setting aside some listening time. Read *Coffee Time With Jesus!*

In my Coffee Time with Jesus, I have been taught to listen and in the listening time Jesus showed me the difference between sympathy and compassion. Ask God to talk to you and reveal things to you. I never used to set down and ask God what he wanted to talk about, but now I do. I had never even thought about the difference between sympathy and compassion and I by myself would have never taken the time to think about them.

Jesus never had sympathy, yes Jesus cried for others but crying is not sympathy when it leads you to enough compassion to lay down your life for others. You want true love, true compassion. Lay down your life and follow my Jesus. Read the life of Jesus and walk as Jesus walked, full of love and compassion for others. Ask God for compassion and you will receive it!

While talking to people who go to doctors, it seems they are driven more by *feelings* than results. That is they say they *feel* he is really going to help. I liked his bed side manor, it made me *feel* as though he cares or I *feel* he really cares about my pain. These *feelings* and emotions are easily discerned and I am sure the doctors really do care! Even though they care, doctors know there are going to be side effects of the medicine. Sometimes, the side effects of the medicine are so horrible that people will continue to go to the doctor until they feel he doesn't care and then they feel they need a new doctor and the feelings just go on and on! They are driven by feelings and not by real results. They have discernment of feelings and they can discern physical things. One example is that they discern that the pain still hurts or they feel this new pain etc. Their discernment goes no further than their own body and is of physical systems they can feel! Then, they are driven by feelings and emotions and not what the word of God says. They have no rock to stand on. They are truly a wave tossed by the wind of feelings and emotions.

I know or discern by faith in my Jesus and my Father in heaven that I can bring Heaven to earth by simply believing in my Jesus and my Father! I can have heavenly peace, wisdom, and be single-minded the rest of my life! The side effect for my belief is peace, love, joy and strength and I will be the one ministering to the hurting and down trodden instead of the one in need of ministry. If your prayers are not answered please ask God to show you where you are praying wrong, because He will and He promised us answers. We must discern our thoughts better then we discern our feelings.

Do you realize our thoughts come from our hearts not our minds? Here is some discernment for you!

Matthew 9:4 But Jesus, knowing their thoughts, said, "Why do you think evil in your hearts?

Luke 5:22 But when Jesus perceived their thoughts, He answered and said to them, "Why are you reasoning in your hearts?

Luke 24:38 And He said to them, "Why are you troubled? And why do doubts arise in your hearts?

There are many places in the Bible where Jesus talks about thoughts come from the heart. Man has to learn discernment. Jesus even said out of the heart a man speaks.

Matthew 15:19 For out of the heart proceed evil thoughts, murders, adulteries, fornications, thefts, false witness, blasphemies.

Luke 6:45 A good man out of the good treasure of his heart brings forth good; and an evil man out of the evil treasure of his heart brings forth evil. For out of the abundance of the heart his mouth speaks.

You see, we store thoughts in our heart and if we do not discern we can store good treasure and or evil treasure. You decide what is in your heart by discernment. Please ask God right now for the gift of good discernment. I hear people say things like, "I believe in God so I can have a new car." I think that is okay but I think God would be more pleased if we believed and used our faith for discernment as to what He needs us to do today. If the thing God needs done today requires a new car you will have it without even asking for it. Jesus has so many promises for us.

Jesus promised to take away our pain, not just physical pain but heart pain. We can have a deep pain in our heart. For example, if you lose a loved one you will experience pain in your heart. If you love and know God in an intimate basis, He will show you that your loved one is in heaven and this knowledge will take away your pain totally. You can actually rejoice knowing your loved one is in the loving embrace of Jesus and has the Joy that surpasses all our understanding. You may not actually feel this Joy physically until you will experience it supernaturally and your heart will respond with rejoicing in knowing where your loved one is! Then your body will respond with the good feelings of love and being empowered to help others instead of feelings of depression and loss of direction in life! That's my Jesus and that's some good discernment!

Jesus conquered death and trampled all the power of the devil to control our feelings! If you allow the knowledge of what Jesus attained at the cross in your heart, you will win over your feeling and emotions. When I say you will rise over feeling and emotions by having a relationship with my Jesus, I'm saying you will actually rise above sadness and depression and their effects. Drugs will only mask or suppress depression and sadness but Jesus will open doors of opportunity for you to share His love and power to others. Physical discernment is fairly simple yet mental discernment can be just as easy if you let the love of God into your heart and ask for discernment of your heart thoughts.

When I mentioned praying wrong in the paragraph above what I mean is that sometimes we pray about the system instead of the root problem. For example, if we pray against depression such as, "Oh Lord I am so depressed please help me" and the problem is that we are not discerning our thoughts. How should Jesus answer that prayer? It would be like, "Oh Lord, my house payment is late and I don't have the money, please help me!" Yet you have plenty of money but you are spending it on everything to impress your neighbors. How should Jesus answer that prayer? The real prayer would be, thank you Lord for the discernment on how to determine who is talking to me about depression and finances. Lord who is telling me to impress the neighbors, or go into debt?

Discernment is important in everyday life and it is the most important tool we have to determine where we will spend eternity. Most people do not want to think about eternity and most people do not think about discernment. They would rather think about the here and now; that they will spend time wanting to impress the neighbors with what they have. And when these desires fall short of satisfying their needs to impress, the need to impress will lead them into being depressed! Then depression will lead them into living on feelings and emotions which is a roller coaster ride of medicine and doctors. To halt all these problems, don't pray to have the depression removed but pray instead to have discernment of your thoughts! Jesus made it so simple! Please listen for His voice and let Him bring you out of the problems by changing your heart from wanting to impress other to being the love of Jesus Christ on the earth.

Discernment is the real key to eternity. We have learned that we speak from the heart and we can have good or evil treasures in our heart. So how do we protect our heart? We must determine what good information is and use discernment of all information we let into our heart. Jesus tells us to protect our heart by guarding what we see, hear and dwell on, you see we have been given by God the choice of what we choose to learn from and believe in. If we watch pornography we are letting pornography into our heart and guess what will come out of our heart. It really is that simple. Guard your heart, your eyes and your ears! Jesus said out of the heart a man speaks and desires. If you lived in a country, where there were no cars at all, I bet you would not desire one. In fact you will not try to impress your friends with one. Guard your eyes and your ears and your heart; for if you guard them, what comes out of your heart will be pure.

Matthew 12:34 Brood of vipers! How can you, being evil, speak good things? For out of the abundance of the heart the mouth speaks.

How can we even think we can have a pure heart when we watch and listen to things that corrupt our hearts? Yes, television and radio, newspapers, magazines etc. will corrupt your heart. And even some Christian music will plant bad seed of doubt. Yes, some preachers have been corrupted. These are just some of the ways the devil has to corrupt our hearts. I am so joyful I have a relationship with my Jesus! In the minds of most this would bring confusion but I have peace and joy in this world because Jesus said if I believe and I do! Jesus said in John 14:27:

John 14:27 Peace I leave with you, My peace I give to you; not as the world gives do I give to you. Let not your heart be troubled, neither let it be afraid.

You see John heard Jesus say these things and believed them! Peace is real when you believe in Jesus Christ and your heart will never be troubled. We have the word of Jesus to believe and we can choose to believe in Jesus and live in peace or to be troubled in our heart, you decide.

John 14:26 But the Comforter, *which is* the Holy Ghost, whom the Father will send in my name, he shall teach you all things, and bring all things to your remembrance, whatsoever I have said to you.

Which one will it be? Peace and Joy or troubled heart and unrest? I choose the comforter! Jesus will teach me all things. Jesus will bring all things to our remembrance. Thank you my Jesus, I love you too!

Have you ever heard old people say 'I'm having a senior moment' or 'my mind just isn't what it used to be' or maybe 'the golden years are just not what they were cracked up to be'. My mind works perfect because I think, I talk, and I live with my Jesus living in me! Who brings all things to my remembrance? Jesus said in John 14:26, "The Comforter will bring all things to my remembrance! " I trust the Comforter!

Who is the discerner?

Hebrews 4:12 *For the word of God* is living and powerful, and sharper than any two-edged sword, piercing even to the division of soul and spirit, and of joints and marrow, *and is a discerner* of the thoughts and intents of the heart.

Who is the Word of God?

John 1:14 *And the Word became flesh* and dwelt among us, and we beheld His glory, the glory as of the only begotten of the Father, full of grace and truth.

We see from Scripture that the Discerner is the Word and the Word was made flesh! The Word came and dwelt among us. The Word is the only Begotten Son of the Father; the Word is Jesus and Jesus is now the Word in our heart. Jesus gave us the word through the Holy Spirit who dwells in us 24/7 if we just invite Him in.

You see the Holy Spirit of Jesus is our Discerner. All we have to do is listen for His voice. Jesus said my people know my voice and follow and a stranger's voice they will not follow. Jesus said He goes before us and we follow for we know His voice.

John 10:4-5 And when he brings out his own sheep, he goes before them; and the sheep follow him, for they know his voice. Yet they will by no means follow a stranger, but will flee from him, for they do not know the voice of strangers."

Discernment goes on all your life. We must exercise our right to discern by exercising our hearing from the Holy Spirit. Recently while hearing from Jesus as we had coffee together, Jesus plainly told me the importance of hearing His voice. Really discerning the voice of Jesus is more important than breathing for me. You know I can breathe my way to hell but I must discern and breathe to reach my heavenly Father and my brother Jesus. Thank You Jesus for the gift of discernment. I will walk and talk and have my being with you because you love me and I know it! I discern that all good gifts come from above as Jesus said and each gift brings me closer to Him!

James 1:17 Every good gift and every perfect gift is from above, and comes down from the Father of lights, with whom there is no variation or shadow of turning.

As you can see, we must have Bible knowledge to help us understand the voices we hear. By having faith in my Jesus, He tells me where to look in the Bible to get understanding.

For example, some people do not discern the difference between knowledge and wisdom. Jesus in his word said good wisdom comes from above.

James 3:17 But the wisdom that is from above is first pure, then peaceable, gentle, willing to yield, full of mercy and good fruits, without partiality and without hypocrisy.

You can plainly see when talking to others if their wisdom is pure it will be peaceful, gentle, easy to understand, full of mercy (not accusing), good fruit, without partiality and without hypocrisy. When you invite Jesus into your heart you really start to discern correctly and you can pass His wisdom to others by presenting the truth of God's word; that is the Holy Spirit will talk through you!

Would you like one more discernment tool? When the apostles came back after being sent out the first time on their own they were excited as they reported to Jesus and said even the devils hear us and obey. Jesus said to them don't be excited about the power over the devil, it is only one small part of our kingdom, be excited your names are written in the book in Heaven.

Luke 10:19-20 Behold, I give you the authority to trample on serpents and scorpions, and over all the power of the enemy, and nothing shall by any means hurt you. Nevertheless do not rejoice in this, that the spirits are subject to you, but rather rejoice because your names are written in heaven."

People, our names are written in heaven when you receive Jesus into your heart and start listening for His voice. In no time at all you will discern whom you are listening to. You can back up your discernment with wisdom from above and really come to know the intimate love Jesus has for you! Then you will be rejoicing with the Holy Spirit in your heart.

Discernment is real, the Holy Spirit is really in your heart and we really do speak from our heart. Please take time to listen to and have conversation with my Jesus. My Jesus died so we could talk to each other, please take time to listen!

Jenny, Ron and Jesus love you all and thank you all for taking time form your busy day to draw closer to my Father.

Changing the world one heart at a time! My Jesus is so patient!

Love you all!

Don't Pray the Problem

When a problem comes, do you pray the problem? If you ask God, "Oh Lord, why did this happen to me? Why do people hurt me like this? Why I am always broke? Why can't I get a good job? Why doesn't anyone seem to care? I want to be a missionary, but I can't figure how to get enough money to go to Africa. My life is a mess. I see people who need help but how can I help? I don't have enough for me. Jesus, your word says you will provide all my needs but you never do. I never have enough. I try so hard, I moved here because I thought you wanted me to. But I must be wrong, nothing has changed, in fact its worse. I love you God, but where are you?"

Actually, we have all prayed like that at some time in our life.

All you see is *I, I, I,* and *but, but, but*; *me, me, me* and *why, why, why!* It sounds so self-centered doesn't it? The devil wants us focused on ourselves. We are easy prey for the devil when we only think of ourselves.

Jesus said when you pray, believe! Do you hear any faith in those prayers? Don't accuse God of not answering prayers. When in reality, you have not prayed. All you've done was to complain to God. Ask the Israelites about complaining. We don't get punished like the Israelites did because we live under grace. Thank God! God told us to come to Him in faith, nothing doubting. James 1:6-7 it says:

James 1:6-7 But let him ask in faith, with no doubting, for he who doubts is like a wave of the sea driven and tossed by the wind. 7 For let not that man suppose that he will receive anything from the Lord;

I believe God wants every prayer to start with your declaration of belief. For example, say you lost your job, immediately say "Jesus, I thank you for finding me a new and a better job. I praise you that our house payment will not be late. I praise you Father that your word says that you are my Provider. I trust in You and know we will find a new job. Thank You, it is done." That is faith. The prayers in the first paragraph are a declaration of fear. Fear is from the devil. I believe God wants us to use His words in our prayers. If you want the devil and fear to flee, focus on Jesus and quote His word. Don't let the devil i.e. fear dictate your prayers. Jesus said resist the devil and he will flee. In James 4:7-8:

James 4:7-8 Therefore submit to God. Resist the devil and he will flee from you. Draw near to God and He will draw near to you. Cleanse your hands, you sinners; and purify your hearts, you double-minded.

Jesus will draw near to you; He wants to be your best friend. Jesus is your brother; He wants relationship all the time, not just in your time of need. If you want Jesus to answer your prayers, pray in faith and quote His word, and thank Him for doing what you asked. Faith is the substance of things hoped for, not the substance of things complained of. Pray the answer not the problem. Praying the problem takes no faith. Jesus told us to come to Him in faith!

Mark 11:24 Therefore I say to you, whatever things you ask when you pray, believe that you receive them, and you will have them.

We enter His gates in praise! I'm sorry, but I did not hear any praise in that first paragraph. I did not hear the word of God in the first paragraph. I did hear 'fear' to the max. It tells me we don't know who we are in God. When you know for a fact that Jesus' Holy Spirit dwells in you, then fear is defeated. You can't say, "I can't" when the "I can" dwells in you. You can defeat everything when you know the Holy Spirit dwells in you! Faith in the devil is unbelief, and when you know who you are in Jesus Christ, unbelief is a thing of the past. Belief in God is our act of loving God. You can say that you love God, but when you pray the problem you

58

prove you don't believe. Believe God for all His Word. For the word is God.

In the first paragraph we ask God, "Why is this happening to me? Why do people hurt me?" We need to know in our hearts that Jesus loves us. When you know that Jesus loves you, you cannot be hurt by others. You will no longer need the approval of others. You cannot be hurt by the world. So what if you lose your house, cars and status? Jesus said in Mark 8:36:

Mark 8:36 For what will it profit a man if he gains the whole world, and loses his own soul?

Notice the word "own"; the only thing we own in life is our own soul. We are all working so hard to make a profit and provide for ourselves, and in doing so we lose sight of what is really important, our soul. When we seek after the things of this world we can lose sight of our Father's promise to provide everything for us. Then when we lose a job or whatever, it is real easy to start complaining and ask God WHY! Jesus is our Provider, when we are working day and night to provide for ourselves, I believe Jesus is asking us "WHY"?

I believe we have missed the message. We have no idea how much we are worth to God. Jesus said:

Luke 12:7 But the very hairs of your head are all numbered. Do not fear therefore; you are of more value than many sparrows.

The hairs on your head are numbered. To me that means every detail of our life is provided for. Let God love you. The sparrows to me are worthless birds, compared to a human life, yet God provides a home and food for them. Jesus wants to spend eternity with us. All we have to do is trust in Him! We must be worth a lot to Jesus for He paid the ultimate price, His own life! I mean, He died for me! The greatest lesson in the Bible is the love that our Father, and Jesus, and the Holy Spirit have for us.

I used to work 60 hours a week providing for my kids. Now they do the same thing. If only, I had known to teach them to love and depend on Father God. Teach them they are very important to their Father and He will and has already provided for them. Now I praise Him for providing time, security, and most of all, for the joy of knowing the Lord and that He has answered my request for them to have a relationship with Him.

Matthew 7:11 If you then, being evil, know how to give good gifts to your children, how much more will your Father who is in heaven give good things to those who ask Him!

The devil gets us trying to provide for ourselves. Jesus wants us to do the work of the kingdom. You know, heal the sick, raise the dead, cast out devils and preach the gospel. If your goal in life is kingdom work, your needs are already taken care of. Your goal in life should be to spend time seeding God's Word. Fulfilling God's work in the world will fulfill your kids, your wife and your life. Jesus is love and so are you. So be fulfilled in Jesus, die to self and live to love others! Expect nothing at all from others, and the devil can't hurt you.

When you pray for others, don't point out their faults. In your prayer for others, never ask them to repent for a sin issue that you think they are dealing with. I never saw Jesus do that! He is our example. You cannot make the love of Jesus conditional! When you pray for others, do you love them? I know you do, and you love them even in their sin. Jesus said if you, being evil, knows how to give good gifts to your children, how much more will Jesus give good things to them He loves.

Jesus' love is unconditional. Jesus only sees us as the finished work of the cross. Jesus forgave us our sins and if there is something to repent for I believe Jesus will reveal that to them personally. We are not judges, Jesus in the flesh never judged anyone. We are not to judge anyone or we will be judged. Jesus just administered love to everyone! Jesus is our example!

When we are born again, we are free of our past. When the apostles received the baptism of the Holy Spirit, it was not conditional on them being perfect. Some were fisherman. I'm sure they had bad days where they even cussed. They were human. In fact, they probably didn't feel any different until they started talking and walking in the spirit. We must walk by faith, and by the Spirit that dwells in us. Like the apostles, we can walk and talk in the Spirit. If the Holy Spirit would bring up a sin issue, repent for that sin issue in your life, and then walk by faith knowing they are removed, forgiven, and forgotten. You cannot be an ambassador for Jesus if you are constantly looking backward at sin issues.

Curses, sins, faults, shortcomings were all in the past. It'll make you feel bad, worthless and unforgiven, and worse of all it takes your mind off of the love that Jesus has for you. Tell me those thoughts are not of the devil. I guarantee you, only the devil, will want you to dwell on past sins. Forget about your past sin issues; don't let them hold you back. The devil wants you to think about the sins of your parents, and curses being handed down, door points etc. Everyone knows that Jesus came to justify us, but the devil wants to condemn us. When you dwell on your sins of the past you come under condemnation, which is never from God. You cannot walk in love towards God or others while under condemnation. The two greatest commandments are:

> Mark 12:30-31 And you shall love the Lord your God with all your heart, with all your soul, with all your mind, and with all your strength.' This is the first commandment. And the second, like it, is this: 'You shall love your neighbor as yourself.' There is no other commandment greater than these."

There is no condemnation in the two greatest commandments is there?

How can you love your neighbor as yourself if you are always looking at sin issues that make you condemn yourself? If you do the work of the kingdom, you are guaranteed joyfulness? Move on, knowing Jesus loves you and wants a personal relationship with you. You have to know you are worthy. Jesus took the beating, the crown of thorns, shed His blood and died on the cross, not for you to listen to the devil and condemn yourself by looking at past sin issues. Jesus said He justified us, the word "justified" means just as if it never happened. I think it means to stop looking back at sin issues and look forward to a new life of service to the one you love!

Just talk to Jesus and you will be surprised. He will be so happy to hear your voice. He will cry tears of joy for you. Jesus wants you to experience His love on a personal level so the two of you can be as one! Jesus is not looking at your history, and saying, "if only that had not happened." Jesus only looks forward. You know how I know that? The only one who benefits from our past shortcomings, is you know 'who'. So look forward! We only wake up every morning by the grace of God, so we can look forward. Jesus is our example, He never said to His Father, "no, I'm not going, look at what they have done. What they did is just too bad, they are too far-gone, and I'm not going." Jesus came to earth because He was looking forward. Jesus just looks forward, forward to the day when He can say, "I love you" and holds you in his loving embrace and cry tears of joy because you looked forward and saw who you can be in HIM! Letting your past sins hold you back is from the devil.

Start today to dedicate your life to who you are in Jesus! Jesus dwells in you. Jesus dwells in you! The Father dwells in you! The Holy Spirit dwells in you! There is nothing we can't do. Say it, until it's the only thing you think about. Jesus died to dwell in you. There is nothing you can't do! Bring Him glory by looking forward, by thinking forward, and by living forward with Jesus every minute of the day. The future is here today. Start loving the Jesus in you! How on earth can you hate yourself when you know Jesus Himself wants to live in you and dwell in you! Do not worry about your past and invite Jesus into your heart right now! Say dearest Jesus come into my heart and talk to me and live with me so we can be as one.

You know Jesus never labeled us sinners. He told us "go and sin no more" but Jesus never called us by our sin. Jesus asks the woman "where are your accusers" and notice he told the men there "you without sin cast the first stone". Think about that Jesus never put guilt on anyone, even at the cross where He commanded His Father to forgive them for they know not what they do! Notice when Jesus also prayed for the sick or the demon possessed or to raise someone from the dead He never ask His father to do it, He just commanded it to happen and His Father made it happen.

We literally need to command and Jesus who said come boldly to the throne room, commanded and His Father granted His request. Jesus loves boldness; Jesus loves us to be as bold as He was. Boldness is not being prideful – it is knowing our identity. Boldness is commanding in the name of Jesus. Jesus knew his identity is or as a Son of God and He told us we were to be Sons of God and we are so praying like it. Don't complain to God, don't beg God and don't ever ask why? Get your identity from knowledge in God not earthly knowledge like diplomas. Ask God to teach you how to walk and talk and be like Jesus and you will receive knowledge, wisdom, understanding and the most important gift of all Jesus in your own heart.

Jesus came to show us who we can be in Him. Jesus is love and love is unconditional forgiveness, so forgive yourself and just let the love of Jesus into your heart. Love is Jesus!!! Love is who we are to be! Love unconditionally loves others! Jesus is love! Love is who we are to be! We are to be Jesus on the earth. Christian means 'Christ-like'. Christian almost spells like 'Christ-I-am'. When you are a Christian, everyone should see the Jesus in you! After all Jesus dwells in you!

So let us pray: Father, we thank you and praise continually. Your words of praise will be forever on our lips. Father, I am just now starting to understand what Jesus did on the cross. I thank you Jesus for forgiveness of sins, and for sanctifying me. Thank you for revealing to me how much you love me, for revealing how much You want me, and for revealing that you need me. The fact that you need me is an awesome revelation to me. Yes Jesus, I am only now starting to realize my worth to you. I want to see everyone the way You see them. You see our potential to preach the gospel, and to win souls to you. We can break the bondage of the devil and set people free. We can heal the sick, raise people from the dead, and cast out devils, just by believing in the power in the name of Jesus. Jesus you are awesome!

We must be very important for Jesus to pay such a huge price for us. Jesus took all those stripes for me. He wore the crown of thorns for me. Thank you Jesus for the grace that gives me time to understand what You did for me. Jesus the life you lived and the example you set for me, is totally over the top of any one's expectation. We literally can do all things in the name of Jesus. All we need is faith in that name. The respect I have for you Jesus has no boundary, like what we can do with faith in the name of Jesus. There are no limitations on your love, your power and what Jesus can do through us. People are healed, raised from the dead, and set free from evil demon spirits. That is really cool, Jesus!

Jesus gave me a new word today. That word is "impossible". Any time you see something that looks impossible you know you are listening to the devil because Jesus said, "all things are possible to those who believe."

Mark 9:23 Jesus said to him, "If you can believe, all things are possible to him who believes."

You see how the devil turns everything that Jesus said around, or I should say he tries to. Study the word and you will discern whom you are listening to. All things are possible!!! Do not allow life to define you, you define life!

I leave you with this thought: Why is it so hard to believe someone that never lies? I love you Jesus, and thank you for all truth!

Jesus lets have some coffee.

Loving you unconditionally, Jenny and Ron and Jesus.

Earthly Desires

I heard of a couple that won an award for cleaning a church for 42 years straight. That was really great of them to sacrifice their time and it is a job that needs to be done and they did it without complaining. They did not seek any reward and although the pastor wanted to give them some recognition it did not change the fact that they have a heart of love for Jesus and that is why they cleaned the church. They experienced the Joy of the Lord while doing a job most people probably would not volunteer for. A lot of learned people would not be able to see the Joy of the Lord in cleaning the church for 42 years, but thank You Jesus some do! I believe this couple enjoyed watching people worshiping Jesus in a clean church.

Jesus said we are all part of the body, each with different functions and none is more important than the other. Like a car, everyone wants to be the steering wheel and no one wants to be the muffler but without all the parts working together the car would not function. I want to thank everyone who have given of themselves to do the jobs almost no one else wants to do and I believe Jesus wants to thank you also.

Jesus said to bring heaven to earth and so having heaven while on earth must be possible. I believe when we stand before Jesus for judgment, if we hear the words well done my faithful son, we will be so full of the Joy the Lord and the peace of the Lord the world could not contain it. So to me, heaven is Joy. Yes, the Joy of knowing a loving God and the Joy of being in His presents! I know we can experience His heavenly joy right here on earth. We can also enjoy the peace of the Lord right here on earth, along with the power of the Lord and the company of the Lord right here on earth. The Joy of the Lord is our strength and His joy is contagious. So today, go give some contagious Joy of the Lord to everyone you meet. In fact, go and have some fun and infect everyone with His Joy! Tell them the Jesus season is not like the flu season. Tell them the Jesus season is year round and the Jesus season is strength to overcome, tell them this is one infection you want year round, in fact you will love it year round!

If you want to catch the Jesus infection you might need to put down some earthly desires. An earthly desire is desiring anything that might take you away from God instead of leading you to Him. We read in the Bible and see even back in biblical days the comfort our earthly desires gave. These earthly desires could keep you from following Jesus Christ. Today, just as back then we Christians are not willing to lay down our earthly desires to become Christ-like. Jesus talked about a man that came to him and asked, "teacher what must I do to gain eternal life" Jesus answered in Matthew 19: 16 through 22.

> **Matthew 19:16-22** Now behold, one came and said to Him, "Good Teacher, what good thing shall I do that I may have eternal life?" So He said to him, "Why do you call Me good? No one is good but One, that is, God. But if you want to enter into life, keep the commandments." He said to Him, "Which ones?" Jesus said, "'You shall not murder,' 'You shall not commit adultery,' 'You shall not steal,' 'You shall not bear false witness,' 'Honor your father and your mother,' and, 'You shall love your neighbor as yourself.'" The young man said to Him, "All these things I have kept from my youth. What do I still lack?" Jesus said to him, "If you want to be perfect, go, sell what you have and give to the poor, and you will have treasure in heaven; and come, follow Me." But when the young man heard that saying, he went away sorrowful, for he had great possessions.

I'm afraid today most Christians probably would not fare too well under Matthew 19:21. For most of us would not be able to sell all we have to give to the poor. Yet, we know someday we will die and lose our possessions, we even create will's to try to control our positions after we have left this world. I see why so many non-Christians call us hypocrites. I wonder how many Christians could answer as well as the young man in Matthew 19:20 did?

Empty possessions!

I see Christians working so hard to have a good life for their children and yet end up like those people I see in the campground, just filling up the day by being busy. Their empty business is killing them because their life is empty and void of purpose. One couple I talked to while they walked three dogs said yes we have grandchildren and we set aside a half hour every Saturday to call them, but most of the time they are too busy to talk to us. So if they cannot set this time aside to talk to us what are we to do? Change our whole life to accommodate them and their schedule? Sounds like a pretty empty life to me! I am not judging but I am recognizing the emptiness in their hearts. Their dogs cannot and will not fill that emptiness either.

The grandparents in the paragraph above represent the relationship I had with God years ago. That is if I gave God any of my time it was on my schedule and it was when I wanted to spend time with God or when it was convenient for me. Unlike the grandchildren who did not have time to talk, God was still ready to meet me on my time schedule but all I did was complain and then hurry off to my job. I never took time to listen to God. I saw God as a go-to-God and as a God that would fix my problems. My prayer life was a list of problems and ended with something like "okay I have to go and I'll see you later." I never listened for an answer from God and if He tried to talk to me, I was too busy complaining to listen.

Also like the grandparents above I chose who or what to give my love to. I never chose dogs as they have but I did choose who would receive my love and when I would give my love.

You see I was like them. Everything was about me, they chose to give their love to dogs because they need some love back and dogs do give back the love. I think people choose to love dogs because dogs forgive and dogs don't know how to hold anything against you. You can kick a dog because he is in your way and two minutes later you say, "Come here, Skip" and Skip will wag his tail and come running. Dogs are easy they can demand but if you're not in the mood to play they will just go off and do something else. If your dog barks, you can tell it to shut up and it will. You can even send your dog to obedience school. Try that with your grandchildren!

I think people have an earthly desire to love something. That is why some people like object. For example, Jenny liked light houses. After I bought her a couple light houses she said, "That was enough, don't buy me anymore." Some people get obsessed with their objects, but objects cannot give love back. When you think about all these earthly desires we have and how momentarily these are, it is no wonder there is so much depression in the world today. There is really nothing on this earth that can compare to a loving relationship with Jesus.

Thank you Jesus that has all changed for me. I have put off my earthly desires and I Joyfully proclaiming the relationship I have with my Jesus is so ongoing, and I have Jesus dwelling in my heart 24/7. Jesus is living in me and I never go to Him with problems anymore. I know He has already taken care of my problems. I spend my time thanking God for making me into His image and likeness. I thank God for showing me how to wake up every day and be Jesus conscious and not sin conscious. I wake up every day and ask Jesus, "What are we going to do today?"

Have you ever wanted something so bad that all you could think about is that thing? I remember being young and wanting to buy a motorcycle. Mom and dad said no to the motorcycle. So I made a list of reasons why I should be allowed to have it. I presented my list to my parents and they still said no. I took my list of 10 reasons and made them into a ten day crusade. Every day I would have some reason to say, "You see if I had my motorcycle I could go to the store for you and save dad a trip". My point is I made getting the motorcycle my focus and that is all I could think about.

Well that is where I am with my Jesus now. All I *want* to think about is Jesus and how I can be more like Him. Talk about true Joy, true peace and a life full of purpose. Try Jesus and you will see He is ready to spend time with you because you are that important to Him. The earthly desires that were so important to me years ago are empty to me now. My earthly desires have been replaced with the love of Jesus in my heart. Like I said I wake up and ask Jesus, *"What are we going to do today?"* I guarantee you something will happen and you will deliver the love of Jesus to someone. It is that simple!

When you simply believe and you simply ask Jesus, "What are WE going to do today?" you are simply asking God what He needs to be done today and God will set you up for the two of you to have a great day! The really amazing thing about asking God what you need done today is He might say go to the football game with your friends. You might think, "Wow, I wanted to go to the football game with my friends." While there you might get to demon straight the love of Jesus to someone. Life really is that simple when you give your heart to the Lord. There is a Joy that is unexplainable to human understanding but it is real! The cool thing about the love of or Joy of the Lord is we can live in that loving, Joyful place 24/7. You will have strength like you never knew before and along that strength will come boldness. It is this boldness that will enable you to do whatever it is God will ask of you that day.

When I hear people talk about their blessings from God, like a new car or house or whatever material thing they thought would bring themselves happiness, I actually have sorrow in my heart for them and I think how they have missed it! You see to me the true blessings are freedom from that stuff. The true blessing is knowing Jesus is in your heart and knowing Jesus truly wants to see you experience His kingdom right now! I'm telling you the kingdom of heaven we can experience is the pearl or peace of great price and once you experience it, you will joyfully sell everything that would get in the way of a closer relationship to God.

There are people on earth that live to impress others all their life. I pray they come to the knowledge of knowing Jesus Christ as their best friend. The best impression one can make and the only impression one can have that truly satisfies is having the Joy of the Lord to give away. All other means of impressing other is to look what I have, look at my new car etc. but with the love of Jesus you impress others because what you have you love to give away! You will be so secure in your love of Jesus, that material minded momentary happiness will totally fail by comparison.

Jesus impressed everyone and yet He had nothing by earthly standards. Even the clothes on His body were stripped away at the end of His life. By our standards, He was not successful. In fact at that point, Jesus looked like a total failure. Most of us will go to the doctor if we feel any pain and by our standards Jesus would have looked like a fool to take on that much pain. Yet look what an impression He has made on the lives of us all that choose to believe Him.

Jesus is so smart that He wrote one book that can educate you from birth to death. Jesus lived a life that reveals to us a way to live above the earthly desires and shows us that nothing on this earth is worth working for except giving His love and His strength to all we meet. Jesus revealed the things of this world will pass away and yet we will do everything to keep positions and have positions. Ask Jesus to have the Father give you revelation as to what is really important, and then live to live the life He reveals to you! The life Jesus has revealed to me is simply I can have heaven's Joy right now because I can experience the love of the Father and Jesus through the Holy Spirit every moment of everyday.

That is right! You can live in heaven right now and have the Joy of the Lord right now. Jesus said not to worry about tomorrow. And when you receive Him in your heart and you believe Him to be in your heart you will not worry about anything. Jesus is alive and well and just wants someone to flow through. Jesus is our example of how to live, so ask Jesus to help you live the life He lived and you can have the mind of Christ and the heart of Christ and be the Love of Christ. Now that is amazing and the best part is you will not have to tell anyone about your love affair, because they will see Jesus in you. That is right! They will see the new you and they will see the image and likeness of my Jesus in you! The new you will be enable you to share the love of Jesus to all.

I believe emptiness and business has no place in the heart of a Christian. The most joyful people I have ever met have the joy of the Lord in their hearts because they give themselves so much that giving is a lifestyle. I believe when Jesus changed water into wine at the wedding feast, His joy level was off the charts. I know the first time Jesus flowed through me to perform a miracle I was blown away for weeks. If there was such a thing as a joy meter, my joy meter would have exploded! I believe that Jenny, in her limited capacity at the time was feeling the excitement also. I believe joy is what Jesus was talking about when He said we could bring Heaven to earth. Peace on earth and the Joy of Jesus through you to all on earth.

The other day, I heard some women talking about the millions of dollars people spend on trying to look young and stay healthy. If you are trying to stay young and healthy, please read this: I believe Jesus has the answer for the people who want to stay young and have a youthful appearance. Jesus actually tells us how. Yes Jesus wants you young.

Please ask Jesus to come into your heart and you will watch compassion come into your life. You will see purpose that brings Joy and strength that is overpowering aging. You will truly be young at heart. You will see life more abundantly, you will not be doing things to fill up your day and you will not have enough time to get everything done. Your day will not be busy, but your day will have a purpose. You will have peace and you will know your life is pleasing to God and you will have rest. With Jesus in your heart life has meaning and no worries and the purpose of your life will become so real that sharing the love of Jesus will totally overcome all fear! I know because Jesus said His perfect love will cast out all fear. If you have fears of anything, try letting the love of Jesus in your heart and watch His perfect love kick out fear. The love of Jesus is that perfect!

For example, I met a woman that was working two jobs because she had a special needs child and she needed two incomes to pay the premium on an insurance policy that would provide for her son in the event she died. She was literally working herself to death trying to provide for her son. In doing so, she was taking on the responsibility of her son's wellbeing herself. She was totally living in fear and she was also missing the joy of being with her son. Please rest in the fact that Jesus said he will never leave you or forsake you. Jesus did not give that son to her to see her kill herself trying to provide for him. If she knew Jesus, she would know His love would see her through and in that love she could shine like the sun on a bright new morning. We can either be a vessel of Faith and love full of life with peace and Joy or be a worried, tired, exhausted, drugged, depressed, human being that is just barely hanging on. Choose Jesus and worry-free! Know that my Jesus loves you!

Can you imagine Jesus telling His Father, "I wish I had time to talk to you Dad, but I am working two jobs so I can provide for my son? I'll pray later if I am not too tired. Praise you Daddy, I love you daddy and by the way where are you when I needed you!" I don't think Jesus ever had a relationship with His Father like that and neither should we! If you can't think of words like that coming out of the Mouth of Jesus, it is because you recognize Jesus had a relationship with our Father and I hope and pray you have a relationship like that with our Father also.

Please just get up every day and ask Jesus what it is that He has for you to do today and I guarantee the two of you will have purpose and at the end of the day you will not need a sleeping pill. At the end of the day you will not need to put on beauty stuff because Jesus Himself will make you new with His love and that is pure JOY! Try to find that in a bottle of whatever.

Why do we go to church?

Do you realize Jesus never said for us to go to church to find Him? Jesus never went to church to find His Father.

John 8:28 Then Jesus said to them, "When you lift up the Son of Man, then you will know that I am *He*, and *that* I do nothing of Myself; *but as My Father taught Me, I speak these things.*

Jesus never went to the synagogue to learn; He went to teach what His Father taught Him and all that heard Him marveled at His wisdom. Jesus taught from the wisdom of His Father and He did so as Jesus the man. In John 8:28, we see Jesus was taught by His Father. Now by His Holy Spirit; Jesus and His Father will teach us all things!

I tell everyone to ask God into your life. Please ask God into every detail of your life. Jesus as a man said, "I do nothing of myself". I believe the words 'nothing of myself', would cover everything Jesus did. So Jesus asks His Father into everything He did! Jesus had a relationship with His Dad and so can we! We can do everything Jesus did by just asking Jesus into our life. Ask Jesus to teach you all things and He will!

The word 'church' is found in 79 verses in the New Testament and not once does the word church even remotely come close to referring to a building. The word church is not mentioned in the Old Testament. In all 79 versus the word church is referring to the people of God. I believe Jesus saw the people of the Old Testament go to the synagogue's to learn of Him. I believe Jesus came and literally became our teacher for all time. Jesus is our example and Jesus never once went to the synagogue to learn anything! The Bible is very clear: Jesus went to the synagogue to teach! Jesus himself said He went to the Father and as the Father taught Him so He speaks.

We too can go to the Father in the name of Jesus Christ. Jesus the man took time to listen to His father. We too must take time from our busy lifestyles to set down and listen for our Father's voice.

Jesus talked to His Father all the time. Jesus is our example of how to communicate with Him. Jesus never led anyone to a church building to find Him. We are to be like Jesus and live like Jesus and our example will make people want to be like Jesus. The apostles wanted the Joy they saw in Jesus. They wanted the love they saw in Jesus and Jesus gave it all to them not because they did something to deserve it but simply because he loves them. Jesus will give it all to you simply because He loves you! I want to add one more thought: I believe when I communicate with Jesus on a personal level I get the best results when I speak out loud. I believe when I talk out loud to my Jesus I hear best and I believe Jesus likes us to talk to Him out loud. You know speak boldly the word of Jesus!!! You will hear yourself proclaiming His word boldly even in your quiet time with Jesus.

Do you have an earthly desire to change the people of a congregation or are you spirit lead trying to change a church congregation? Some church splits are caused by well-meaning people trying to change the church leadership! Please be very careful if you feel you are being lead in that direction. I want you to consider the fact that every time I have seen a transformation in anyone, the transformation of that person was painless and the person actually wanted the transformation because of the love they saw in the person (Jesus' representative) bringing the changes. The

73

most powerful force on earth is the love of my Jesus and Jesus loves to flow His love through people like you and me. Just make yourself available to Jesus and watch transformations happen right before your eyes. Want proof?

2 Timothy 2:25 in humility correcting those who are in opposition, if God perhaps will grant them repentance, so that they may know the truth

Notice that we give instructions in meekness to those that oppose themselves. I believe those that oppose themselves are people that do not discern their thoughts and sometimes listen to the devil.

How do teach boldly and remain in meekness?

2 Timothy 2:22 Flee also youthful lusts; but pursue righteousness, faith, love, peace with those who call on the Lord out of a pure heart.

Again we see Jesus is our example to follow. We must flee our youthful lusts (earthly desires) and follow Jesus with boldness for the world to see and we teach in meekness as Jesus taught, righteousness, faith, charity, peace, and listen to the Lord with a pure heart. I believe these are the gifts of following Jesus! These gifts are not to be held on to but to give away! Jesus gave these gifts to everyone that would receive them and so can ourselves! These are the treasures that moths and rust will not destroy. Give them to your children as an inheritance!

2 Timothy 2:26 and *that* they may come to their senses and escape the snare of the devil, having been taken captive by him to do his will.

You see 'they may recover themselves out of the snare of the devil' you as a farmer for the Lord, will plant the seeds of righteousness, faith, charity, peace, and you will teach them how they themselves can listen to the voice of God and God will purify their heart. God brings the increase.

Just as the apostles gathered together from time to time, for a time of refreshment, we should go to a church building for fellowship with likeminded people. They should help us in our quest to live like Jesus. Together we should edify each other and encourage each other with testimonies. If the people in your church building are not like minded or are not seeking Jesus then thank God for sending you there. To gently show them Jesus and to give them the Joy of the Lord that flows out of you in abundance. We are to be the love of Jesus and the example of Jesus to everyone in the world and to everyone in the church building.

We do not go to believers or future believers to give sympathy to each other. Sympathy is the devils counter fit of God's compassion. Sympathy never raised anyone from the dead, sympathy never healed anyone, and sympathy never casts out a devil. Sympathy is actually giving people permission to be less than God created them to be! Sympathy will never lift someone out of the snare of the devil! Sympathy is an earthly desire to show you care but in reality it leaves the person in the same or worse shape than when we found them.

The compassion of Jesus healed, cast out devils and raised people from the dead. Compassion is love in its purest form. Compassion is Hope walking into the room. Compassion is knowledge of God living in your heart and it is giving the love of Jesus to everyone that will listen. Compassion is not an earthly desire; it is doing God's desire here on earth. Compassion comes from a pure heart and God's compassion brings life to all you give it too! Jesus was compassionate not sympathetic. We are His compassionate representatives here on the earth so get...

BOLDLY COMPASSIONATE

The apostles were not in a church building when Jesus called them. They were working. They were busy and had obligations but they saw something in Jesus that they did not see in the synagogue.

Jesus calls us the same way He called the apostles. When Jesus went to the synagogue, He brought His Father's knowledge with Him. He spoke and the high priests were amazed with His knowledge. We too can be amazing and we too can change people's lives, by listening to and for the voice of God in our heart and we change lives by letting Jesus humbly flow through us. We change in our hearts by simply letting Jesus teach us all things. We use our brain to figure out who we are listening to *(discernment)*.

Discernment is a tool from God that we must exercise continually. Jesus said take every thought captive to the obedience of His word.

> **2 Corinthians 10:5** Casting down arguments and every high thing that exalts itself against the knowledge of God, bringing every thought into captivity to the obedience of Christ

Casting down imaginations is taking every thought captive. All sin starts with thoughts. No one has ever done anything without thinking about it first. Sometimes, a simple picture or a glance at a person can lead someone into a sin of lust. Television is an amazing tool to create earthly desires. It uses two of our senses, eyes and ears at the same time. Television is a very dangerous thing to watch.

And bringing into captivity every thought to the obedience of Christ. To do this we must have a relationship with Jesus. I personally cannot watch television because the thoughts come so fast that I cannot discern them, so I simply choose not to watch it. I believe we must make choices. Do we let our earthly desires dictate our life or do we let the desires of Jesus dictate our life?

If I am doing anything that brings thoughts to me too fast for me to decide what I am thinking in my heart, I simply will not listen or watch. Does the thought of bringing earthly desires such as wanting to make myself happy or satisfied or does the thought bring peace, Joy of the Lord, glory to God, or shame, guilt, condemnation? Discerning of our thoughts is so important. Discernment is one of the biggest and most important weapons we have in our battle of earthly desires. Please ask Jesus to help you discover the intimate relationship you can have with Him. Jesus will teach you how to discern your thoughts if you make a conscious decision to turn away from wanting to be entertained, to a yearning for Him! Jesus said to seek Him with all your heart and mind and spirit.

Discerning our thoughts can sometimes be manipulated by our motive. I met a man that wanted to start his own church. His motive might have been pure and there might have been a real need in the area he lived in. When he asked my opinion, I simply said, "If you heard from the Lord then go for it." I know Jesus has told me change one heart a time and that is what I do. I know I heard from my Jesus so I don't need a second opinion.

Please never try to change anything in church or church leadership on your own strength. If you become a willing vessel for the love of Jesus to flow through, you will walk out of the church after the service and know you made a difference. If you humbly and patiently be an example of the love of Jesus, after a while the church leadership will come to you and ask you to be with them in their meetings, and they will want your opinion. When that happens you will know it is nothing you said that brought them to you but it is the love of Jesus flowing through you and it is now time to share the love of Jesus and share what God has shared with you. Remember Jesus called the apostles and they humbly waited until Jesus told them to go preach the gospel to the world.

If you continue to give yourself to the Lord and wait for His prompting the church leadership will be willing and eager to listen. On the other hand if you are trying to change your church and they are not listening, the problem could be you are not waiting on the Lord. You might even step out and try to start your own church with this new knowledge you have. I really do not think America needs another church, America needs more Jesus and if you just let the Jesus in you flow out of you; the world will see Christianity differently. The church will see the difference in you and your example of letting the love of Jesus flow through you will help all people everywhere to experience the love of Jesus! If you want a beautiful America again, change one heart at a time to the love of Jesus Christ by being the Love of Jesus to everyone.

Jesus has told me to change one heart at a time. In doing so, we will be able to flow the love and joy of the Lord to the world and we will be beautifully giving the love and the Joy of the Lord to everyone everywhere!

Our source of knowledge is Jesus and our focus has to be Jesus. When we focus on Jesus we see life through His eyes and feel with His heart. People will actually see Jesus in you and you can portray Jesus by living like Jesus and you might not even need to speak a word. Now that is a life, like the life Jesus portrayed to the world! It is a life that is filled with purpose and Joy and strength and most of all love. If you think the churches are filled with hypocrites; it might be because you are not letting the love of Jesus flow through you and into them! You know the hypocrites need love also, so let us pray for them to come to know Jesus on a personal level.

John 14:23 Jesus answered and said to him, "If anyone loves Me, he will keep My word; and My Father will love him, *and We will come to him and make Our home with him.*

We worship Jesus by being like Jesus. We love Jesus by keeping His word. How do we love Jesus? *'If a man love me he will keep my words'* – we keep the words of Jesus in our heart because Jesus said from the heart a man speaks. The words of Jesus are also the commands of Jesus, so we are keeping His commands by living like Jesus lived. Jesus did not break any commands of His Father. In fact Jesus said to can keep all the commands of His Father by being the love of His Father to all we meet. When you know your Father loves you and you are absolutely sure He loves you, sins of hate, unforgiveness, envy and jealousy, and lusts will be removed along with thoughts of the past because the love of Jesus will overwhelm you and thoughts of the bright future you have with Him will overtake you! The love of Jesus is that strong. Jesus proved it by going to the cross first.

Can you imagine going to the bank for a thirty year loan on a house and after the banker hands you your check for the amount of the loan, saying here is a receipt marked paid in full? You look at him and say, "What is this?" He says, "I just want you to know I trust you" to which you say, "I don't believe this!" Do you realize that is what Jesus did for our life? He handed us a lifelong receipt, marked paid-in-full. I trust you to live up to your end of the New Covenant and if you miss a payment, I have grace for you. In fact my love for you will be new every day! Please try to understand this love of Jesus has for your heart by letting Jesus in your heart and then watch Jesus take away worry, stress, condemnation and guilt and replace them with Peace, Love, Joy and Strength! The best part is there is no strings attached, no fine print, and no payment books, just the love of my Jesus who wants to be your Jesus, so let Him!!! Don't worry, He is MY Jesus but I am into sharing!

How do we get the word of God in our heart? Read on and you will see. We simply ask Jesus into our heart. Jesus is the word. "If a man love me he will keep my words." Jesus and Father God Himself will come into your heart if you ask them! Do you see that in the Scripture *and we will come to him*. Just think Jesus and Father God will make their abode in us.

Please focus on Jesus being in your heart. Focus on Him being in every situation because He is in every situation. Loving God and receiving God into our hearts is more important than how big your house is and how many cars are sitting in your driveway. I make that comparison because I know how hard I used to work to have a house and cars. If I would have spent half that many hours seeking the Lord my heart would so full of the Joy of the Lord I could not contain the Joy. Having the Father and the Son make their abode with me is very important to God and if it is important to God I would be a fool if I did not make it important to me. Please make hearing and discerning the voice of God your highest priority.

Here is a situation that came up:

When you lay down your desire for earthly desires, and as people realize how different your life is and as they see the joy in your heart, you may get challenged from time to time. Don't worry, you have the Creator of the universe on your side. Sometimes we are challenged by people who quote half a scripture. For example, the other day someone said, "Jesus said anything you ask in my name I will do it for you, right?" I said, "Right". The man then said, "Ask your God to give me a million dollars." I said no. Then he became so proud of himself and said, "Is your God a liar?" I said, "Let us look at the word of God and I will prove my Jesus is a God of His Word."

> **John 14:13-15** And whatever you ask in My name, that I will do, that the Father may be glorified in the Son. 14 If you ask anything in My name, I will do it. "If you love Me, keep My commandments.

As you can see John 14:13 clarifies John 14:14. Just giving away a million dollars – which is an earthly desire – is not going to glorify the Father in the Son. I didn't even get a chance to ask him if he was keeping the commandments. As you can see, if someone is trying to trip you up or they have laid a trap for you, don't worry. The Holy Spirit will tell you the truth and the Holy Spirit ever so gently will lead you to the knowledge to help the person understand how they quoted the scripture incorrectly.

Generally speaking, Jesus probably will not be glorified by giving you a million dollars, but I do know of people that have asked for a million and received a million dollars. Jesus gave Pastor Sumrall a million dollars because the pastor was being obedient to the wishes of the Father and keeping the commandments. You see Jesus had asked Pastor Sumrall to buy something and it cost 1 million dollars. It took a lot of faith for Pastor Sumrall to put his name on a contract saying he would have one million dollars in 30 days. It was humanly impossible and Pastor Sumrall had never done anything like that before but 30 days later he had the money. Only Jesus could make it happen and it took a lot faith for Pastor Sumrall to trust God.

I pray I never lose focus of my Jesus and what He needs done. I believe on Judgment day what we have done to glorify the Father in the name of the Son is going to be important! I pray to my Jesus I will always see how important keeping the commandments are to pleasing Jesus. I pray to never be distracted by an earthly desire! I pray for a desire to always seek Jesus and keep His words so the Father will love me for who I am. You see at the end of the day I have peace knowing my Jesus loves me and there is nothing else I need.

I think I need to say this again!

John 14:23 Jesus answered and said to him, "If anyone loves Me, he will keep My word; and My Father will love him, and We will come to him and make Our home with him.

Then Jesus went on to say, "And my Father will love him and *we* will come to him, and make our abode with him." Isn't that too cool? I mean I have Jesus and Father God living in me. I have the mind of Jesus and the heart of Jesus and I see as Jesus sees. You cannot earn these gifts, you cannot work to deserve them and you cannot clean yourself up to get ready for them but you can have them just for believing the word of Jesus. You see, to believe Jesus is to love Jesus and to love Jesus you must trust Him literally with all your heart.

Jesus is calling us into an intimate relationship with Him and our Heavenly Father! Just simply believe the pure heart of Jesus, the pure mind of Jesus and the pure eyes of Jesus are ours for the asking and believing Jesus will honor His word. I believe when we put aside our earthly desires and we open our heart and mind to receive the image and likeness of Jesus we will receive them! To put aside earthly desires read your Bible and believe in your heart the words are true. I get a little upset when I hear people say they are in search of truth and for Jesus very plainly said to seek Him and in doing so we have truth. Your desire to hear from the Lord should be so strong that you will put all your earthly desires aside and follow Him. In doing so I know you will have more Joy in your heart then you have ever experienced from any earthly desire.

John 8:32 And you shall know the truth, and the truth shall make you free.

How do we know truth? What is truth? Who is truth? Does truth have a name?

John 14:6 Jesus said to him, "I am the way, the truth, and the life. No one comes to the Father except through Me.

The truth is Jesus! The name of truth is Jesus! The only truth in the world is in the word and person of Jesus Christ of Nazareth! We are to seek Jesus and truth is a byproduct!

Matthew 6:33 But seek first the kingdom of God and His righteousness, and all these things shall be added to you.

Seek you first the kingdom of God! Not truth. When you seek the truth you will be led astray because the only way for us to judge truth is by our own knowledge. When you seek the kingdom of God who is truth, you will automatically be in truth. God – who cannot lie, is one hundred percent Godly truth. There is no earthly desire that can satisfy like being loved by someone that cannot lie, and says I will never leave you or forsake you! That is the truth and Jesus said it so I believe it!

If you have a desire to be loved in ways that bring true hope and peace that the world cannot understand? Then try a relationship with intimacy and the true love from God.

I can tell you how to know if you are in an intimate relationship with God. It is when you do not let the circumstances of the world dictate your joy or lack of it. If you are looking for the approval of man, if you need compliments from fellow humans, if you are looking for a status symbol to fulfill your life, you literally have not gotten the truth of Jesus in your heart.

You can be the best missionary or the best pastor in the world and receive all the complements in the world; yet they do not make you happy! The problem is you do not know how much God loves you!

Please ask God to help you realize that only the love of Jesus can get you past all the earthly desires of being famous, smart, rich, popular, or even being a good mother or father, parent, pastor, Christian, or any other earthly desire you might be striving for. Lay them all down and just seek to be the representative of Jesus and you will have the Joy of the Lord, the peace of the Lord flowing through you and true joy and strength of Jesus!

I pray for anyone who reads this to come into agreement with the word of God that says we are actually predestinated to be in the image of His Son. In the Bible, the firstborn of any family had special rights and was handed the family inheritance. Now we can all be the firstborn in the kingdom of God. Our inheritance is bought and paid for with the prepaid promissory note in our hand.

> **Romans 8:29** For whom He foreknew, He also predestined *to be* conformed to the image of His Son, that He might be the firstborn among many brethren.

Please spend time listening to my Jesus and learning to discern His voice. You will not regret it, in fact you will love it. My Jesus loves me and I know it! My Jesus loves you and I pray you know it.

May the peace and Joy of the Lord be your strength as He is mine and may you call on the name of the Lord, walk with the Lord and live the life Jesus came to show us? Joy and peace really do exist, just trust in MY JESUS!

Jenny, Ron and my best friend Jesus!

Faith

What is faith? Where does faith come from? Faith is mentioned in 231 verses in the Bible. Only two times in the Old Testament is the word faith used and yet 229 times in the New Testament. I believe Jesus came to show us faith and to demonstrate faith. Jesus is walking and talking in faith. Jesus is our example of how to live a God pleasing life here on earth, so how can faith be so misunderstood? There has to be an answer to the question 'What is faith?'

Hebrews 11:1 Now faith is the substance of things hoped for, the evidence of things not seen.

Hebrews 11:6 But without faith *it is* impossible to please *Him*, for he who comes to God must believe *that* He is, and that He is a rewarder of those who diligently seek Him.

Could faith be a spirit? Is a spirit a substance? Let us look at what Paul said in Ephesians about faith:

Ephesians 3:9-21 And to make all see what is the fellowship of the mystery, which from the beginning of the ages has been hidden in God who created all things through Jesus Christ; to the intent that now the manifold wisdom of God might be made known by the church to the principalities and powers in the heavenly places, according to the eternal purpose which He accomplished in Christ Jesus our Lord, in whom we have boldness and access with confidence through faith in Him. Therefore I ask that you do not lose heart at my tribulations for you, which is your glory. For this reason I bow my knees to the Father of our Lord Jesus Christ, from whom the whole family in heaven and earth is named, that He would grant you, according to the riches of His glory, to be strengthened with might through His Spirit in the inner man, that Christ may dwell in your hearts through faith; that you, being rooted and grounded in love, may be able to comprehend with all the saints what is the width and length and depth and height— to know the love of Christ which passes knowledge; that you may be filled with all the fullness of God. Now to Him who is able to do exceedingly abundantly above all that we ask or think, according to the power that works in us, to Him be glory in the church by Christ Jesus to all generations, forever and ever. Amen.

Ephesians 3:12 *in whom we have boldness and access with confidence through faith in Him.*

Here we see some of the substance of faith. By faith in Jesus, we gain boldness to proclaim His Word to every nation, and by faith we gain access to God. Through faith, we can have relationship to God the Father through Jesus by faith. Faith is a substance and the substance is a desire to know God or a desire for knowledge of God in your heart not just head knowledge. Faith is the substance gained by knowing God intimately!

If you like a sport, you want to know all the names of the people that are on the team you like. You will read and study the status of that team. Then you will proclaim that knowledge to everyone boldly. You will receive self-esteem in return for your knowledge. People will raise you up to others, "He is an expert on the Cincinnati Reds ask him anything about the Reds and he can tell you." Self-esteem brings you momentary happiness, momentary pride, the kind of pride that puffs you up. Self-esteem gives you self-worth as long as the people you hang with are interested in the sport you like. Actually, self-esteem will limit you to seek friends you can impress. I know a man that had a nice boat. Someone asks have you ever gone to the lake so and so. He said yes but I won't go back because everyone there has a bigger boat then mine. He said I only go to the lakes where I have the biggest boat. You see there is a substance gained through knowledge and the substance gained is not always a good substance.

Unlike Godly knowledge that brings Glory to God, earthly knowledge brings self-esteem. Self-esteem brings on a desire for more self-esteem and it never ends. Self-esteem is a devil that steals your time and limits you to where you go and the people you meet. Building self-esteem robs you of time that could have been used to learn about God and how to bring Glory to God. Self-esteem steals your heavenly reward and the Joy of knowing the Creator of the universe. Unlike momentary happiness of self-esteem; faith brings the everlasting substance of Joy!

Ephesians 3:17 That Christ may dwell in your hearts through faith; that you, being rooted and grounded in love

Now we know that faith is a substance and we receive it through love. I think we can all agree that love is a spirit. Knowledge is a spirit that brings a desire to know Jesus, but like everything else in life, the devil has a counter fete spirit of knowledge that brings self-esteem. The devil has a counterfeit to the spirit of love which is called lust. The difference is God's spirits bring glory to God and a lifelong everlasting relationship with God to us.

Galatians 5:22-23 But the fruit of the Spirit is love, joy, peace, longsuffering, kindness, goodness, faithfulness, gentleness, self-control. Against such there is no law.

These are gifts which money cannot buy! These gifts cannot be achieved! God gives these gifts freely and they are meant to flow through us, not just to us. But the only way to receive them is by faith. You have to believe that God freely gives them to you and you must believe they are meant for you! You cannot earn them! You cannot be good enough to deserve them they are free gifts from God. When I hear people talk about financial blessings I cringe. I mean if God had a list of the top 100 gifts He has for us, money would not even make the list! Please read Galatians 5:22-23 again and realize they are all about the peace and joy and love! We can give these gifts to others to bring Glory to our God. They are easily seen in us and will enable us to shine the light of God everywhere and to everyone! I believe money does not bring glory to God or if it does the gift of money is momentary like happiness and does not truly fill a void in our life.

Galatians 5:24 And those who are Christ's have crucified the flesh with its passions and desires.

When you surrender your life to God you are saying I will walk and talk in the faith of God. God's gifts "the fruits of the spirit" will give you power and enable you to crucify the flesh "the devil" with his affections and lusts. Just think for a moment; about what life would be like if we just stopped seeking material junk and just spent our time seeking God. I guarantee you Joy beyond your understanding because God promised us Joy beyond our understanding. Just believe!

Galatians 5:25 If we live in the Spirit, let us also walk in the Spirit.

Living in the spirit and walking in the spirit is more Joy than humanly possible. Just believe!!!

Galatians 5:26 Let us not become conceited, provoking one another, envying one another.

Today, Galatians 5:26 would read let us not be desirous of self-esteem, putting down someone else to make us look good and envying each other's possessions, wanting a bigger boat, or house, or camper and the list goes on!

For me, vain glory, provoking one another, and envying one another are all gifts from the devil that give you self-esteem! They require no faith. In fact they destroy faith and they steal from you! They will kill your desire to love one another by giving you self-esteem and this self-esteem will destroy the gifts or fruits of the spirit of God.

We all know when we desire to truly love one, our love for them will continue to grow forever and we continue to seek the person we fell in love with. I believe when we allow the spirit of faith into our heart; faith will grow forever; as long as we seek

God, the giver of faith! We have all seen people fall in love and out of love. Faith is the same way. I know I have had great faith in God and then something started chipping away at my faith and caused me to doubt. The apostles did the same thing and they ask Jesus.

> **Luke 17:5-6** And the apostles said to the Lord, "Increase our faith." So the Lord said, "If you have faith as a mustard seed, you can say to this mulberry tree, 'Be pulled up by the roots and be planted in the sea,' and it would obey you.

The sycamore tree was a very big, tough and strong tree. So with the apostles, that would seem impossible. Yet by faith, Jesus tells them it can be done! Jesus was showing them the power we have with faith in a relationship with Jesus. Jesus then goes on to tell the apostles how to get more faith.

> **Luke 17:7-10** And which of you, having a servant plowing or tending sheep, will say to him when he has come in from the field, 'Come at once and sit down to eat'? But will he not rather say to him, 'Prepare something for my supper, and gird yourself and serve me till I have eaten and drunk, and afterward you will eat and drink'? Does he thank that servant because he did the things that were commanded him? I think not. So likewise you, when you have done all those things which you are commanded, say, 'We are unprofitable servants. We have done what was our duty to do.'"

Here, Jesus is telling the apostles if you have a servant that works for you all day, do you reward him by fixing him dinner, or do you tell him to fix your dinner and do you thank him for doing the things he is told to do? I think not. So when you have just done all the things you are commanded to do, you will not even be thank, in fact Jesus calls you unprofitable servants.

I believe Jesus is talking about the law that is if we continue to keep the physical laws of the Old Testament we will not even be thanked. You see keeping the laws of the Old Testament does not build faith and will not build the kingdom of God. It just keeps us busy trying to please God by showing him how we can obey, you still spend your time trying to remember every law and then have endless debate of how to keep the law. Jesus plainly said without faith it is impossible to please Him. You cannot make God love you more, God's love for you is so complete that there is nothing you can do to can make Him love you more. BUT you can please God by seeking relationship with Him. Just believing you can have a relationship with Him takes more faith then keeping all the laws perfectly if were possible.

In America, you can keep all the driving laws perfectly for years and years and one day you miss a stop sign and you get a ticket because you broke the law and now you are a law breaker! The law doesn't care about all the years you stopped at the stop sign in fact the law doesn't have a name of the person that keeps the law but it sure has a name for you when you miss the stop sign one time. Maybe you are just an unprofitable servant!

Jesus came to reap sons and daughters that serve Him in love and faith through relationship with Him. Jesus shows us faith in Him is more important than just serving Him as servants. Servants just keep the laws of the master whereas the Sons of God will go out and keep the spirit of the law but also bring glory to God by spreading the good news and the truth of Jesus! Sons will think and act like Jesus. Being Son is faith that Jesus is real and faith pleases God. Jesus said without faith it is impossible to please Him.

Hebrews 11:6 But without faith it is impossible to please Him, for he who comes to God must believe that He is, and that He is a rewarder of those who diligently seek Him.

By faith, you will know Jesus will love on you and bless you with more knowledge. Godly knowledge will build the kingdom of God to earth and bring Glory to God! Godly knowledge brings love and Joy, Peace and Rest to all that seek relationship to Him. Faith is the substance of belief. Faith is waking up every day excited to see how God himself will flow through you. Yes it takes faith to believe the Holy Spirit of God dwells in you and by faith I know I am pleasing to my Father. I know by faith I cannot make God love me more but by faith I believe I am His favorite!

You can serve him by keeping his laws if you want but I want to be the Son that he is proud of. I want to be the one that if I stray Jesus will leave the 99 and go get me because I'm His favorite! I believe by faith that I am his favorite and so I believe there is nothing I cannot do! Do you see how believing builds faith and faith pleases God, you better believe I will walk and talk and please my Jesus by faith today. By faith I will keep all the commandments and by faith I know that if I miss one stop sign *(sin)* I am not labeled a law breaker in God's eyes because I will repent and I will and I am still a son of God! And instead of paying fines, I will have Jesus picking me up into His loving arms and He will dust me off and say stay with me and Jesus will show you the narrow path. I will hear the words, I love you son! By faith I am forgiven!

Being servants takes no faith and being unprofitable to God is not a good place to be. It kind of sounds like servants that just keep the laws out of fear might be servants in heaven. For when they come in out the field they will have to fix dinner for the master. I ask you: if I keep the law and don't eat pork how does that build the kingdom of God and bring glory to God?

Jesus said by faith we will do bigger and better things then He did.

1 Corinthians 12:7-13 But the manifestation of the Spirit is given to each one for the profit of all: for to one is given the word of wisdom through the Spirit, to another the word of knowledge through the same Spirit, to another faith by the same Spirit, to another gifts of healings by the same Spirit, to another the working of miracles, to another prophecy, to another discerning of spirits, to another different kinds of tongues, to another the interpretation of tongues. But one and the same Spirit works all these things, distributing to each one individually as He wills. For as the body is one and has many members, but all the members of that one body, being many, are one body, so also is Christ. For by one Spirit we were all baptized into one body—whether Jews or Greeks, whether slaves or free—and have all been made to drink into one Spirit.

Notice the words ONE SPIRIT or SAME SPIRIT, throughout these Scriptures. Faith is a spirit of believing in Jesus. Without the spirit of faith we are as unprofitable servants, but with the spirit of faith we are SONS OF FATHER GOD. For by one spirit we are baptized into one body! When Jesus was baptized; Father God said with a loud voice from Heaven.

> **Matthew 3:16-17** When He had been baptized, Jesus came up immediately from the water; and behold, the heavens were opened to Him, and He saw the Spirit of God descending like a dove and alighting upon Him. And suddenly a voice came from heaven, saying, "This is My beloved Son, in whom I am well pleased."

We receive the same spirit of faith and we can hear in our spirit the words of God THIS IS MY BELOVED SON IN WHOM I AM WELL PLEASED. Don't wake up just trying to please God by keeping some law! Wake up in Faith knowing you are His beloved Son in whom He is well pleased! Yes, Jesus came to forgive us our sins but Jesus did so much more! In so many churches I've been in the message is Jesus came to forgive our sins and that forgiveness is a bus ticket to heaven, just do works of kindness and bring the sick a bowl of soup. Please look beyond the bus ticket and look what Jesus really did! By the spirit of faith I am a Son of God and a brother of Jesus! By the spirit of faith that works in me I can do all things and in that revelation knowledge I *do all things!* By the spirit of faith, I heal the sick, I raise the dead, I control the weather, I cast out demons... Anywhere in the Bible you read Jesus did something, put your name there. Ron raised Lazarus from the dead. Now that takes faith and that faith pleases God so go do some God pleasing today. Jesus came to show us faith. In Romans, Paul said anything that is not faith is sin.

> **Romans 14:23** But he who doubts is condemned if he eats, because he does not eat from faith; for whatever is not from faith is sin.

In chapter 14, Paul was showing us how to live in peace with our brother. Paul tells us not to Judge or we will be judged by our own standard. Paul ends Chapter 14 by telling us if we doubt we are damned for not living in faith and whatsoever is not of faith is SIN!

I believe that in chapter 14, we learn not to judge and not to offend our brothers in Christ. I believe that in chapter 14, we learn what true love looks like. I believe faith is love in Jesus Christ of Nazareth. That is why faith is so hard to explain. Faith is love and like love, it is so hard to explain. Jesus said there is no greater love than this that he lay down his life for another.

> **John 15:13** Greater love has no one than this, than to lay down one's life for his friends.

If you want to know what faith is, replace the word love with the word faith in John 15:13. You see, it is love for your brethren to lay down your life for them but it also takes faith in the love of Jesus to believe enough to lay down your life for another. Jesus gives us the reason to lay down our life. If I were a non-believer I would not have the reason to lay down my life for another because this life is all there is to a non-believer. I would not have faith that Jesus conquered death and I would not have love for Jesus. Faith in Jesus changes everything. Because of my love for my Jenny, I believe her words of love for me are true. I have faith that Jenny would never cheat on me or better put Jenny would never sin against our vowels. Because of my love for Jesus I have faith that every word of the Bible is true.

> **Hebrews 11:6** But without faith it is impossible to please Him, for he who comes to God must believe that He is, and that He is a rewarder of those who diligently seek Him.

Without faith it is impossible to please him. I think Jesus explained to us what faith is by how He lived. Jesus came to show us the Father is love and that Jesus and the Father are one in love. In love, I am one with Jenny and Jenny is one with me. Love is powerless to make us one with each other without faith. Without faith love disappears like the wind.

Faith is a spirit of love!

As newlyweds, if I *thought* Jenny had cheated on me in our marriage, my faith in her would have been broken. So is our faith or love in God. Our love for God is very fragile at first. Knew that faith that is only in our love of God can be very weak. Faith like love starts with a desire to know someone or to know God.

Jenny and I took our marriage vows to each other very seriously. In the beginning, just a *thought* could break my faith in our vows. Jenny and I had to prove our love to each other over the years and in doing so our love grew for each other until our new for a fact we were in love. When you know that you know your love is true, love changes into complete trust! Now if someone came to me and said Jenny was cheating on me and I would not believe it, I would not even entertain the *thought!* I believe that love will become trust at some point. As love grows, it actually becomes trust. I have trust that Jenny would never cheat on me and in the beginning my trust was very fragile and just a *thought* could break my trust. But as the years go on my trust in our love and our devotion to each other grew into knowing Jenny's heart was pure and Jenny knows my heart was pure.

Faith is a spirit of pure love and pure trust in God.

Our love for each other was still growing and that growth brought us to a place where we would expect each other to do what we said. Our words have meaning and for love to grow we need to mean what we say. I knew for a fact if Jenny said she would do something that something would happen. I had absolutely no doubt. Jenny's words were true, whatsoever she said I could believe in and therefore I could love and trust in the pureness of her heart. Yes I could trust Jenny's heart because Jesus said out of the heart a man speaks.

Faith is pure love and pure trust in the word of God with full expectance that what God said is true and will come to pass.

All of that adds up to an expectance of knowing God as someone with a pure heart, someone I can trust and love forever. God is someone who means what He says so you can expect Jesus to do what He said. That is how God explained faith to me. You see, new love can be broken by a thought but love that has grown into trust and into Faith will not be broken from just a *thought.*

Faith will not be broken! Faith is real love! Faith is real trust! Faith is pure and with faith in God we must come to Him expecting Him to perform to His word. Speak the word of God out of your heart and Jesus promised it will not return void but it shall accomplish that which will please Jesus and we will prosper.

> **Isaiah 55:11** So shall My word be that goes forth from My mouth; It shall not return to Me void, But it shall accomplish what I please, And it shall prosper in the thing for which I sent it.

The words Jesus spoke have all come true. Jesus spoke the words light be and we have had the sun shining forever, Jesus spoke the world into existence. Have you ever thought what would happen if Jesus just kept these thoughts in His head but never spoke them? The sun, the moon and the earth would not exist! I don't know about man because Jesus never spoke us into existence. In Genesis, it says that Jesus formed us out of dust and then breathed life into us.

> **Genesis 2:7** And the Lord God formed man of the dust of the ground, and breathed into his nostrils the breath of life; and man became a living being.

One more thing to think about: Jesus told Adam not to eat the fruit of the tree of good and evil or he will surely die. When Adam ate the forbidden fruit, death entered the earth and mankind but Adam did not die physically. His relationship to God died. Jesus came every day in the cool of the evening to talk to Adam, but after Adam ate of the tree of good and evil Jesus stopped coming. So the relationship with Jesus is what died! Now Father God wanted to restore that relationship and did so by sending His only Son. You may not believe that but I do. By Faith I believe!!!

Father sent his only Son Jesus! In doing so, look what He reaped. More sons conquered death, true forgiveness for sins, He defeated the devil, and most important of all He gave us a new life! A life of communication with Him. He gave us an example to follow and freedom from sickness, devil position and death. Jesus brought Heaven to earth and we can walk in it all by FAITH!

Some people ask me if I have faith then why Jenny is not healed. I have people tell me I *must receive* the healing and I think I understand what they are saying. I think if it was just receiving God's healing, then healing would require no faith. I know there are examples in the Bible where Jesus just gave people healing and they had no faith but they did receive their healing. I don't want to play down receiving healing because I believe for me it would be hard to get healed if I do not receive it. Jesus always seemed amazed at people that through faith expected healing. Like the lady that spoke the words out loud if I could just touch His garment I will be healed. She went and touched his garment and God the Father flowed through Jesus into her by faith in that touch and she was instantly healed. Jesus did not even talk to her nor did He know who it was that touched Him for healing. That is faith and faith is expecting! So when you pray, expect God to honor His word. God does and always will honor His word. I know for we have His Word on it!

Faith in God is like marriage here on earth. We start to know Him and we fall in love with Him. By faith, we start to realize He is real. As Jesus becomes real to us, we start to seek Him for relationship. Our relationship to Him will turn into love and love will turn into trust and trust will turn into faith and with faith we can expect God to flow through us all the time.

Another aspect of Faith is hearing a word from God.

Romans 10:17 So then faith comes by hearing, and hearing by the word of God.

If you look at Paul's writing in chapter 10, he is talking about preachers teaching the word of God. The preachers teach by talking and you learn by hearing, but faith or believing comes by hearing a word from Jesus himself in your heart. Some call it a word of knowledge for someone they just met. For example I met a family the other day. They were sitting at a picket table as I approached them. We started talking about God and God prompted me to ask their ten-year-old son if he had pain in his body. He looked surprised and said yes I have pain in my foot and I cannot walk without pain. That was a word of knowledge from

God, sometimes the word from God is general like that and sometimes it is very specific. P.S. God did heal that boy's foot that night and it was really awesome to watch him run and play without pain! When your relationship with God grows you will hear from Him all the time. I have asked God "where are my car keys?" and I hear him say, "They are in the trunk lid where you left them." Faith comes by hearing and hearing by a word from God.

Galatians 3:2 This only I want to learn from you: Did you receive the Spirit by the works of the law, or by the hearing of faith?

How do you build the kingdom of God? Do you build a kingdom by keeping the laws of the Old Testament, say not eating pork or worrying about who can do the burnt sacrifice? Or do you build the kingdom of God by doing what Jesus did and by doing what He sent His apostles out to do, "Heal the sick, raise the dead, cast out demons and preach the word boldly, by the hearing of faith!" That is how we RECEIVE you THE SPIRIT!!!

Galatians 3:5 Therefore He who supplies the Spirit to you and works miracles among you, does *He do it* by the works of the law, or by the hearing of faith?

I know it is by the HEARING OF FAITH. Can you prove your love by taking your wife out to eat every day? Or could that be telling her you do not like her cooking. Or do you prove you love her by listing and responding to her needs? Both are works and both require some of your time, but one is building a relationship. One is more loving because you are HEARING HER and BY FAITH she is expecting a response. The reward is the joy of love in both your hearts.

I love to go out and find people to pray for. There are so many people who need God's love, you won't have to look too long. Some of them are healed right away and some later. When I get a word from God about the person I have targeted I get excited and I look out for God is on the move and their hearts will be changed. When Jesus brings people to me for prayer I really get excited because I know He wants them to experience His love.

Most of the time, they have already prayed for before so the seeds of healing are already in place. It is a gift from God to witness the awesome power of God and it is a privilege to get to pray for people and watch God bring the increase. We just have to be willing to do the work of the kingdom that is we must stop what seems important to us and be available to God. If however, you are trying to keep the laws of the Old Testament, you will probably be too busy interrupting the laws to do the work of the kingdom! If you live in the New Testament, you will find that doing God's work is pure Joy and more fun and more satisfying than anything you can think of that brings happiness, for happiness is momentary and Joy is everlasting!

Jesus said faith without works is dead.

James 2:14-20 What does it profit, my brethren, if someone says he has faith but does not have works? Can faith save him? If a brother or sister is naked and destitute of daily food, and one of you says to them, "Depart in peace, be warmed and filled," but you do not give them the things which are needed for the body, what does it profit? Thus also faith by itself, if it does not have works, is dead. But someone will say, "You have faith, and I have works." Show me your faith without your[a] works, and I will show you my faith by my works. You believe that there is one God. You do well. Even the demons believe—and tremble! But do you want to know, O foolish man, that faith without works is dead?

In James 2:14, I believe the scriptures are saying that we can talk about faith all day but until we prove our faith by action it is dead. You prove your faith like Jesus did by acting on it. You can say I believe in healing but until you go out and command healing into some one, your faith is dead, and you cannot save him!

In James 2:15-16, for an example, you can walk by a baby crying in a crib and you say I love you but if you don't change his dirty, stinky diaper you have not shown him love. What does your love profit the baby?

In James 2:17, in other words if your faith is inside you and never comes forth to change your world then it is dead. It would be like Jesus only thinking, I would like to make a new world and call it earth but never speaking the words, there would not be an earth. If faith is just in your mind it will never help anyone!

In James 2:18, until we speak our faith into action and command it to work nothing will happen

In James 2:19, if you just say you believe in God but never give voice to your belief; you are no different than a devil except they at least tremble at the thought of God.

In James 2:20, you are a vain man if you put your pride above the works of faith. If you say I will not speak my faith because someone might think I am nuts, if the miracle doesn't happen. If every miracle I commanded to happen; happened what faith would I need to continue?

Faith without works is DEAD! We must get out there and command Satan to go away and command healing to come. We must raise people from the dead, but most of all we must have faith in the name of Jesus to preach the gospel to all the nations. Jesus said faith comes by hearing and if we are to busy to listen we will not hear!

My faith tells me I can raise the dead and heal the sick and cast out devils and do all the things I read in the Bible and my faith also tells me I am my Father's favorite! If you meet someone that does not walk with the Lord, you can first pray that God calls them into the relationship and that God allows you to demon straight the love of God to them and to give them the heart of God and then by faith; you will know they will be saved. My faith tells me that by being the love of God on the earth now I will hear the words 'job well done my faithful son that served'. I love my Jesus so much; I don't need self-esteem; I don't need diplomas, I don't need people to tell me how great I am, I have a relationship with my Father and my Brother and that is all I need! I simply believe and I simply love my Jesus and this belief simply opens the door to relationship and trust! Thank you Jesus and I love you too!

So what is faith? Faith simply put is knowing God loves me and because I know He loves me I can continue on and do the work of His kingdom. I am not a denomination. I am not a religion. I simply believe! I simply trust in My Jesus and I let Jesus light my path!

I live a simple life and I am in peace knowing that God has called me.

The love of Jesus and my Father be with you all. Please don't worry about being Father's favorite, I have that covered!

Jenny, Ron and Jesus love you!

Thank you Jesus for faith and I love you too!

Fat and Ugly

The other day while visiting some friends, I was asked to go to a Bible study. After arriving and meeting the other people there, we started talking about God when a lady came to the door and I'll call her Pam. Pam was invited in and she was crying and pretty broken up. Apparently, she came to the Bible study crying before. She was in her forty's and was divorced for a number of years. Her boyfriend had called her fat and ugly and she was also having problems with her disrespectful teenage children. Everyone started consoling her and I could tell by the jest of comments that they had pretty much written her boyfriend off, as a not-so-good influence for Pam. In a little while Pam calmed and as she looked around the room and apologized for interrupting and said, "I am sorry, but he is the only boyfriend I have." As they consoled her, I sat and ask my Jesus what He wanted to say to her.

Then our eyes met and she looked surprised to see me. She asked me if I was the guy whom she met in Bob Evans Restaurant and prayed for her about a week or so ago. I said yes. She asks me if I would pray for her again. I assured I would but I need to ask you some questions first. She agreed and so I asked her, "What would you say if I called you fat and ugly?" Her mouth dropped open and so did everyone's mouth in the room, and not to mention there was dead silence in the room. Then Jesus told me to asked her, "Why does it upset you so much when I call you fat and ugly?" Jesus was prompting me through this conversation. I am not a person who would normally ask these questions. Then I asked her, "If Jesus was standing in front of you right now, would He call you fat and ugly?"

Pam answered, "No way!"

Then I said, "Why do you think I asked? I want you to know that Jesus is a loving God and He would never call anyone fat and ugly."

She said, "You are right!"

Then I asked, "So what does that tell you about your boyfriend? Do you think we need to pray for him? Will he come to this Bible study?"

She said, "No way!"

I said, "Let us focus on you for a moment and we will come back to him later."

From your answers, I know you are sure God would never call you fat and ugly. You know God well enough to know He is a loving God. Then you should know you are made in His image and likeness, that is you are made to be the love of Jesus here on earth. There is only one reason you would listen to the comments from your boyfriend. For the same reason you let those comments hurt you and break you. If someone walked into this room right now and said to me, "Ron you are fat, ugly, stupid, and no one loves you, your comments to Pam are out of line, get out of here" what do you think I would say? Do you think I will be hurt? What is the difference between you and I?

There is one major difference in us. Spiritually, I have a personal relationship with my Jesus. I don't have to tell you I have this personal relationship with Jesus because it shows! That is why you ask me to pray for you in Bob Evans the other night and why you ask me to pray again tonight. I am going to pray for you!

I will pray for you to start developing a personal relationship with my Jesus. We all know if someone called Jesus fat and ugly, He would not be broken and in need of prayer. The reason Jesus would not be broken is He had a relationship with His Father! We too can have a relationship with Jesus! And with our Father through Jesus, this relationship will be our source of strength and Joy. As this relationship grows our strength will grow to a point where we can be beaten beyond recognition, have a crown of thorns, be nailed to a cross and watch all our friends abandon us and after all we gone through we will be able to say, "Forgive them Father for they know not what they do."

My friend Dan once said, "The devil has a problem when he puts you in a trial because the trial the devil is trying to break you with, the devil runs the risk of making you with." Every trial we have is designed to take our mind of Jesus and his love for us. If the devil can get you to ask God why or why me, or worse, get you to curse God, the devil wins! But if we turn to God like Jesus did in His trial or time of need we win!

I have a friend who has a two-year old boy with Down syndrome and a newborn baby girl when her husband walked away out of her life. Two years have passed since he left and now my friend lives in a camper. The water lines freeze in the winter and the camper does not heat very well. She does chores on her dad's farm to pay the rent. She has not filed for divorce, or for child support, but she has asked God to turn her pain into a passionate love for Jesus. On her first anniversary without her husband she spent the day thanking God for her two little ones! What the devil was trying to break her with she has let her Jesus make her with. She asked Jesus to turn the trial into a passionate love of God and He has! The devil lost big time! Her trial goes on day after day but she is totally committed to a loving relationship with my Jesus and our Father. She is totally joyful and full of strength and is a loving light to the world. She is not broken. She is very outspoken and speaks of her love of God in her actions and her words. Her heart is aglow with the warm fire of Jesus and if you meet her you will know because being around her your heart will also glow.

Pam, will you receive the love and healing Jesus has waiting for you? Just open your heart and receive the love of Jesus in your heart by seeking Jesus and I mean really seeking Jesus! To know what Jesus thinks of His creation we must hear His voice, know his will and be available to him 24/7. The simple truth is we all need to spend time listing to God talk to us. You ask me to pray for you because you don't think God counts your prayers worthy. That makes me cry. The devil has deceived us into thinking we are not worthy. Pam would you buy something if you knew it was not worth the price you paid or does the price determine the value. I know Jesus paid a huge price for Pam and I know Jesus was not deceived into paying too much. I know in this case we could say the price does determine the value and we should never let any devil tell us we are not worthy.

I believe that like most people in the world today, you have gotten your self-worth from what others say about you instead of what God says about you. Pam please know that if the truth was known there are others reading this right now who are trying to get their self-worth by what they say and what they do and by what others say about them. I would say most people put value in what others say and think about them. It is a very fragile place to be! The devil can and will attack us wherever we are weak. The answer is simple: We just put our life, our self-worth, our trust and our love into having a personal relationship with Jesus! Like you said Pam, Jesus would never call someone fat and ugly and may I add, neither would anyone who has the love of Jesus in them!

Would you like a personal face to face encounter with Jesus? Would being with Jesus on a daily basis and communing with Him every day be important to you? Do you know it is important to God for Pam to have this kind of relationship with God? Pam you can have a face to face encounter with Jesus everyday by simply reading His word. That is right! You can commune with God everyday by spending time with Him in His word. And, it is God's highest priority to have a daily, personal relationship with Pam! You are that important to Him!

I believe God wants us to express our needs to Him but only one time and not every day. And I believe we are to stand in faith that Jesus heard us and will perform to His Word. I believe we must make ourselves available to Him. Have you ever asked God what does He need to be done today? Are you available to God to do His work? I can tell you that the Pam that walked in here tonight was not available to God. When we are broken in our spirit and walking in self-pity, we are not going to be too useful to anyone. I can tell you I believe the Pam I am looking at right now will be available to God before she leaves here tonight. To be ready to serve God we must accept Him into our heart and be ready to sit and listen for His voice. We must have a desire to hear from God just like you want God to hear you when you pray. I see a new strength coming into Pam, I see the Joy of the Lord working as we talk.

How on earth do we hear from God? Answer, we must discern His voice! Jesus said "My people know my voice and follow me."

John 10:27 My sheep hear My voice, and I know them, and they follow Me.

The voice of Jesus is real! Pam you already know God well enough to know Jesus would not call you fat and ugly. How did you receive that knowledge? You already know God answers prayers or you would not ask for prayer. How did you receive that knowledge? The problem is you don't think God answers your prayers. Where did that idea come from? Maybe I should ask, what the devil told you that? I believe we can establish that you are hearing from God and the devil so all you need to do is discern your thoughts better. The truth is we all need to discern our thoughts better!

Pam we must look to God as our source of knowledge, wisdom, understanding and discernment. Jesus taught the apostles and Jesus is still our teacher and our comforter today. Please read "The Comforter." I know you listen to God because you know Jesus would never call you names! You already hear His voice, but you do not receive all God says about you! When you start receiving all God says about you and living in the revelation of the love of God, no one will hurt you ever again! To receive you must believe and discern your thoughts. Knowing who is talking to you is just as important as breathing! If you are not discerning the voices you hear, life will become confusing and what good is breathing without the Joy of believing! That is why we have so many suicides in America. People are just breathing, or just alive to please themselves. They are not experiencing the Joy of believing! Please read "Discernment".

Notice that in John 10:27, Jesus asks us to follow Him! Follow Him not just worship Him. I see people sing worship songs and praise Jesus in church and those are good things but they are worshiping Jesus, not following Jesus! I believe worshiping is doing the will of God to bring Him glory. Just singing to God about how great He is usually will not change our life into a life of Christ.

Singing is a form of worshiping but our actions will bring huge glory to God. For example, I could have sung songs to Jenny all day long but if I did not bathed her and feed her, she would stink and die. We must let Jesus feed us and bath us in His word every day; we must let Jesus love us every day. We must listen for His voice, His love and walk in faith every day.

Jesus said that without faith it is impossible to please Him! Faith is doing the works of God! Faith is going out to the demon and straightening the love of Jesus like Jesus did! Faith is knowing God is walking with you, faith is knowing God Himself will talk through you to others. Faith is letting God protect you! Faith is fearlessly relying on God for everything. Faith is being the voice of God and the actions of God and the love of God even in the face of many trials! I believe that asking God what He needs done today and then doing it is more important to God and brings Him more Glory than just signing to Him every Sunday morning. Please don't take me wrong; singing praises to God is very important but don't let that replace glorifying Him with your actions. We are to follow Jesus and in doing so we lay down our life to be who He created us to be! Who did Jesus create us to be is written very plainly in His word. Jesus is our example to follow. Jesus said I only do what I see my Father do. So Jesus was following the example of His Father. Everything Jesus did, He did it out of love so we know His Father is love so we must be love. For me life is so simple and I just live to be the love of Jesus Christ to everyone I meet!

1 Timothy 1:5 Now the purpose of the commandment is love from a pure heart, from a good conscience, and from sincere faith

You see the end of all our efforts of following Jesus must come from a pure heart – a pure heart that does not expect anything in return. The Love of Jesus is defined as charity, giving and sacrifice and Jesus clearly gave and never asking anything in return for His love. A clear conscience (*never doubting God*) and done in faith unfeigned (*a sincere faith, a faith not compromised by doubt*). When we start living this way no one can hurt us. We will pray for people that call us fat and ugly and we might even weep for them, because they are so lost and have missed everything Jesus did for us.

We should only do what we have seen my Jesus do. Love others unconditionally! The apostles only did what they saw Jesus do, they loved everyone unconditionally. Head knowledge cannot love but let heard knowledge become head knowledge by asking Jesus into your heart and you will become love in action! Asking Jesus into your heart is asking to become the love of Jesus on the earth. When we walk out and know that Jesus is in our heart, we will turn this world upside down. We can only walk out heart knowledge and not head knowledge for when we open our heart to God and let Him flow into us and through us. The love of God will dominate our thinking and what we speak. That is right! Following Jesus is walking in His revelation full time. We don't just pray for people while we are in church! We are His church and we are to manifest Jesus' love to everyone 100% of your life. By following Jesus we receive His love, His Joy and His pure heart but these gifts are not to keep for ourselves but to give to everyone!

I remember seeing people wearing bracelets that said W.W.J.D. or *What Would Jesus Do?* That question should have been settled in your mind before you put on the bracelet! In fact you really should not need a bracelet! We must live like Jesus lived, and that is we must be willing to give our life to save others. We will not lay down our life for others if are not sure if God exists. Let us settle the question then! When our trial comes let us be able to say forgive them Father for they know not what they do. So if someone calls me fat and ugly, I will pray for them that to come to know the love of Jesus because if they receive the love of Jesus into their hearts they will become Christ-like and all their sins will melt away like dirty snow on a hot day.

Pam, you know there is power in prayer. I believe we must pray for each other and there is power in praying together. Jesus said, "Wherever two or three gather together to pray, I will be also."

Matthew 18:20 For where two or three are gathered together in My name, I am there in the midst of them."

When we pray together we can expect God to perform His word so you are right to ask others to pray for you. There might be some doubt in your mind that God does not answer your personal prayers, so you ask others to pray for you. Jesus asks us to pray with expectance or faith in Him with nothing doubting. If God does not seem to answer your prayers then the right prayer might be, "Jesus how am I praying wrong?" This is where your personal relationship becomes so important. You will not even ask such a question if you do not hear or discern His voice on a regular basis! Discernment is so important! You see, if you pray and you hear 'you are not worthy', I know you are hearing the voice of the devil because God will never call you unworthy. Pam you are a child of God, an heir to the throne of God and you are the bride of Jesus! These are just some of the ways Jesus sees you.

Pam, please read in the book of Matthew 23 where Jesus had to tell the Pharisees what they were doing wrong and listen as you read and you will hear how much it hurt Jesus that the Pharisees did not listen. There is real pain in the words Jesus spoke and they seem so out of character for Him, yet they needed to be said! I pray to be a better listener every day! I think it is a very good prayer!

How do we recognize the voice of God over the voice of the devil? You must desire a personal relationship with God! You must devote time to Him like you would a boyfriend. If in every conversation you had with your boyfriend was a list of needs and wants and if you never listened to his needs and wants, how long would you expect him to stay around? Jesus calls love Charity (*giving and sacrifice*) in the Bible and yet most of us think of love as receiving blessings from God. Again, relationship is asking God what He needs us to do today. I believe God delegate's work for us to do every day. How will you know what work He has for you today? We must be able to distinguish His voice from the enemy and in order to do that, we must listen!

Jesus gave us the Bible as a tool to learn from. We must ask God for discernment before and every time we read His word. Jesus tells us in His word that He is our teacher.

John 14:26 But the Comforter, *which is* the Holy Ghost, whom the Father will send in my name, he shall teach you all things, and bring all things to your remembrance, whatsoever I have said to you.

You see the Holy Spirit of Jesus is the comforter and our teacher. How will Jesus teach us if we never set time aside to listen to Him? How will Jesus comfort us if we are too busy to wait upon an answer? Notice that Jesus said, "He will bring all things to our remembrance, whatsoever I have said to you." How will Jesus bring anything to our remembrance if we are too busy to listen? Jesus put His thoughts in our hearts, for out of the heart a man speak! Pam, instead of asking for a boyfriend ask God for discernment, understanding and ask God to transform you into the best you that you can be! No one can take what God says about you away but we can lose sight of His thoughts and His value for us by not discerning our thoughts. We are told to discern good from evil so we must be able too! Jesus asked Adam who told you, you were naked? Discernment is so important; if we don't know who we are listing to; we are lost and we will sin.

Genesis 3:11 And He said, "Who told you that you were naked? Have you eaten from the tree of which I commanded you that you should not eat?"

When someone is listening to the devil and not discerning their thoughts, they could repeat what they heard in their head like *'you're fat and ugly'*. Why should we, who know who we are in Jesus Christ listen to the devil speaking through someone? Fat and ugly comments should run off us like water on a duck's feathers. We should discern who is speaking and say that is not what my Jesus says about me and I believe Jesus and I will pray for you to become who Jesus created you to be! That sounds like forgiveness to me and it is a lot better than crying and letting the devil beat me up. The Joy of the Lord is my strength and I will forgive, because I am to live like my Jesus. And my Jesus said "forgive them Father for they know not what they do" or should I say for they know not what devil they are listing to! Please ask God for discernment!

Hebrews 5:14 But strong meat belongs to them that are of full age, *even* those who by reason of use have their senses exercised to **discern** both good and evil.

Unlike earthly teachers who have agendas, God's only agenda is to bring us closer to Him through trust and faith. It is called childlike faith in the Bible and putting your childlike faith in God and not man. It is the most adult act of faith you can do. Yes, Jesus has work for us to do and the reward for doing the things that Jesus needs done is Joy, Peace, understanding, and knowing He loves us! I want you to understand these gifts come through the love God has for us. Everyone knows Jesus said that without faith it is impossible to please Him. Faith pleases God so we please God when we walk in faith but faith doesn't change his love for you.

In other words we need to know that Jesus loves us now the way we are. We cannot earn His love by what we do but we can please Him by what we do. You please God by having a relationship with Him but He still loves you even before you open your heart to Him. I have three children and I love each one the same, but the one that spends the most time with me is the one I am most pleased with. My son will clean and wax my car because he knows I like my car cleaned and waxed. It pleases me to have a clean car, but my son cleans my car because he knows I love him and he wants to please me. He does not clean the car to make me love him. I love him and he loves me so much that we want to please each other. The most pleasing act of kindness we can do for each other is to spend time together. A clean car brings happiness until it is dirty again, but spending time together brings Joy and Joy strengthens our relationship. I believe my Father and Jesus what more than any act of kindness is to spend time with me! How do I know this? I discern my thoughts and I have heard this from my Father and my Brother! Please discern your thoughts and you will please your Father and your Brother; spend some time with them every day. Please read Coffee Time with Jesus!

To walk in the gifts of Joy, peace, love and strength of the Lord might seem almost humanly impossible on a daily basis. But these gifts exist and they are ours and they are real. If we only believe and trust and hear from God on a daily basis, we will walk with them daily. Jesus tells me I am beautiful every day, so I don't need to hear it from you. If you tell me I am beautiful, I will thank you but if I need you to tell me I'm beautiful I am not walking in the fullness of who Jesus says I am.

We should never put expectations on another human being. Needing another person to compliment me is a recipe for disaster because at some point they may not fill my need and I will be disappointed in them. If they put an expectation on me, I am sure in time we will both fall short and they will be hurt also. Pam if you need your boyfriend to be a certain way for you to be happy, that is where the devil will attack because we make ourselves vulnerable. Put your trust in God and expect your prayers to be answered. That takes faith in God and God truly loves Faith, God honors faith. Faith is our way of showing God we trust Him. No wonder God loves our faith! I have my Faith, my hopes and my trust in God and I will never be left down. I have His word on it. Pretty simple life isn't it. My childlike faith is in Jesus, the only one who has already died for me! I love you, Jesus!

Can I pray for God to give you a new boyfriend or to change the one you have into a man of God? Can I pray for God to make your boyfriend so loving and so perfect that you will be in love with him forever? Yes, I can pray that way! And that prayer request will line up with the will of God. I believe you will be better off if I am praying for God to make you perfect *'sinless and spotless before Him'*. What makes you perfect? Knowing and believing the love God has to us! What will give you boldness on Judgment day? Knowing God is love and the God of love dwells in you and you dwell in Him! Knowing Jesus on a first name basis! What did Jesus mean when He said, "As he is, so are we in this world?" Jesus was sinless and spotless and as He said "as he is, so are we in this world." Who are *'the we'* Jesus is talking about? It's you and I! We can be sinless and spotless if we are smart enough to repent and smart enough to believe and smart enough to trust and love in the word of God. I didn't make it up read it yourself. You see when someone can call me fat and ugly, I will pray for them.

1 John 4:16-17 And we have known and believed the love that God has for us. God is love, and he who abides in love abides in God, and God in him. Love has been perfected among us in this: that we may have boldness in the day of judgment; because as He is, so are we in this world.

I believe that Godly men are attracted to Godly women. So I will pray for you to become a Godly woman (*helpmate*) with a purpose of bringing Glory to God and focusing on God! I believe you will receive a help mate that together you two can bring Glory to God. Aim high for in God all things are possible!

God saw Adam was lonely and He created a woman for Adam and together they bring joy to each other in a human way but their purpose and goal is to bring Glory to God! Never lose sight of your purpose. If your life is all about you or anything that does not bring glory to God, you have already lost sight of your purpose. Thank God for grace and time to get it right, refocus and start Glorifying God! Being called fat and ugly will not hurt you when you see it as a way to bring Glory to God. Bring Glory to God through forgiveness for that person and pray for them to come to know Jesus.

I believe Jesus wants us to have a good marriage here on earth and a good helpmate is in the will of God. So yes, I will pray for you to be a Godly woman that hears from God every day. A woman that can discern her thoughts and receives her identity directly from what God says about her and not from what man says about her. Then, a Godly man will fall in love with her and the two shall become as one.

When we pray in the will of God, we can pray with faith and believing God heard our prayer we can now start thanking God for being our perfect helpmate. After you make a request to God for anything start thanking Jesus for honoring your prayer. You know, Jesus said pray in faith with nothing wavering. You see, if you ask over and over, all you are doing is asking! Asking takes no faith. Thanking God for granting you your request is a prayer in faith. Faith is the substance (*what you ask for*) of the things hoped for and the evidence of things not seen. Thank Him before you have your request because that shows faith, that takes faith, and that is faith. Remember your prayer request has to line up with His word. To know if your request lines up with His word, you must know His word.

Jesus did not write the Bible for us to just set it on the coffee table in the living room for others to see and so they will think we are spiritual or we could look spiritual. The Bible is the word of God and His words need to be in our heart, not on the coffee table. The Word of God needs to be in our hearts and if it is up to me, coffee needs to be on the coffee table! ☺

WE ARE TO READ HIS WORD!!! BELIEVE HIS WORD AND LIVE HIS WORD, GLORIFY HIM WITH OUR ACTIONS AND HIS WORD!!!

I can guarantee that when you pray this way and you are in the will of the Father and you will be transformed to His image and likeness so fast that you will be giving this message to some other hurting person in the near future! That is right! You can be ministering to others in no time at all. Talk about joy! Think about ministering this message to other people! Helping broken people get the strength of the Lord is the most rewarding purpose of life because it brings Glory to God!

Jesus says the Joy of the Lord will be your strength! Jesus is our teacher still today! The strength of the Lord sure beats being in need of sympathy! There is no joy, no strength and no lifting up of your spirit from sympathy. The compassion of Jesus will bring you to a place where His true Joy will smash sympathy into last week's garbage and the compassion of Jesus will take the pain of someone calling you fat and ugly and allow you to forgive them for they know not what they do. Forgiveness of the Lord will turn pain into laughter and Joy of knowing Jesus loves you! Instead of hurt you will have the strength to pray for that person! I love your compassion Jesus!

Which do you want? To be the broken one in need of prayer or to be the strong one that gives the love of Jesus to others because you know the strength that God gives you. I know for a fact God told us to heal the sick and we can when we pray in His will! Jesus told us to be His ambassadors here on earth and we are if we let Him flow through us. Please make yourself available to Him and then watch Him work through you. Life is amazing. God is amazing and Pam, you will be amazing too when you allow God to flow through you.

Pam, I also want to talk about your children for a while. You know, these teenagers are testing your will right now. When problems come up with your children, is it your responsibility to solve them? I believe it is your responsibility as a parent to guide them and teach them how to solve problems by having a relationship with Jesus. You are not here to solve every problem they have. When a child is small you tie their shoes but as they grow you teach them to tie their own shoes. When you have a Best friend and He is in love with you and you know He loves you down deep in your heart, you will call on Him and you know He will give you an answer because He will.

Pam, your children need to know that mom does not have all the answers, but mom knows who has the answers and how to get them. Direct your children to God for answers. Teach them how to solve their own problems with their relationship with God. Pam, Jesus is your best friend and you need to call on Him 24/7. You need to hear from Him! Let Jesus teach you how to solve your own problems. If you can convey this knowledge to your children, they will go to God for answers and not man. They will derive their self-worth from God and not from man, and they will live in the knowledge of being in love and being loved by Jesus. Bring your children up in the ways of the Lord and be a model for them to see Jesus in you. They will live in the knowledge of Jesus and be confident Jesus is their source of self-worth.

When your children see you ask Jesus for help, when they see your strength and devotion to God in your time of trial, when you rise above the problem because you surrendered the problem to God When you walk in the joy of the Lord and knowing Jesus is your helpmate, the victory is yours just for believing in the one who said I will never leave you or forsake you! Put your faith, your trust and hopes in the love of Jesus and watch Jesus love on you!

Pam, let us talk about your boyfriend. To be a friend, girl or boy, there must be some common morals, some common beliefs, common desires, and common goals but most of all you must see his desire is to be Christ-like! Without these truths in common, you two will have a hard time finding peace and love and there will be no lifelong commitment. For example, if you and your friend do not share the same moral values, you will find it hard to do anything with that person. Say you went shopping with your friend and your friend went shoplifting. What if he didn't have a get any problem by shoplifting and even tried to get you to share his belief by saying that the stores build the cost of shoplifting into their pricing, so you are paying too much for the goods you buy, it is like they are ripping you off. So you might as well go ahead and get a discount. Pam you have a decision to make.

You must pray for God to open his heart to hear the Word of God and you must also pray that God gives you the words and the wisdom to gently move his heart to have the desire to seek God in all his ways. God will allow you to show him and give him the desire to understand the need to seek God. Then, you will see a change in him and you will not even have to point out his sins or tell him shoplifting is wrong. Jesus said that it is His goodness that leads a man to repentance not our preaching.

Romans 2:4 Or do you despise the riches of His goodness, forbearance, and longsuffering, not knowing *that the goodness of God leads you to repentance?*

You see people will argue with words and never settle a thing. I have yet to see a debate change the other person's heart. But our actions will change a heart only when they come from our heart. Jesus said we can be His heart, we can see as Jesus sees and we can love as Jesus loves! Jesus in His Word called love Charity and the greatest of these is Charity.

I believe we will lead people to Jesus Christ more by our example than anything we can preach. I believe when people come to Jesus from meeting Jesus in us, there is a deeper spiritual relationship started and they will be hearing from God very soon. When they see the righteousness of God they will want to repent and they will succeed in repenting because they will focus on Jesus and not the sin.

You see if you try to change someone in your own strength, by telling him shoplifting is wrong, he will probably not listen to you. He will come against you with a million reasons why he is right and you are wrong. It is like fixing a flat tire by putting more air in it every day and never repairing the problem. You will wear yourself out teaching morals instead of bring him closer to God. Remember that it is the goodness of God that leads thee to repentance. Remember goodness is from the heart and to the heart. Don't try to change the habit (shoplifting) change the heart and the habit will flee! Focus on God not the problem. Don't wear yourself out arguing over the sin. Bring the focus on Jesus and win! Change the heart!

Changing habits is frustrating and often will bring you down. Instead, bring him to God, the teacher of understanding, the God of truth, the God of wisdom who came to set the captives free. Remember, Jesus will bring the increase. We are to lead people to God by our example not just our words. When we walk with the Lord and talk with the Lord, we set an example of Godly living and that allows the Lord to flow through us to others. Pam, you as a Christian could never shoplift? You don't shoplift because it is wrong. If shoplifting was just wrong, someone like your boyfriend could come along and maybe persuade you to shoplift. Pam, you will not shoplift because you have a relationship with Jesus and you know you would hurt or grieve your heavenly Father and Jesus your Brother. There is nothing loving in shoplifting and no love equals no Jesus in your life.

Pam, when your love for Jesus is on display, your boyfriend will notice something beautiful about you and he will receive a desire to be Godly! This new Godly desire will compel him into seeking God and when a person has a desire the size of a mustard seed to seek God, look out for big changes are on the way. The mountain will move and be cast into the sea. Believe me! Jesus will transform him into His image and likeness! That is an image and likeness you can fall in love with and together you both can grow in your relationship with Jesus by putting Jesus at the Helm! Glorify God the Father through Jesus by simply trusting God to honor His word.

I believe the devil has us putting Band-Aids on problems. By this technique, the devil wears us out and eventually we give up. You see we have to seek God first and when we do seek God first we will let Him show us the path to setting others free. I think we tend to focus on the problem such as shoplifting and ugly words and try to go into their past and see where this belief got started.

115

Focusing on their past can take a life time and totally drain you of your strength. Instead, we need to ask them to let God in their hearts by being the Joy of the Lord to them. When you walk into the room, Joy will walk into the room. The presence of God will stop people from telling dirty jokes. The presence of God will change the atmosphere in every place you go. The presence of God will convict others around you and your boyfriend will suddenly want to set a good example so he can continue to be around you. Isn't God great? He makes this life so simple! Jesus condensed all the laws down into two simple laws.

> **Matthew 22:36-40** "Teacher, which is the great commandment in the law?" Jesus said to him, "'You shall love the Lord your God with all your heart, with all your soul, and with all your mind.' This is the first and great commandment. And the second is like it: 'You shall love your neighbor as yourself.' On these two commandments hang all the Law and the Prophets."

I believe it is humanly impossible to teach love to anyone except by showing love! You can tell people all day how much you love Jesus and I can guarantee you they will judge your love of God by what you do rather than what you say. How do you love a shoplifter? Easy, you simply ask God how you can show His love to the shoplifter. God will show you how to love the shoplifter and you will see God work. God will ordain a set of circumstances where you can demon straight the love of God and through His love for you, your boyfriend will see why shoplifting is wrong. Your boyfriend will see how ugly words are wrong and he will also see how your love of God changed your life and your need was provided for in a supernatural way. You do not need to preach to your boyfriend that shoplifting is wrong. All you need to do is ask God to show your boyfriend that shoplifting is wrong! Focus on Jesus and problem solved!

Never label the sinner. Never refer to your boyfriend as a shoplifter, for in doing so you are speaking that over them. Jesus never told the woman at the well what her sin was, Jesus never called or defined her by her sin. He simply gave her the love of forgiveness by saying go and sin no more. It was the righteousness of God that led her to repentance! Jesus never even called her accusers sinners. It was the righteousness of Jesus that led them to walk away and not throw any stones. Jesus only did what He saw his Father do! I know His Father and I know Him as my Father and I feel His gentle corrections all the time. I thank God for those corrections but most of all I love that we are so in love that I also feel His forgiveness! This means that I want to please Him and so if I fall short I know it, because I am in a relationship. I hear His voice and I love it. I cry out, "dear Jesus! Make me whole that I may bring Glory to God. Make me one with you Jesus. I want your thoughts, your mind, your eyes, but most of all make me your love here on earth!"

I am in a relationship with my Father God and Jesus all the time. He is my best friend and my best friends can correct me! You see, I love God and I am loved by God so I never want to hurt my Father or my Jesus or let them down. He really is my best friend and I love having Him so close to me we become one with each other. That is pure Joy, a pure heart, and purely being in love with someone that has laid down His life for me. I will seek Him with all my heart forever.

When a bird has eggs, the mother bird will sit on the eggs and keep them warm until they hatch. The mother bird will nurture them and feed them tirelessly. But the best mother bird in the world cannot make her baby birds fly. She has to pick the right time and then kick them out of the nest. They will either fall to the ground dead or fly. Her reward for stepping out in faith is seeing her birds set free of the confines of the nest. What a glorious time that must be for her! Take this lesson from the mother bird. You cannot teach the love of Jesus to others but you can demon straight it and the others will receive it and the reward for being the love of Jesus is pure Joy of watching freedom from the confines of our earthly desires. Pam, you must ask God for discernment! There is a time when we are told to shake the dust off our feet if some ones heart doesn't change. Sometimes we demon straight the love of Jesus and if the recipient does not respond we are to move on knowing God will raise someone else up to change their hearts.

Pam, I will fly and I will pray that you do too! I am out of the nest! I am set free and I am the love of Jesus for all to see! I know my Jesus loves me and I pray you know the love of Jesus too! Welcome to the love of Jesus! Welcome to my home! You are welcome to share His love to the entire unknown! To soar on the wings of eagles simply trust in my Jesus! Until Jesus calls you home!

Fear

What is fear? Simply put, it is faith in the devil. When you are afraid of anything, you are really saying, "I don't believe Jesus can handle this." Anything you do not surrender to Jesus, you're in bondage to. If you're in bondage to something, that thing has control over your life. It has the power to make you afraid, unhappy, raise your blood pressure, and control you.

I hear Christians singing God is good all the time and He is. So who is bad? It's the *devil*. So when we believe a bad thing can happen, then we believe in the devil. God is good all the time; devil is bad all the time. God is faith in the word and that good things will come to us that believe. The devil is fear that bad will come to us. So choose well! The difference is heaven or hell!

Are you in heaven or hell right now? Yes heaven is listing to and believing Gods word right now. Hell is listing to the devil right now. You will reap sickness or health, being poor or having prosperity, being carnally minded or spiritually minded, loving life or hating life, loving yourself or hating yourself, sowing love or sowing hatred.

This is an example of how the devil comes to kill steal and destory:

Let's say you're afraid to go into the water because you almost drown when you were young. So for the rest of your life you will not go near water. You don't go swimming, boating, skiing, water sports, etc. and every time someone asks you to do one of these things, your blood pressure goes up! You have anxiety, you are even unhappy. Your peace leaves you and you feel you have to tell them why you will not go near water. So to explain why you don't like being in water, you relive the near drowning incident all over again. When you relive the incident, you are actually reinforcing the trauma in your mind. I have heard of someone who actually moved to a cold climate, so no one would ask him to do water sports.

You see how one little fear can dictate an area of your life. You say, I have just learned to live with it. Fear is of the devil, so what you are really saying is, "I have learned to live with the devil." You have actually surrendered to the devil in that area of your life. The devil will never be satisfied. You see in our example, that person was afraid of drowning. At first, he was afraid of going under water. Then came fear of just going into water, then fear of boating and water sports. Then came fear of people that liked water sports, then for fear that they would ask him to participate with them. Eventually, he moved to a cold climate to escape being around water sports. So the fear of drowning changed his lifestyle, limited his friends and control where he lived.

The devil will not stop there. He wants to control you more, so he will eventually get you afraid of the rain and driving a car in the rain. Now he has limited your time outdoors, and when you can only drive. He will also get you afraid of bathing or showering. When that happens, people will not want to be around you. So you become isolated and alone to the point where all you can do is live by yourself. You might even think of suicide! I know I took this example to the extreme, but the devil does work that way. He likes to isolate you from loved ones, so he can fulfill his mission which is to kill, steal and destroy.

He killed your spirit, stole your freedom and destroyed your life by isolating you from others all because of fear. That is faith in the devil.

From our example, you can almost drown. But this time let us say your parents have knowledge of how the devil works. So the first thing they do is cast out the demon of fear, and start praising God your alive and free of fear. You start swimming again right away. You have the joy of being in the water again and you did not lose anything. That little act of casting out the devil will stop everything that followed in our example. I can almost guarantee you this. If you are on a public beach and your son almost drowns and you start casting out a devil of fear, people will look at you like you are being weird. At that moment we will find out if you have a fear of mankind. For if you do have fear of mankind, you will say to yourself, "I will cast that devil out later, when no one is around." So the demon of fear is dictating your life and now is getting a strong hold in your son's life.

In reality, you are passing your spirit of fear on to your son and he will probably pass his spirit along in the future if he will have kids. Yet the whole cycle can be stopped with the knowledge of God's Word.

Jesus in His Word said my people die from lack of knowledge. In our example you can see how God's knowledge would have changed your life, and your eternity.

> **Hosea 4:6** My people are destroyed for lack of knowledge. Because you have rejected knowledge, I also will reject you from being priest for Me; Because you have forgotten the law of your God, I also will forget your children.

When we receive knowledge from the Lord we must act on that knowledge. If we reject the knowledge, Jesus said He would also reject us. You see to reject knowledge is to reject God's truth. Jesus said he will protect us, but we are rejecting Him and His protection. It is real easy not to be rejected by God. Just accept all the written Word of God as true. Don't read the Bible and wonder if this is true. Read the Bible and accept that it is truth. Jesus said in His word He cannot lie.

> **Titus 1:2** In hope of eternal life which God, who cannot lie, promised before time began.

Let's say you pray for someone's eye to heal. Then you look at the eye and say it didn't change. So you assume your prayer didn't work.

God's word says He cannot lie! God's Word says He will heal all! God's Word says speak to the mountain and it will move. Remember that God cannot lie. So why is the eye not healed? Is it fear? Is it doubt? Jesus said have faith! So what is faith? We think, we must have faith in our faith to move the mountain. Jesus told us to have faith in the name of Jesus, for it is faith in the name of

Jesus that made all miracles come to pass. Usually we speak the words of faith and then look to see if the thing spoken came to pass. When nothing appeared to happens, our faith dissolves. We start looking for excuses why it didn't work.

Then we blame ourselves. That sounds like the work of the devil, and it is! Jesus in His Word said stand firm, in your confession. So command the thing to happen and praise God it did happen, no matter what we see with our senses. Then stand firm that it did happen and it will happen for sure. Faith is the substance of things hoped for and the evidence of things not seen. So isn't Jesus tells us that we might not see it come to pass right away? So stand firm to your healing words and don't be deceived. Praise God for the miracle, no matter what you see and you will have it.

Don't let the devil steal the miracle. Stand firm to your confession! Realize that when you plant an apple seed, it takes a while to become an apple tree. You don't walk outside the next day and say, I guess it didn't work, I don't see an apple tree. You know it takes time for the apple seed to become an apple tree. When you sow a healing seed it might take time to become healing. Jesus wants us to stand firm. Nothing doubting because doubting is of the devil.

You know it might be that when we first step out in faith, the healing seed we sow is our own healing tree. Just like the apple tree, we must let our faith in our healing tree grow and become a healing tree before we bear healings. The apple tree doesn't bear apples overnight and our healing tree might take some time before it bears healings.

To plant an apple tree we must first open up the ground and plant the apple seed. So we must open our heart to plant the word of God in our heart. When the apple seed is planted we must let God perform the miracle and transform the seed into a seedling with roots going deep into the earth. So we let God perform a miracle to transform our hearts and let His Word take root deep into our heart! God will lead the roots of the apple seed to just the right nutrients to pop it out of the ground. We need to let God teach and lead us to the right truths of His Word so we can pop out into our surroundings. The apple tree is very fragile at first and it must be given care and protection that no one breaks the

122

seedling. We also need God's protection to protect our hearts from worldly teachings.

As the apple seedling grows, others will recognize it as an apple tree because of its leaves and the bark of the seedling. People will start to recognize us by our faith in God. One of the first gifts from God is peace and joy. People will recognize these gifts and as we grow people will start asking you where does this joy come from? They might even recognize the fact we have special gifts from God in our heart. I know there will be some big differences between us and the apple seedling. For example, God's seed of faith can be planted in us at any stage of life. The results will be the same if we are 10 years old or 60 years old. The miracle of God's transformation will take place in our heart at any age. People will recognize the difference in us and when we allow the truth of God's word into our heart, God himself will transform us.

The apple tree will continue to grow and with God's protection it will blossom and bear good fruits. It needs the protection of God in all of its life. You know there can be insects that will come and can attack the tree and rob it of its goodness. The apple tree will need constant care and nutrients. There are outside forces at work to steal the goodness of God from us also. We need to have a relationship with God all our life. God gives us Joy as our strength and just as we will have great joy when we see the love of God flow through the branches of the apple tree into the fruit of the apple tree! We will experience great joy when we see God's great love flow out from us to others. God transforms the tree into branches and branches will have leaves and blossoms and blossoms will transform into little apples and with just the right mixture of sun and rain and most of all love the fruit will be good.

God will see that the tree will become strong enough before He lets it have apples. God's protection will keep the tree from having too many apples at one time and thus keep the tree from being overburdened and having branches breaking from the load of the fruit. All these miracles take place because someone planted a seed in faith knowing that God would bring an increase.

We too will experience the joy of God's love flowing through us and we too will watch His love transform other lives into beautiful blossoms and then into fruit for the kingdom of God. God said He is the vine and we are the branches. It is the exact same nutrients in the vine as the branches. We are fed by God and we become so God like one cannot tell where the vine stops and the branch starts. God said He will live in us, dwell in us and the two of us will become as one.

The apple tree does not try to have apples to prove it is an apple tree. It was an apple tree when it was a seed. We too are a seed of God's love! We don't become love as we grow. We were God's love when He made us! Original sin can make it hard to see the love of God with us but God also gave us baptism to remove the original sin and let His love show. Like the apple tree that grows stronger everyday so does God's love in us. The apple tree will need to be pruned every so often to get rid of unfruitful branches. So it is with us, we need the forgiveness of God for our sins or unfruitful actions in our life. A big difference in our life with God is we can start out new with the baptism of the Holy Spirit. Unlike the apple tree we can make discussions and God gave us a free will to make those discussions with.

The secret of a good healing tree is to grow and stand in faith knowing just like when the apple tree did not produce apples right away. We must know in our hearts that by faith, our healing tree will bring good fruit by the decisions we make. In our mind, we knew it was an apple seed we planted, so we had faith that we would get the apples someday because we know we planted an apple seed and by faith we know that the apple seed turns into an apple tree!

We need to plant the seed of God's word in our hearts and in faith we water it with more of God's word and by faith we know God's Word will turn into God's love. We know that it will take years before we will have apples so we let the apple seed mature and eventually the seed became a tree and eventually we had apples! The tree did not have apples to prove it was an apple tree. We knew it was an apple tree because we planted it! God is love and we want to be His love to everyone we meet, so we plant His love in our hearts. The cool thing is with God there is no waiting! We must plant the truth of God's Word in our hearts and we will watch the love of God explode in everyone!

124

Just as you watch the apple tree grow and blossom, your faith in that the tree will bring good fruit grows. When you see the apple tree blossom you do not say I wanted apples not flowers on my tree. Again, we know that the blossom is one of the steps to being an apple. We know that from knowledge, the blossom will turn into great fruit. We also know that from Knowledge of God's word, we will blossom and people will notice and we will see good fruit for the Kingdom of God.

We must know in our heart we have the Word of God in our heart and we must know God cannot lie. With that knowledge in our hearts, we start to speak God's word (healing) into existence. When the tree popped out of the ground, we got excited even though we knew it would take years before we had apples. When we speak the Word of God out of our mouths, we get excited to see God perform to His Word! Unlike the apple seed that didn't change into an apple tree over night, we are a healing tree the moment we received the word of God into our hearts. The first time we speak God's Word out of our mouth we will be planting seed of God's love! Yes, we will blossom into a mighty healing tree as we grow in faith but we have to stand in faith that even if first time we speak healing words into anyone and the healing did happen whether we see it or not.

This analogy of the tree verses man actually is in the Bible.

Matthew 12:33 "Either make the tree good and its fruit good, or else make the tree bad and its fruit bad; for a tree is known by *its* fruit.

We are not apple trees but 'faith trees'. We either bear good fruit, faith in God's word or we can bear fear in the devil's word, bad fruit. So take the mustard seed of faith and turn it into a mountain moving word of God! Jesus said that all things are possible! Jesus in His words says so and I choose to believe it! So read the word of God and quote the word of God out loud, so your inner ear can hear and deposit the truth in your heart. Remember the song, "I want the *joy, joy, joy, joy* down in my heart, where, down in my heart?" To have that joy you must make deposits.

Day by day we make deposits of the word of Jesus or words from the devil, and then we speak from that abundance of the heart. I want to make my heart full of Jesus, I want the mind of Christ, and the Spirit of Christ, and the love of Christ to manifest in my life every minute of every day. I believe to have manifestations of Jesus I must make deposits every day! I wake up every day and ask my Jesus, *"What are we going to do today?"*

A fearless life is really not that hard. We either choose to believe in Jesus and live fearless or we choose to listen to the devil and live in fear. If you are in fear of anything, then you are listening to the devil. It only takes a little faith to counteract the devil. In the swimming example, you see how just a tiny bit of faith in God could have cast out the devil right as he came in. We know from the Bible, the devil will steal the good seeds we plant as soon as possible even before they have time to root. You see how just a little knowledge could change that whole picture from bondage and fear of water to freedom that Jesus came to give us.

In our example, you see how we gave into fear without a fight. The devil started dictating our lives, and we just caved in because of our lack of knowledge. Do you realize the whole time we could have been going to church and singing songs and doing nice things for others? But don't ask me to swim. We can explain to others our fear of swimming and sometimes they – other Christians – will reinforce our fear by telling us about their fear. Fear loves to feed on other people's fear.

Freedom from fear is a total life change. You can have freedom from fear at any time. Jesus gave us power over the power of the devil.

> **Luke 10:19** Behold, I give you the authority to trample on serpents and scorpions, and over all the power of the enemy, and nothing shall by any means hurt you.

Use your God given power to break free! Freedom from all fear is true freedom. Jesus promised us true freedom. Just believe that Jesus came and died for you! He loves you! Prove that you love Him by simply believing in Him! There is so much in His Bible I cannot explain or understand but I choose by faith to

126

believe it. To prove that I believe, I walk my beliefs every day. I believe Jesus walks with me every day. I believe the two of us are one so how on earth could I fear. Most people fear death and yet they are in church they sing songs about, "How I want to be in that number on that glorious day" or they say "Bring the rapture, I am ready!" But if the doctor says you have cancer, they are in every healing line they can find. I believe the devil is laughing at him and Jesus is saying, "Just believe and be set free."

I know people that worship Jesus every Sunday by singing and being at church but the minute they leave the church they start talking about their problems! I believe true worship is being Jesus on the earth. Jesus called us to be ambassadors! How do singing praise songs change anyone's life if you do not believe what you sing? Believing is being Jesus and being Jesus on the earth is worshiping 24/7. Can you imagine Jesus being in fear about anything? Yet the Bible tells me Jesus was tempted in every way we are tempted. Jesus was tempted to fear but I cannot even think of anything that might have given Jesus the man any fear.

Why is it so hard for us to have faith in God who never lied, and is the Author of Truth? And yet, it is so easy for us to have faith such as fear in the devil who is the author of lies? The stated mission of the devil is to kill, steal and destroy lives here on earth and for eternity. Jesus is the Author of Truth, and the Author of Eternal Life.

What is faith? Faith believes in God. Jesus said we could do all things if we believe. Jesus said that nothing is impossible. Maybe all things are too general for you and maybe you even think, "Yes, God said all things but what about my cancer?" Maybe you think, "Yes, God healed my friend's cancer but I am not as good a person as her so I am not sure He will heal me." I know as you read those words out loud you heard the doubt in your spirit. Speak out loud and you will hear your own doubt in your heart and then counter with the words of Jesus out loud and watch doubt and fear disappear.

Mark 9:23 Jesus said to him, "If you can believe, all things are possible to him who believes."

The only reason we have fear is we come into agreement with fear and let fear come into our lives. We have to come into agreement with it to have it! Why do we tell people we have fear like it is so natural? We should break that agreement by drawing near to God and then agree with God in faith that His word is true. In other words, believe in the One that never lied and the One who wants to be one with you!

> **James 4:8** Draw near to God and He will draw near to you. Cleanse your hands, you sinners; and purify your hearts, you double-minded.

Cleanse your hands you sinners. Guard your eyes, and your ears. Guard what you see and hear. Be careful what you put in your heart. News, television, radio, internet, and even the preacher on Sunday morning can be sources of fear! Fear and distrust comes with everything we hear and see on television. I had to stop watching television because I could not discern my thoughts as fast as the thoughts and pictures came at me. I had to choose my friends well because friends will take you up or down but they never leave you where they found you.

Purify your hearts you double minded. Junk in and junk out, God's word in and the love of Jesus Christ out, you choose. A little of both in and a little of both out, and you are double minded. Really, how hard is it to turn off something that is giving you fear. I know fear comes from so many sources and I know we all have access to the Bible! The Bible is our source of Joy, Peace, and love! The Bible tells us how to live without stress and worry! Don't read the Bible to see if it is true! Read and believe it is true! Ask your Jesus to be your source and He will be! Please read *Freedom from Self!*

Now, let us say your fear just came upon you today, because you just walked out of the doctor's office and he told you have cancer. What should you do? You cast out fear of cancer, break the words the doctor spoke over you and don't come into agreement with the lie! Then praise God for His word that says you are healed and you have power over the devil of cancer. Jesus in His word says, whose report are you going to listen too, His that says we are healed or the doctor who says you have cancer? Praise God and

128

tell everyone you have freedom from cancer. Walk by faith not by sight. Jesus never lets you down, believe and receive His good side effects.

If ever you're in doubt about any of God's word, check your prayer life. When you have that personal relationship with God, there is no doubt. Faith comes from hearing and that is you speaking the word of God over yourself and more importantly taking some quiet time to listen to Jesus. When you hear yourself say it, it comes to life a lot faster than if you listen to another person say it. When you listen to the voice of God when He talk to you, His truth gets into your heart and manifest in your body (*healing*) in your mind (*set free, renewed*) and in your spirit (*one with God, peace, love, joy, freedom, and that list goes on*).

Now, you want to know the best part. Freedom from fear is freedom from you. Now you can go out and do the Word of God (*heal the sick raise the dead and cast out devils*). That is freedom – freedom to tell yourself how you feel. Get up in the morning and tell your body to come into alignment with God's Word that says, "Jesus took away my pain, sickness, and disease!" You will be pain-free and sickness-free, and disease-free when you believe in God's word. Believing God's word is a decision we must make! Choose well! Be a good tree! Remember that we are a good tree because we choose to believe. Yes, we must choose to believe Jesus and His word!

One more thought about trees. You know fruit trees usually only bear one kind of fruit, where we are being the fruits of Jesus can bear all kinds of good fruit. Healings, casting out devils and raising people from the dead are all good fruit but the best fruit we can bear is to transform people with the love of Jesus Christ! A good fruit tree will bless us with a good apple and the apple will put a smile on our face while we eat it. But good Jesus fruit will put Joy and strength in us and through us to others forever! For more on being a tree please read *Fruits*.

To be a son of God and a Jesus tree bearing good fruit you do not have to fight fear or the devil. You simply become an ambassador for Jesus! Set your mind on Jesus and you will be fear-free!

Freedom From Self

It was March 7th of 2012, and I was walking Jenny in her wheelchair when a couple came up alongside us. We started a conversation as we walked together and upon learning that we were full time campers, the man told me about his new gun that is the ultimate knockdown weapon. The man asks, "What kind of gun do you carry for protection?" Then I told him "I carry a big gun." He wanted to know what kind it was. I told him, "I don't know, I bought it used but it is big and it takes big bullets." He wanted to see it so we walked to our camper and I went inside to get my gun.

When I came out with my Bible the man's wife looked at me and said, "You think you're funny don't you?" She then went on to tell me about some missionaries who trusted God for protection and they are now dead. She said, "I'm glad God told my husband to carry and use a gun for our self-defense."

I told them, "I carry my faith for protection." They thought I was kidding, and they asked me, "What if someone broke into your camper and pointed a gun at you and you could tell that the gunman was serious and he was going to kill you and Jenny?! What would you do?" I said, "I would stand on faith that God is my protector." So they asked, "So you would not defend yourself?" I answered, "No. I would not defend myself. Jesus is my Defender. I know God said to be absent from the body is to be present with Lord. So I would be at peace knowing the words of Jesus are true."

2 Corinthians 5:8 We are confident, yes, well pleased rather to be absent from the body and to be present with the Lord.

She went on to say, "You can have your faith in God for protection, but those missionaries that had faith in God's protection are now dead!" She continued, "I know God has told my husband to protect me with a gun." I answered her, "I know of missionaries that are dead, and I can see why people think God did not protect them. We all have the right to choose. You know God created us with a free will to choose what kingdom we are listing to. God will not go against our will! The gunman has a choice and so do I." Then the couple said, "Don't be a foul man. We are talking about some really bad people out there!" I said, "I know there are some really bad people out there, but when you know Jesus dwells in you fear is not in your vocabulary."

If someone wanted to kill Jenny and me, at that point, I have a couple options. I could go into fear and trust a gun to be my protection. And that would be like saying "Jesus, I cannot trust you to handle this, so I will."

Jesus has a couple options also and I explained. The gunman could kill us and I know we will be with Jesus that very second. Praise God we got the express ticket. We would be in instant Joyfulness. The gunman could go to jail and have a chance to be saved, Jesus and Jenny and I win. Or the bullets could go right through us and do no damage. In that case we should be able to lead the gunman to Jesus because he has just witnessed a miracle. Wouldn't that be cool!

On the other hand, if I had a gun and killed the man, everyone would know that it was self-defense. I might even get praise from fellow men for taking a killer off the street. I could go about life as usual, and actually be happy from the notoriety which I received from the news media. The problem for me is this: I do not know the relationship the gunman had with the Lord. I would assume he went to hell. By killing the man, I'm actually helping the devil put another person in hell. That would make me really sad because God's Word says in John 15:12-13:

John 15:12-13 This is My commandment, that you love one another as I have loved you. 13 Greater love has no one than this, than to lay down one's life for his friends.

I would have missed my express ticket to heaven because I didn't allow Jesus to be my protector. It would only prove that I don't believe God's word. Guilt, shame and fear would be mine to wear until I realized I needed to repent for killing the gunman. Jesus would forgive me I know, but it would be really hard for me to know I was working for the devil. I really don't like it when the devil wins! I know some people get hung up on John 15:12-13 because of the word friend. I believe we can have the eyes of Jesus and the heart of Jesus if we believe in faith that we can receive it. So to me, I want to see everyone as the perfect children of Jesus, even someone pointing a gun at me can be my friend. I believe the love that Jesus showed us while He was here on earth is proof that we can love as Jesus loved! If we just open our heart to His love.

As for Jenny and I, the choice is very clear. The Most High JESUS CHRIST and his army will protect us! Faith and not fear controls us. The mind of Christ motivates us and not guilt. And proclaiming the love of Jesus, not shame, keeps our motor running. Jesus we love you and praise you until the end of time. ALLELUIA!!!

What if the gun was not physical? It could be a spiritual demon firing spiritual bullet at you. Do you have a spiritual gun to fire back? Yes! We have the power over the enemy spiritually when we have the Holy Spirit in us. Jesus said that our battle is spiritual and spiritually we don't surrender. We are to fight spiritually and we do so by calling on the Name of Jesus for we are told everything will obey when we command in the name of Jesus. Jesus commanded the storm to stop and the pigs into the sea and devils to leave and sickness to go but He never commanded another person to obey Him. The only exclusion is another human. Jesus showed us love and gently tried to change our heart but He didn't and cannot use this God given authority over your free will. You see we have a choice in believing or not and Jesus left the choice up to us. We are commanded to love one another not to beat each other in to submission. You see by letting the gunmen kill me I am showing him love and if he receives it into his heart, his heart can be changed because Jesus teaches me that it is the goodness of man that leads a man to true repentance not ministry. I pray if someone does someday kill me, he will see that my act of kindness and the love will touch his heart and I will see that man in heaven someday.

Jesus will tell us what to do and when to do it if we just trust Him with our life. How can we not trust the one that has counted the hairs on your head? We cannot add one second to our lives. I mean get real, Jesus is real and alive in my heart. I live to be like Jesus and that is real life! Happiness is so overrated and so monetary but Joy is beyond our understanding and Jesus said so! Joy is something that no man can take away from you and it lives inside you. I actually have great Joy in my heart to think I can be Christ like and lay down my life for another.

> **John 15:12-13** This is My commandment, that you love one another as I have loved you. Greater love has no one than this, than to lay down one's life for his friends.

I believe in Jesus and my life is simple. Jesus is transforming my life and purifying me to new standards of His love that I never thought possible. He will do the same for you if you just let Him. Please give God permission to transform you into His image and likeness. His perfect love will remove all fear a life without fear is wonderful! Yes, there is real peace in putting your trust in the one true God who sent His only Son to renew our relationship to Him. Yes, Jesus came to remove our sins, but just as important Jesus came to show us without a doubt we can live without fear of death. Jesus conquered death and fear at the same time. Jesus showed no fear when he was going to the trial, the beating, and the cross. Jesus showed us His perfect love when they nailed Him on the cross and Jesus said in Luke 23:34:

> **Luke 23:34** Then Jesus said, "Father, forgive them, for they do not know what they do." And they divided His garments and cast lots.

That is true peace, true love and it is yours if you just ask Father God to be his Son. That is right! We are Sons of God if you only believe! Peace and love are yours for just believing! The only physical thing Jesus had to His name was His clothes and He gave them His clothes. Can you imagine? Jesus was giving His life for the people that were trying to make a profit on His clothes! Jesus gave His life for people who didn't understand Him, who didn't believe Him, who didn't receive Him! You can say that I am crazy to put my life down for another and I say, "I am in some pretty good company. I am a son and I am forgiven and I am loved by my Heavenly Father and my brother Jesus! And if that is crazy to you, then it is okay with me because I AM A SON WHO SERVES!!! JESUS is real and He is making me real. I ask Him into my heart and He is my heart!"

John 1:12 But as many as received Him, to them He gave the right to become children of God, to those who believe in His name:

Romans 8:14 For as many as are led by the Spirit of God, these are sons of God.

Galatians 4:6 And because you are sons, God has sent forth the Spirit of His Son into your hearts, crying out, "Abba, Father!"

Yes, I am a Son of God and you can hear my spirit crying Abba Father, for my Abba Father wants us to hear His voice every day and He wants to be in everything we do and say! Please don't say 'Father, have mercy on us all' that takes no faith. Instead, say *"Father has mercy on us all!"* and praise Him for His mercy because that is faith! Pray in faith and praise Him by being like Him. Thank you, Abba Father!

Last night, I was talking to a nonbeliever and after being prompted by Jesus, I told him a couple stories. It took a while because of interruptions. Then he summed up the evening by saying, "You have some really different beliefs but they serve you well. I think you are a sweet person." Then, he gave me two big hugs and shook my hand as we parted.

Just be available to Jesus and love some with your gift of time and Jesus will make that time count for His kingdom.

I will lay down my life for you, the decision has already been made. THE LOVE OF JESUS ALWAYS WINS!!!

Love from Jenny and Ron and Jesus.

134

Fruits

In the beginning, Jesus spoke the world into existence. I find what Jesus said about fruit trees to be very interesting and how we are likened to a tree so often in the Scripture. Jesus also talked a lot about fruits while He was here on earth.

Genesis 1:11 Then God said, "Let the earth bring forth grass, the herb that yields seed, and the fruit tree that yields fruit according to its kind, whose seed is in itself, on the earth"; and it was so.

Notice the fruit tree will yield fruit after his kind. The word '*his*' is an interesting term for a tree. The seed is in itself, just like the seeds of humans are in humans.

Genesis 1:12 And the earth brought forth grass, the herb *that* yields seed according to its kind, and the tree *that* yields fruit, whose seed *is* in itself according to its kind. And God saw that *it was* good.

Jesus spoke it and it was good. How do we recognize whether the fruit is good or not? Here we read, "God saw that it was good." Jesus is judging His creation and saw that it was good. In Matthew, Jesus said He will judge a tree, and we will recognize the tree by its fruit! We are not judges, we only recognize. We will recognize ourselves by the fruit we produce.

Matthew 7:16-17 You will know them by their fruits. Do men gather grapes from thornbushes or figs from thistles? Even so, every good tree bears good fruit, but a bad tree bears bad fruit.

Here, Jesus is talking about men and not actual trees. A good man will bring good fruit. How does this happen? It happens by sowing good spiritual seeds. Every Scripture is a good spiritual seed. It is truth and brings good to whoever receives it. I believe most sowing is done without saying a word. Most sowing is done by action or deed.

1 John 3:18 My little children, let us not love in word or in tongue, but in deed and in truth.

What Jesus talks about is if you see someone naked and you say Jesus loves you and you don't clothe him you have not loved him. Notice the deed (physical action that is healing or clothing them) comes first. The person cannot receive very well if they are hungry, naked or in need of healing. If you feed them, clothe them, and heal them, then believe me they will be able to receive the love of Jesus. Jesus healed before he preached most of the time.

Matthew 7:18-19 A good tree cannot bear bad fruit, nor can a bad tree bear good fruit. Every tree that does not bear good fruit is cut down and thrown into the fire.

In Mathew 7:19, Jesus says 'a tree that brings forth not good fruit is hewn down and cast into the fire'. Jesus doesn't tell us to hewn down and cast into the fire. He does the casting down because He is the Judge!

Matthew 7:1 Judge not, that you be not judged.

We recognize them and we can shake their dust off our feet. We forgive them and we are to recognize the anti-Christ but Jesus judges them not us!

Matthew 7:20 Therefore by their fruits you will know them.

Notice that in Matthew 7:20 it says "therefore by their fruits you shall know them'. You see, we'll recognize them by their

136

fruits." Notice that there is only good fruit and evil fruit not bad fruit. Notice also there are good trees and corrupt trees not bad trees. I am not sure when evil fruit became one as bad fruit in our language but it seems that we are always watering down the gospel. Evil is evil and we should call all evil, evil! In my mind, the word evil congers up the works of the devil but the word bad congers up rotten like this apple is rotten.

We have made bad or rotten a description for children that are doing something cute. We even say they are rotten to the core, meaning what they are doing is really cute. I never hear anyone say they are evil to the core unless they mean evil as in evil. I think we need to choose our descriptive words we speak over our children wisely. Another example is calling our children as kids. The Bible refers to kids as baby goats in 43 verses, so I am going to ask God to put a check in my spirit to call children, children and baby goats as kids.

I believe Jesus likened us to fruit trees because we bear fruit. Our fruit will be judged by God, to be good, evil or lukewarm. Jesus said, "if your lukewarm I will spew you out of my mouth."

Revelations 3:16 So then, because you are lukewarm, and neither cold nor hot, I will vomit you out of My mouth.

As humans we can inspire other humans to be good, evil or indifferent (lukewarm). We will actually attract good, evil or indifferent by what we say and do with our lives. If you look around today, you will notice how indifferent has become the norm. We call it being tolerant, (that's okay you believe what you want and I will believe what I want). If being tolerant is okay then why did Jesus come and why did he die for us? How is this for the indifferent, lukewarm or tolerant (I think it is a woman's right to choose)? What happened to 'thou shall not kill'?

Jesus wants us to take a stand. Being tolerant of evil in the name of peace or getting along is admitting that you have no spine, no courage! And Jesus has no tolerance for cowards! Jesus said proclaim His word boldly! NO ONE has the right to choose to let an unborn baby live or die but if someone makes that choice and sometimes later ask for forgiveness, then we have no right not to forgive.

That is right! We are commanded to forgive, and I have no right to judge but I am commanded to forgive. Jesus forgave all that repented. Jesus is our example of how to live so we must forgive! We are here to set the captives free, not to judge them! I believe the love of Jesus will touch everyone and change the heart of everyone that has not hardened their heart by life circumstances (listening to the devil). I believe even Hitler could have been saved if just one person would demon straight the love of Jesus for him.

Forgiveness is not tolerating! Forgiveness is cleansing of your heart. It is forgiving them for they know not what they do! Forgiveness is giving them the love of Jesus and the truth that sets them free. The truth will set you free because when you accept the love of Jesus in your heart the world is a better place. No one can take that love away from you! When the devil comes to kill, steal and destroy that love, you, simply say, "I know the love and forgiveness of Jesus has for me and Jesus came and died for me so I can start out new every day." In other words just love Jesus because you know He loves you! Now that is freedom to the maximum! Freedom is good fruit! Forgiving is being a good tree because Jesus said you will know a tree by its fruit. Be a strong fruit-bearing tree of forgiveness and set others free!

Luke 6:44 For every tree is known by its own fruit. For men do not gather figs from thorns, nor do they gather grapes from a bramble bush.

I believe Jesus is comparing us to trees because an apple tree cannot bear a plum or a cherry. We cannot be evil in our heart and bear good fruit. Just as a tree needs a good root system that will pump water up to the top of the tree for life and good fruit. We need a good heart to bear good fruits. We all know that a good heart has Scripture written on the tablet of our heart. Good from evil is easy to recognize in actual fruit from trees but is it not always easy to recognize in humans. Sometimes, it is actually very hard. Unlike an apple, we cannot peal a person to see what is inside. But Jesus did give us some great ways to recognize or discern good from evil.

> **Luke 6:45** A good man out of the good treasure of his heart brings forth good; and an evil man out of the evil treasure of his heart brings forth evil. For out of the abundance of the heart his mouth speaks.

That is right! We store treasures in our hearts. Our good treasures bring forth righteousness, health, love, pureness, kindness, and all the fruits of Godliness.

I know doctors that say the heart is a blood pump and nothing more but they are totally wrong. Jesus said, "for the abundance of the heart a man speaks." Sometimes, people with heart transplants have huge personality changes and the doctors cannot explain why? It is so simple to explain if you believe God. And I believe in God!

> **Matthew 12:35** A good man out of the good treasure of his heart brings forth good things, and an evil man out of the evil treasure brings forth evil things.

Jesus said good and evil comes from the heart. I believe Jesus and I believe that our heart is a little more than a muscle that pumps blood! THANK YOU JESUS!

> **Galatians 5:22-23** But the fruit of the Spirit is love, joy, peace, longsuffering, kindness, goodness, faithfulness, gentleness, self-control. Against such there is no law.

These are the good fruits that God gives us just for loving Him. When we manifest these fruits then we are manifesting Jesus! Manifesting Jesus should be our goal and not just going to heaven. You see, if your manifesting Jesus, you will be filled with the Joy of the Lord and you are already in heaven!

Galatians 5:24 And those who are Christ's have crucified the flesh with its passions and desires.

But for an evil man, out of the evil treasures of his heart will bring forth evil, hate, sickness, and lust! I hate, hate, hate evil! I hate sickness. I hate lust. I hate the works of the devil and I hate when I manifest any of these because I am manifesting the devil. The good news is I do not wage war against the devil and let him dictate my thoughts. I just dwell on the Good News of Jesus and keep my focus on Jesus and the devil is defeated!

Wow! I just realized that the news media are doing the work of the devil every day. They will tell you the evil news. In fact, the more evil the news is, the more they like it. Evil news brings in fear, doubt and a feeling of helplessness. The devil is coming into your house every time you turn on the television. I remember when I would tell my children to shut up because I was trying to listen to the news. I bet that the devil was laughing his you know what off as he watches me watching how the devil is manifesting on my television and telling my children to let me listen to it.

Thank God I stopped watching television about ten years ago. I can tell you this: if I was still watching television I would not have the time to write this. I would not be full of Joy right now. I would not have a relationship with Jesus or a heart full of hope, a life full of love. And I would not be a house fit for a King. If you want Jesus fruits, then be a Jesus' tree! When Jesus trims your tree, there is no pain because Jesus took away your pain. There is no suffering but just the Joy of knowing the Lord. And most of all there is no despair or hate – there is only love, hope and faith! It is easy to see these virtues in Jesus and it will be easy to see these virtues in the Spirit of Jesus in you! That is some real good fruit!

Do you know good has a name? Do you know good has someone to follow? Do you know good has someone to look up to? Do you know good has someone to be proud of in life? Do you know good has a name? His name is Jesus, the Name above all Names!!! Notice how the devil will hide behind you. Jesus never hides behind anyone! In fact Jesus went right into the sinners houses boldly! Boldness is a fruit of knowing Jesus. Being a coward is a fruit of knowing the devil!

The devil will never use his name, but he will surely use yours if you let him. For example, Hitler listened to evil and manifested evil everywhere he went. People could see the evil and decided to stop him at all cost. I believe the problems of America today are still the devil at work but the devil learned a lesson when Hitler was killed and decided not to manifest his evil with one leader, instead he manifest in hundreds of little leaders and that is a lot harder to fight. Who is leading the fight for abortion? In no-prayer in school? How about open sex and making it legal to kill the mentally handicapped or using them for experiments? For taking prayer out of America? Who is corrupting our movies, news media and our government a little at a time? Who do you think is doing it? Who is responding to it? And who do you fight? The devil, that's who!!! Try to put a name on him now days. That's some evil fruit!

The answer is still the same. Stay steadfast in your beliefs. Center your life on Jesus and how he didn't pay attention to the circumstances. Be God-centered and not problem-oriented! Pray for America! We pray to manifest Jesus every day in every way! Change hearts one at a time!!! Jesus wins every time! Our fight is not flesh and blood – it is in our spirit that dwells in us. It might seem simple minded but we win one soul at a time. The devil learned a big lesson when the massive movement of Hitler was shut down. The devil realized it takes longer but he can corrupt the world one soul at a time almost even without a fight. If we all wait for some big bomb to go off and destroy evil, we are wasting all the opportunities we have here and now of today! How does a tree bear good fruit? Answer: by one blossom at a time! Bear good Fruit, one soul at a time. The answer is to do the work of the kingdom in one soul at a time! Just be a good spark! I know every forest fire started with a spark somewhere! Sparks can be gooooood fruit! The farmer that never planted seeds, never had a harvest!

In this fight, we cannot go by our physical senses since they are easily deceived and manipulated as we will see in the father-in-law story below. So what do we go by? First, we have to seek the truth in the Word of God and deposit or plant that truth in our hearts. Then we nourish the truth by listening for the voice of God and discerning who we are lessoning to and then living the truth and proclaiming the truth boldly everywhere you go! We do all that by just asking God into our life – by asking God for his manifested presents in our life! That's some gooooood Fruit!

We are to be in the world and not of the world. Then we can distinguish good from evil and others will distinguish us from evil. We must be born again to receive the gifts of the Holy Spirit. That is gooooood fruit!

At first I thought we should study evil so we could recognize it but Jesus made me realized that if you know the truth, that will set us free then you will recognize the evil that keeps us in bondage. We will recognize evil in all its forms. We are to study God's truth. The truth is we are to trust in God and put our faith in God and believe in God with all our hearts. Our heart must be where our spirit is because we are told to write His word on the tablet of our heart.

Proverbs 3:5 Trust in the Lord with all your heart, and lean not on your own understanding;

It is our own understanding that gets us in a lot of trouble! Don't try to understand every teaching of the Bible, just accept that it is true! Trust God, I mean trust, TRUST GOD!!!

James 1:13 Let no one say when he is tempted, "I am tempted by God"; for God cannot be tempted by evil, nor does He Himself tempt anyone.

Jesus said he tempts no man and so we should not tempt any man. Some of the ways we tempt others are so accepted that today we call temptation a joke. The devil has trust torn down to a point where some of us don't even trust GOD! Some of us don't trust our own spouse or our loved ones with stupid stuffs like money! How are we going to trust them with our hearts? Trust is a precious fruit from God!

For example, I knew a man who tempted his future son-in-laws. He would ask them to trust him. Then he would blind fold his future son-in-law and place a dirty stinky diaper full of poop under his nose. He then asks him to stick out his index finger and while holding the diaper under his nose stuck the finger into another diaper covered in peanut butter. He then asks the son-in-law to stick his finger in his mouth. That seems very innocent. I mean, it is just a joke.

In Proverbs 3:5, Jesus said to lean not on your own understanding. Here, we see that his own understanding is all the boy has to lean on and you can see how easy it is to deceive our senses. Sight, smell, touch, and taste were all deceived in seconds. I believe that is why Jesus said He will tempt no man.

In James 1:13, it says that 'let no one say when he is tempted, "I am tempted by God"; for God cannot be tempted by evil, nor does He Himself tempt anyone'. Jesus wants us to have our complete faith in Him and not in our own understanding. But if Jesus tempted us, how could we trust him? I believe when Jesus was in the desert, Jesus knew it was the devil tempting Him because He knew for a fact that His Father would never tempt him. Knowing God, He will never tempt us. It is a great discerning truth that no temptation is from God. I believe sometimes we tempt God without realizing it. For example, say we tithe to the church because we are told by some preachers that we will be rewarded 100 fold. So we give to God because we expect Him to return of 100 fold. Isn't that tempting God to make good on His word? I believe we are to give out of the goodness of our heart and knowing that God loves us and not tempting God to show he loves us! It is like living to love others so God will love us. That is backwards. We love others because we know God loves us and we are to be the love Jesus here on earth. God never tempts us with His love. God gives us His love freely! God tempts no man!

Want another discerning truth? Fruits have to be developed over time, whereas works need to be accomplished! Like the fruit of a tree is ripened from a seed to a blossom to a tiny fruit to a full-grown fruit over time and with the proper care and nourishment. Works would be to pick the fruit and use the seed of the fruit to plant another tree.

At this point the son-in-law has to figure out whether or not to trust his father-in-law. He has to figure out what is in the heart of the father-in-law. The father-in-law had totally deceived the senses of the boy. How will he recognize truth? The real test here is whether the father-in-law has presented himself trustworthy to his son-in-law. If he will have the son-in-law will put his finger in his mouth without any hesitation. The problem with this harmless joke is the father-in-law has now lost the trust of his son-in-law because the son-in-law knows the father-in-law will sell his trust cheap to get a laugh. Harmless joke with a big price, and evil fruit, these can be the fruits of our jokes?

Proverbs 3:6 In all your ways acknowledge Him, And He shall direct your paths.

When our trust is in God without compromise we know Jesus will direct our paths. So we can rest in God knowing that He will never tempt us. We can trust in God knowing God will direct our paths. These are some gooooood fruits!

If the father-in-law has not proved or presented himself as a trustworthy person to the son-in-law, he will not put his finger in his mouth. This is actually a stupid test because if the father-in-law has done this as a joke and the finger has poop on it, the son-in-law will never trust his father-in-law again. Pretty high stakes if it is just a joke. Also part of a father-in-law's role will be to direct the path of the new marriage. Without trust to his new son-in-law, he probably will not even ask the father-in-law for advice. The consequence of the joke can have some pretty far reaching effects. I believe the father-in-law heard the voice of the devil in his head saying this is just a harmless joke and that it will not hurt anything and he acted on that voice. Not being able to discern whose voice we are listening to is a very dangerous place to be in life. I know because I lived there most of my life.

2 Timothy 2:22-23 Flee also youthful lusts; but pursue righteousness, faith, love, peace with those who call on the Lord out of a pure heart. But avoid foolish and ignorant disputes, knowing that they generate strife.

Think about the harmless joke above. Did it lead to righteousness, faith, charity, peace or a pure heart? No way! It led to strife. Jesus said to avoid foolish and unlearned questions. I would call that joke a fine example of an unlearned question.

When you meet people for the first time and they do not want to talk about Jesus and His kingdom, lesson for their heart and don't be afraid to plant seeds of God's love. You will never know what is in a man's heart without getting to know him.

Without knowing the truth of God's word, we do not have any way to recognize good from evil and we become easily swayed like the wave of the ocean tossed by the wind. We will think that the joke is harmless when it is really the work of the devil.

James 1:13 Let no one say when he is tempted, "I am tempted by God"; for God cannot be tempted by evil, nor does He Himself tempt anyone.

You see the truth is that Jesus never tempts us. All temptation comes from the devil. Life is pretty simple when we know the truth. Jesus set the standard for life! We are not to tempt anyone!

In our story we recognize the father-in-law was tempting the future son-in-law, with his trust. Trust is such a precious commodity and that God said He would never tempt us. Knowing that God never tempts us, it actually builds our trust in God! In the story above, the father-in-law thought this was a harmless joke, but really he was trading his trust for a few laughs. Knowing the truth of God's word and living it will set the standard for life and the fruits will be to set others free. The word of God in us and flowing out of us is a very good way to be an example to others and help them to discern good from evil.

James 1:14 But each one is tempted when he is drawn away by his own desires and enticed.

Here God is saying we will all be tempted but not by God! Remember God tempts no man. So we should never tempt anyone or we are acting out evil and doing the work of the devil. You see

145

how the truth sets us free. If we are tempted in any way, even when it seems harmless, we need to have the truth of God's Word planted in our hearts to make informed decisions. The truth is God tempts know man! Trust is a precious commodity and we should take it as serious as Jesus does!!!

James 1:15 Then, when desire has conceived, it gives birth to sin; and sin, when it is full-grown, brings forth death.

In our story the joke seems so harmless yet, the son-in-law will always question the trust of the father-in-law because the father-in-law was so willing to put his trust in the outcome of a joke! When you recognize that you cannot trust someone, the fruit of the broken trust will be death to that relationship. Remember God never tempts any one. You can always know the heart of God and you can trust God and in Him have life not death.

James 1:16 Do not be deceived, my beloved brethren.

That's a big statement. And it is a bold warning. Trust is such a big gift. Don't give yours away in jokes and meaningless actions. Honor trust for what it is a gift from the Father! Just think if we could trust people as we can trust God we would never need lawyers at all. The saying 'put that in writing' would not exist.

People put their trust in so many places and things. They buy things to make others envious like big cars, jewelries, fancy clothes etc. and to make themselves happy. It is a lie from the devil! The devil will say that these things will make you happy and you must trust him. You buy these things only to find out these are junks and then you ask God why did you let this happen to me and the devil is laughing because he breaks your trust with lust and then gets you to blame God for not protecting you and your investment.

James 1:17 Every good gift and every perfect gift is from above, and comes down from the Father of lights, with whom there is no variation or shadow of turning.

The gift of God's trust is one we must recognize and we can trust God because He has no variableness. God is 100% trust and 100% trustworthy. God will never break our trust in Him, not even a shadow of turning. We can actually live this way. Jesus is the example of how to live a trust worthy life. He chose His words perfectly and showed us trust is a fruit of knowing the truth of His Word.

James 1:18 Of His own will He brought us forth by the word of truth, that we might be a kind of firstfruits of His creatures.

Jesus made it easy for us to know His heart. He will never tempt us or deceive us. He is the truth and nothing but the truth. We can trust God with our heart, our mind, and our soul! Trust is a firstfruit from God and it is with our trust in God that we can bear our firstfruit. Good fruit is not an accident!

What are some fruits that can deceive us? Motive can be a huge area of deceitfulness. Was the father-in-law's motive to be a joke or a test of trust? You see why it is so important to know that God will never tempt us. How could we have trust in someone that might tempt us with a stupid joke? The stupid joke has turned into a lack of trust in both parties. The son-in-law will always see his father-in-law as a man that puts a very low value on trust. The father-in-law has lost the trust of his whole family. I guess we can say there is no such thing as a stupid joke.

When I first got serious about seeking God, I read about recognizing fruits. You know them by their fruits. I was drawn into healing ministries because I needed Jenny healed. I just accepted everything I heard there because I saw great miracles happen and thought this has to be of God. They were quoting scripture all through their teachings and I was studying to make sure they were quoting them correctly. My problem came as I studied – I realized I was becoming more fearful of what the devil could do. I was sin conscious all the time and constantly warring against the devil. I was judgmental. I became aware of all these unknowns. I didn't know Jenny's dad and what sins he had been into. My life was becoming trapped in a little world. I did not become free to love

147

others. On the contrary I was looking at others and studying others to see what their motive was. I was questioning motives all the time. The fruit of that is fear, distrust, withdraw and an unloving spirit. Where is the truth that sets us free?

Then came the scripture about seven more worse than the first will come back and tear you up.

Luke 11:24-26 "When an unclean spirit goes out of a man, he goes through dry places, seeking rest; and finding none, he says, 'I will return to my house from which I came.' And when he comes, he finds it swept and put in order. Then he goes and takes with him seven other spirits more wicked than himself, and they enter and dwell there; and the last state of that man is worse than the first."

When I read these scriptures, I said, "How is that fair Jesus? I mean how do I fight that?" I was becoming so fearful and thinking where is the joy in knowing God. There is supposed to be some joy in knowing God isn't there? If so where is it? I went back to the ministry and saw the same people coming back to fight the devil again and again. I cried out to the Lord, what am I doing? Where is the truth? I mean in the Catholic Church, I was at least happy.

I am so blessed to know God because He answered my prayers. He had Peggy at Be In Health church tell me to get my relationship with God on again. I really hadn't realized I've lost my relationship with the God. I spent so much time warring against the devil. I didn't have time to talk to God. I was trying not to sin. After talking to Peggy, I started renewing my relationship with God again and in no time at all I was talking to God and hearing his voice again and the Joy of the Lord came back and so did MY strength.

I heard about Curry Blake of John G. Lake Ministries (www.jglm.org) and life started changing for me. Curry teaches people that we are to be like Jesus. That was a noble idea for me. I mean, Jesus came to forgive me my sins if I confessed them, right? Jesus is the Father God's Son. Who would even dare to compare yourself to Him. The more I studied and read about the life of Jesus I realized Jesus came to be our example. Jesus is the perfect
148

example of forgiveness and love, caring for everyone, dying to self, mercy, trust, Faith, healing, casting out devils, you name it and if it is good then Jesus showed us how to do it right. I love you, Jesus. This is how you defeat the devil. Life is simple! You fall in love with Jesus and keep Him in your heart and in your mind all the time. The devil problem solved! Jesus said resist the devil and he will flee! That is gooooood fruit!

We recognize them by their fruits. Fruits are not necessarily healings and raising from the dead. True fruits are knowing and having a personal relationship with Jesus! Knowing the truth of God's word is fruit to enjoy the rest of your life! Actually, for eternity.

> Matthew 7:20-21 Therefore by their fruits you will know them. "Not everyone who says to Me, 'Lord, Lord,' shall enter the kingdom of heaven, but he who does the will of My Father in heaven.

So he that doeth the will of the Father which is in heaven will be recognized by God. Like my friend Christopher said, "It is not good enough for you to know God, God must know you!"

> **Matthew 7:22-23** Many will say to Me in that day, 'Lord, Lord, have we not prophesied in Your name, cast out demons in Your name, and done many wonders in Your name?' And then I will declare to them, 'I never knew you; depart from Me, you who practice lawlessness!'

I don't want God to say "I never knew you: depart from me, you that work iniquity." I believe what God is saying here is we can do all these works and still not know God. If we are doing all these wonderful miracles and our motive is self-gratification, then we are doomed. God will honor His Word because He said it and it is true. We can use the name of Jesus to cast out demons and raise the dead, heal the sick and preach his word but if your motives are not to bring Glory to God you can forget life eternal. Your reward could be hearing these words 'depart from me'. The first thing you have to realize is God is love. Self-gratification is not love! Read all of first John.

> **1 John 4:16** And we have known and believed the love that God has for us. God is love, and he who abides in love abides in God, and God in him.

We have to know and believe the love of God has for us and GOD IS LOVE if we dwells in love then we dwells in God and God in us. You see love is the key to knowing God is love and love is the key to God knowing and loving you. Do all things in love and you are becoming God-like. My best friend Jesus showed us love with every word and deed.

> **1 John 4:17** Love has been perfected among us in this: that we may have boldness in the day of judgment; because as He is, so are we in this world.

Boldness in the Day of Judgment, how? By becoming perfect in love as Jesus is love (perfect love) so must we be love (perfect love)! Seek to be the love of Jesus and He will prefect His love in you. When you walk in the love of Jesus, you will have boldness on judgment day because His word says "as He is so are we in this world." That is a perfect fruit! You cannot make yourself perfect but you can ask God to make you perfect and you will become His perfect love. In God, all things are possible. All good gifts came down from above. Jesus is love and so are you if you ask God for the gift of His perfect love to be in you and flow through you to everyone you meet! Die to self and start living, start flowing and be a river of life! That's some gooooood fruit!!!!

> **1 John 4:12** No one has seen God at any time. If we love one another, God abides in us, and His love has been perfected in us.

You want to see God? Then look no further than the mirror. 'If we love one another, God dwells in us and His love is perfected in us'. God is in heaven but by His Holy Spirit, we can have God dwells in us. How do we know God knows us? Here God tells us that if we love one another, then God dwells in us and God's love
150

is perfected in us. Notice we do not perfect our love but God's love is perfected in us. Only God is perfect and so if we let him love through us then His love is perfected in us and through us.

1 John 4:8 He who does not love does not know God, for God is love.

The Scripture tells us God is love. I believe that is why it is so hard to describe love. All through John, the Scripture makes it clear that if you do keep all the commands of the Bible and do not love, your eternal life is hell!

1 Timothy 1:5 Now the purpose of the commandment is love *from* a pure heart, *from* a good conscience, and *from* sincere faith,

Here, Timothy is saying the end of the commandment is charity (love). What is the end of the commandment, to simply do them or perform them, like heal the sick, raise the dead and cast out devils, preach boldly! You must do these things with a pure heart. A pure heart is a heart of love, like Jesus loved not by looking for anything in return for Himself. I believe that is a good conscience. When your motives are clearly just to give love freely as Jesus did then you have a good conscience. Faith unfeigned is sincere faith in the love of Jesus flowing through you. The love of Jesus is through you not just for you. In some Scriptures, Jesus likened love to a river flowing, but if you dam up the river the water becomes stagnant and life in it dies. So is our love. We need to share it everywhere. Just as a fruit tree cannot eat its own fruit, I believe our fruit (love) will become useless if try to hang on to it.

I see in the word of God the Scriptures use the word charity but we call it love. That seems harmless because charity is loving others but the word love now days can also mean to receive love. Charity is giving not receiving! Do you know the Barney Song 'I love you do you love me'? We have turned love into a two-way street. That is sick and downright perverted. Charity or love as Jesus loved was never a two-way street! The life of Jesus was all about charity and nothing but charity! When we look for a return of love we are setting ourselves up for failure big time. Remember
151

you die to yourself by giving yourself is love. But wanting love in return makes giving just about receiving. The devil will have you as an easy target when you want something in return. Check your motives. Be pure! Set your goals on giving and loving just like as Jesus did by dying to self!

Are miracles the manifestation of God's love? Are all miracles signs and wonders? Are all miracles fruits? If so, why would God say, a wicked and adulterous generation looks for signs?

Matthew 16:4 A wicked and adulterous generation seeks after a sign, and no sign shall be given to it except the sign of the prophet Jonah." And He left them and departed.

Matthew 24:24 For false christs and false prophets will rise and show great signs and wonders to deceive, if possible, even the elect.

2 Thessalonians 2:9 The coming of the *lawless* one is according to the working of Satan, with all power, signs, and lying wonders,

So we can see from these Scriptures and many more that the devil can perform signs and wonders. If we are not careful, we will be deceived. How are the devil's signs and wonders different from Gods signs and wonders? One way for sure is to know the difference between God's signs and the devil's signs. That is, the Antichrist will never call on the name of Jesus to perform the signs and wonders. Also, the devil's signs and wonders (miracles) will never set anyone free. I mean, if the signs are from the devil, the person will be in constant fear of the devil coming back to take away their healing. They will spend time fighting the devil to keep their healing. They will be in a constant war with the devil. They will see the devil as someone with all the power to attack them and will say, "I'm under such an attack today." All that fighting and warring and FEAR is of the devil and there is absolutely no freedom in FEAR, warring and constant attacks! If you are in fear, I ask you, "Where is the love? Where is the peace and joyfulness of knowing God? All fear is a lack of trust in God's love for you."

If you are in fear of anything, you do not know and trust God. Knowing that God dwells in you and knowing that no one, not
152

even the devil can pluck you out of the Father's hand. That is peace and freedom! Knowing the gifts of the Holy Spirit are yours to live and walk in, that is love and freedom! Knowing the joyfulness of having a relationship with God, that is joy and freedom! Jesus said, "My truth will set you free!" It does! Intimacy with God is truly the most peaceful, loving, and joyful time you will spend here on earth. Intimacy with God is bring heaven to earth.

Jesus said these signs shall follow the believer and not lead a believer.

> **Mark 16:20** And they went out and preached everywhere, the Lord working with them and confirming the word through the accompanying signs. Amen.

Noticed we are to go forth and preach everywhere and when we do the Lord works with us and confirms His word with signs following us. Where do we preach? Everywhere! At work, at play, in our homes, while shopping, that is being the life of Jesus here on earth. Notice who works through you: the Lord! He confirms everything you do and say with signs such as healing and casting out devils and freeing the spirit in you to desire more of Jesus in your life. When you witness someone sets free, you will be praising God with all your heart boldly and the joy of the Lord will make you sing like never before! That is some real gooooood fruit!!!

Don't just lead them to God, give them God and God will bring the increase! Fruit is not some quick prayer to get them saved and gets them to heaven. It is giving them Heaven right here on earth. Fruit is the renewing of the mind, to accepting the transforming of the mind away from the devil and temptation and to seeing and experiencing the love of Jesus now and forever! Fruit is turning off the past completely! Fruit is seeing a future with the Holy Spirit in you and working through you. Fruit is being with Jesus 24/7.

Fruit is knowing you are a Son of God and we are saved by grace. But we can no longer say we are just sinners saved by grace! We are Sons of God! We have a new bloodline: a new Father and a relationship with Jesus our brother. For me, that is the Good News
153

and along with that is that our past is removed as far as the east from the west. Fruit is knowing you can walk in the same power and love that Jesus did. Fruit is knowing God loves you! And most of all, fruit is intimacy with the Creator of the world and knowing the Creator of the world will spend time with you if you let Him.

My my... That sure beats being attacked every day! Intimacy with Jesus is better than getting up trying not to sin today! What if my past hurts are worse than yours or what if yours are worse than mine? The past no longer matters. All that comparing does is trap us in the past and robs us of our future by constantly comparing! The past will says, "Poor little old me! I'm so tired I just want to get on that heaven bus, and get out of here. Jesus, take me home!" That sounds like the work of the devil to me! What happened to die to self? What happened to doing the work of the kingdom? What happened to the greatest two commandments? Where did love go? I got my ticket so I'll just watch television until it is time to go? What happened to 'the greatest of these is charity'?

I'm in relationship with God now! Intimacy with Jesus is not about worrying about the devil and temptation; it is focusing on Jesus and what we can do today! Just ask God right now, "DO YOU LOVE ME JESUS?" I can guarantee you! In fact, I will give you an extended guarantee that you just heard a YES in your head and you will still hear a YES tomorrow and the next day. I know this because Jesus said He died for us all! If someone willingly dies for you, I would bet they loved you!

When Jesus called the apostles he did not do a background check. So why should you? Jesus is the transformer! Jesus is more than a bus ticket to heaven! Jesus is the truth that sets us free to be gooooood fruit NOW! I love being fruity! Jesus is trimming a lot of my branches and they have been hue down and thrown into the fire, because I am surrendered to trimming. I only desire to be a bearer of goooooood JESUS Fruit!!! IN THE CHARITY OF JESUS, ALL THINGS ARE POSSIBLE! AND WITH JESUS IN ME NOTHING IS IMPOSSIBLE FOR ME OR YOU!!!

Remember the seed you sow today might seem so small like a mustard seed but when watered by the charity of God's love, we can expect it to blossom into a fruit tree. Even the blossoms of a fruit tree are pretty, so be a blossom of God's charity today and watch Jesus bring the increase!!!

GET UP EACH DAY WITH THESE WORDS ON YOUR LIPS: JESUS WHAT ARE <u>WE</u> GOING TO DO TODAY?

Jenny, Ron and Jesus loves you all so be fruitful today! Be charity today and most of all be Jesus today!

God's Best Friend

Dear Best Friend,

Let us suppose your urine burns so you think, "I have a kidney infection. I'll take some cranberry juice." I think we have been programmed to look for home remedies first. We trust ourselves and in our own knowledge. If that fails, we go to a doctor. Then if both of those sources fail, we might go to God. What if you said, "Father what should I do, my urine burns?" I guarantee that Father will answer you, because He is or wants to be your best friend!

I heard a testimony the other day. A young couple went to be missionaries in Africa. After five years, they felt defeated. Their newborn baby was very sick and not doing so well. These young missionaries hadn't made anyone convert to Christianity. They were out of food and both of them were hungry. The young man told his wife, "Pack your bags, we are leaving. But first I'm going to have it out with God!" So he went into the jungle to be alone with God. After hours of telling God what he thought of Him, the young man collapsed and while he lay on the ground in that exhausted state, God said, "I never called you to be a missionary. I never ask you to go to Africa. You have exhausted yourself trying to please me. All I ever wanted was to be was your friend." Jesus asked him 'will you please be my friend?'

I believe we have all been in that exhausted state. I believe we all have a desire to please God but we want to please Him our ways. I believe and think that we already know what will please God.

I remember a story about a young girl, Janie that became very sick and the doctors could not figure out how to help her. By the time she was 20 years old she became so sick she was confined to bed, very limited to what she could eat. She had extreme seizures and her parents had to change her and bathe her frail body. Only after exhausting all human measures did they turn to God. Jesus walked into her room one night and healed her instantly. Yes, instantly she could walk, eat, and showed no signs of being sick! Later, as her relationship with God grew she told God she wanted to be a missionary to Africa. She wanted to dedicate her life to God in thanks for giving her healing. God walked into her room again and very plainly told her no. God said, "I thought you wanted a dog and wanted to throw a Frisbee to him in the park?" She started crying and asked God "You healed me so I could throw a Frisbee in the park?" God said, "Yes. You know Janie, there are no paybacks. I just want you to enjoy the life I gave you." Jesus told Janie 'I am your very best friend!'

I remember when Jesus told me, "There are no paybacks, Ron." If my little Jenny's healing manifested before Jesus told me that, I would have lived the rest of my life trying to pay Jesus back for loving us so much. Then Jesus showed me:

1 Corinthians 13:13 And now abideth faith, hope, charity, these three; but the greatest of these *is* charity.

That is right! We have faith and hope but the greatest is CHARITY! To me, charity is giving and sacrifice and in most cases Jesus is the one giving and sacrificing. We simply cannot outgive Jesus! The rest of the definition of charity is that there are no paybacks. If you look at the life of Jesus, you will see a total giver. Jesus never held anything back and the only thing Jesus wants from us is for us to be His best friend. We become best friends with Jesus when we ask Him into our heart and let Him to dwell there!

When you accept God into your heart by asking Him into your heart, you become one with Him. Your heart is protected. You are safe in His arms and no one can break that bond of friendship except you. God never leaves us or forsakes us. We leave Him usually because we start believing in ourselves. We start believing in others who are preaching the word of God and we slip into trusting them instead of God. It happens so slowly and so innocently that we don't even realize it. Then one day that person falls short of our expectation and we lose faith. So put your faith in God, not mankind and have your best friend back. Oh yea, the young couple from the Jungle made God their Best Friend and put all their trust in God. Now, that whole area became Christians because they no longer just taught about God, they started living the love of God! You see, when God is your best friend other people see the peace and joy in you and want what you have. God's love is contagious. His peace is outrageous. His joy is spontaneous. So go sow some contagious, outrageous, spontaneous love of God to everyone you meet. Tell them God is looking for some best friends!

There is another part of prayer you will come to realize when you have made God your Best Friend. I hear church preachers pray for God to do something and the whole congregation comes into agreement that God should go heal Sally or do whatever we want Him to do. They pray, "oh God! Come down and do something." If you are in the habit of calling God down and asking Him to go heal Sally or if you are in church singing and worshiping Jesus trying to get Holy Spirit goosebumps, then you might want to rethink your prayer life. Why are we trying to call God into existence or into our presence when He does exist and He said I will never leave you! You have to understand your Best friend will never leave you and God does exist!

Hebrews 13:5 Let your conduct be without covetousness; be content with such things as you have. For He Himself has said, *"I will never leave you nor forsake you."*

Jesus said it in His words and I believe it. I don't think I need to call Him down when I know He is already in me. Jesus commissioned us to use His power. So if Sally is sick, it is not up to God to come down and heal her, it is up to us! When you invite Jesus into your heart, He shows up with everything we need to bring heaven to earth and says if you believe in me, go and do the things I did! Just command Sally's body to line up with the Word of God and it will!

Matthew 16:19 And I will give you the keys of the kingdom of heaven, and whatever you bind on earth will be bound in heaven, and whatever you loose on earth will be loosed[a] in heaven."

Notice the word *'thou shalt'* who does it you shalt do it! I believe it means you and I can be the you shalt and do it, if we believe.

John 14:12 "Most assuredly, I say to you, *he who believes in Me, the works that I do he will do also; and greater works than these he will do, because I go to My Father.*

I believe my Jesus is my best friend and as such He lives in me and He dwells in me so why would I pray for Him to go do something he told me to do? Most prayers I hear in churches today are just asking and asking takes no faith! I believe we are told to do the work of the kingdom. We are to represent our Best Friend Jesus and He is our example of how we are to run this earth.

For example, you tell your 14-year old son to take the garbage out. If he started praying for you to take out the garbage and he continued praying for ten years, asking for you, his parents, to take out the garbage. I bet you would want to kick him in the... Well, I won't go there but I wonder if sometimes God isn't thinking the same thing. God gave us the power to change the earth and when we pray for Him to take out the garbage I bet he wants to... Well, He won't go there.

Jesus taught us to pray and go do His will and not to pray for Him to go and do His will. Those same people eventually will say, 'God does not answer prayers' or 'I guess it is not His will'. Some people say God answers prayers but we just don't know when. When Jesus told us to go preach the gospel to all nations, He did not say for us to turn around and ask Him to go to all nations and preach the gospel. The same thing is true when God said in the name of Jesus, heal the sick, raise the dead and cast out devils. He said you go and do these things. When you make God your Best Friend, you will never be alone. So when you go to do his will, His Holy Spirit is with you. Knowing that the Holy Spirit is with me empowers me to do what God commands me to do! I believe the bolder I get commanding things to change in the Name of Jesus, the more Jesus is pleased with me. I hear a comedian say "get-er-done" and I think he is talking prophecy!!! SMILE!

Another fallacy I hear some people say is 'God had to break me before I would listen'. I don't believe God breaks anybody. I believe we break ourselves, and wear ourselves out trying to solve our own problems our own way and then in complete desperation we ask God where is the peace and strength you talk about in your word. We become so dependent on ourselves and what we think we are accomplishing that we never stop to listen until we have broken our own spirit. I remember a song by Frank Sinatra where he sang 'I did it my way'. I remember people quoting 'just grab yourself by the boot straps and pull yourself out of that mess'! I didn't realize I was hearing from the devil! I didn't realize I was trying to do things my way and in doing so I was actually telling God to go away, that I don't need God and I'll do it my way. I wore myself doing it my way!

If you had a best friend named Ron and your best friend stopped listening to you or he started doing things you know are wrong, you would very gently try to change Ron's mind but if you were rejected time and time again, you would withdraw. You might pray he needs you someday and you hopefully wait patiently for Ron to want your friendship again. You can watch Ron go down the wrong road, and it grieves you. But if he is unwilling to listen, your hands are tied. If you really are his friend, when he hits bottom you will be there to help him up. You did not break Ron and it was really painful for you to watch Ron makes bad choices. The pain of watching a loved one go down their own path is extremely severe! You know God did not make Ron go down the wrong path and God did not make Ron hit bottom and God did not break Ron.

Ron just stopped listening to God and Ron thought he know a better way to travel the road of life. I believe when we choose to walk our own path, God sees us making bad choices but if we had never really wanted to have a relationship with Jesus, we have never had a relationship with Jesus or we closed off our communications with Him. In a way we could say we have turned our heart away from Jesus. When we decide to walk our own paths and we close communications to our Jesus, guess what? The ever-patient Jesus will still watch over us for He said in His word that He will never leave us or forsake us so I know for a fact that God never left Ron but it was Ron who chose to make his own path. Jesus will actually bring His ambassadors into our path and they will gently show us the love He has for us and the freedom that comes from following the Jesus path. Jesus said His path is the narrow path but He never said it was hard. In fact Jesus said my path is narrow but my yoke easy and my burden is light.

> **Matthew 11:28** Come to Me, all you who labor and are heavy laden, and I will give you rest.

Jesus is asking us to come to Him. How many times are we in need of rest? Anytime you are weary from a heavy load you are working on your own strength. The promise is "I will give you rest" so we can live in His rest. Make yourself available to God and let God set the goals. Ask God every day *what are we going to do today?* and let God set the goals!

> **Matthew 11:29** Take My yoke upon you *and learn from Me*, for I am gentle and lowly in heart, and you will find rest for your souls.

Jesus is asking us to take upon ourselves His yoke and not our yoke. When we think we need to do something to please God we have just picked up our own yoke and laid down His yoke. God said 'Follow Me' and the moment we try to lead we are out of His will. When I ask God "what are we going to do today?" I have never heard God say 'go to Kroger and stand by the door. The woman that gets out of the blue car with four cigarettes in one hand, two vanilla ice creams in the other hand, a purple hat with three feathers in it, and no shoes, I want you to buy her some dog food and tell her God loves her'. God has never talked to me that way and I know that is not God because it would takes no faith to buy that woman dog food and tell her God loves her! I could even get confused and think, "Did Jesus say three feathers or two? That woman only has two feathers so maybe God made a mistake or maybe one of her feathers fell out? Or maybe I should go look in

161

her car to see if there is a feather in there. Gee, maybe I should just wait for someone with all her feathers. I mean maybe that woman was a decoy and doesn't have a dog and if she doesn't have a dog I would look stupid giving her dog food."

When I ask God 'what are we going to do today?', I have never heard an answer. I know by faith I have just made myself available to God, so I go about my day as usual. I know by faith that God will lead me to something He needs to be done. At the end of the day, I know by faith that God used me somewhere. I might have brightened someone's day by just smiling at them. My yoke is easy and my burden is light, I know because God said so! By faith I rest knowing that I will make myself available again tomorrow. There are some days when God had me preach the Good News to people and it's awesome! There are days when I have Coffee Time With Jesus all day and I truly love it. There are also days where Jesus wants me to write a book and I sit in my camper all day and type. There are days where I get to witness God flowing into someone to transform their lives and all of those days are truly amazing but I never try to make them happen. You see, I rest knowing by faith I am in the will of God by letting him set my day. I rest knowing that God is changing the world one heart at a time, I rest knowing that I am doing His will here on earth! I rest because I know it is the will of the Father for us to represent His love and I do because I am resting in Him. Yes I rest knowing Jesus and I are best friends. We walk and talk together 24/7. I rest for in Matthew, Jesus said:

Matthew 11:30 For My yoke *is* easy and My burden is light."

I never worry about tomorrow. Jesus said 'do not worry about tomorrow' so I don't.

Jesus proved that He had a relationship with His Father every day of His life. Jesus chose to have His relationship with His Father! We have to choose to be in relationship with Jesus and choose to listen to Him before we can hear His voice.

In the early part of my journey with Jesus, I would pray a list of needs to God every day and then say, "Thank you God, please take care of that for me," and then rush off to my next meeting. And then I rush to lunch with whoever and then rush to and then and then and then just rush rush rush!!! If I never have any time to listen to God's response, I am like Ron in the paragraphs above. If we are always doing and never resting, we should check what voice we are listening to and why. Jesus said 'I will give you rest' and now I tell you I rest because God is my Best Friend. Make Him yours and you will have a rest too!

Jesus said 'to die to self'! How do you die to self? Simple! You give up your rights. Let's say you get married and your desire is to bring all you have for your spouse to make her happy. Your personality will change from *what I want* to *what we need*. You share your time and recourses to make your marriage work. You no longer work for you alone. You are now working for the two of you. A good marriage is a great reflection of a relationship with Jesus. The two of you become one. You share things in common. There is a uniting together that brings great joy and peace and commitment! The wedding day is a day of new beginnings. The first year is a whole year of firsts, like 'this is the first time we did this together'.

The marriage couple literally dies to themselves to become the perfect helpmate to each other. They protect each other, provide for the needs of each other and material things that might have been his before the marriage are now theirs. They even become best friends!

I just described some of what a relationship with Jesus should look like. There are some major differences I did not describe. Jesus said seek yea first the kingdom of God and His righteousness and all these things shall be added.

Matthew 6:33 But seek first the kingdom of God and His righteousness, and all these things shall be added to you.

Even in marriage, we should seek God and His righteousness first over our wife and children. Read about Job and Abraham! If they had not been seeking God and did not have a relationship with God, they wouldn't be strong enough to withstand the terrors of the devil. Their trial would have turned them into crying wimps and asking God 'why did You let this happen to me?'. Seek God with all your heart, mind and soul. It is not just a cool thought, it is a statement of love, faith, commitment, and accepting God into your heart to be your Best Friend now and forever.

Please study the words of my Jesus in the Bible. I know there are a lot of different Bible translations and especially now people say 'how do you know which one to go by?' I remember the words of Jesus in John:

John 14:26 But the Comforter, *which is* the Holy Ghost, whom the Father will send in my name, *he shall teach you all things*, and bring all things to your remembrance, whatsoever I have said to you.

The phrase 'He shall teach you all things' come to my mind every time someone tries to tear down the word of God because of the different translations. I love my Jesus and by faith I believe my Jesus will bring His true love to me and direct my path because my Best Friend says so! Please read with discernment and you will understand how God protects His loved ones.

One more thing to think about the gifts of having earthly friends in high places are self-esteem, you being puffed up, and the gift of a false sense of security. These gifts are counterfeits of God's gifts. These are all momentary and actually bring strife, hopelessness and bondage to the receiver. I know a lot of Americans who think freedoms come from our government and in reality what governments can do is to limit freedom. Some limits are needed and some are truly the government imposing their will on us. My Bible tells me where true liberty and true freedom come from.

Galatians 5:1 Stand fast therefore in the liberty by which Christ has made us free, and do not be entangled again with a yoke of bondage.

You see freedom comes from our relationship with God. Relationship with God truly removes bondages. For example, you could be best friends with President Obama and because of your relationship with him you would maybe be given some special privileges. But President Obama has no power to give you freedom from anything. If you derived your self-esteem from your relationship to President Obama and one day did something that broke that relationship your self-esteem would be gone. True self-worth comes from God! True wisdom comes from God, and true freedom comes from God.

Knowing God and having a relationship with God the Highest of the High is totally the opposite of knowing people in high places here on earth. The gifts of knowing God are self-worth, wisdom and real security. Jesus describes His gifts:

Galatians 5:22-23 But the fruit of the Spirit is love, joy, peace, longsuffering, kindness, goodness, faithfulness, gentleness, self-control. Against such there is no law.

If we all lived in the revelation that these gifts are from God, we really would never need freedom limiting laws!

Jenny, Ron and Jesus love you all now and forever!!!

Healing Revealed

Over the last couple days while I was having my coffee time with Jesus, He has revealed to me a lot about Jenny's healing. I've been saying for years now how Jenny tears down the walls and opens doors for me to pray for people. What I mean by that is this: If I am all alone by myself and approach people to pray for them, there seems to be an invisible wall that comes up between us. People seem to wonder what I am up to. They will ask themselves, 'what is my motivation?' I mean, most people will not approach you to ask, "Can I pray for you?" People walk around with a wall up. Most don't even think about this defense and they just try to protect themselves. The door to their heart is locked. It will be really hard to break down these walls and unlock their hearts to let the love of Jesus flow into them.

If I approach them with Jenny the wall comes down and the door opens and the love of Jesus can flow in like a river. You can literally watch God work. You will see them transform right before your eyes. Jesus will tell you what to say to them and the Joy of the Lord fills their hearts. When you witness the Joy of the Lord flowing into them and watch that joy transform them, you become so joyful. And you cannot contain that joy! Really, you don't want to contain it and you want to give it away again and again and again!

Jesus has revealed to me that He tears down the wall and opens the door to let His love flow through me into others. I have been giving Jenny the credit for doing the work of Jesus. This correction from Jesus was so gentle and so full of love that it proves to me that Jesus is love! Even His corrections are love! I felt no guilt or shame; just a soft need to repent and then an urge to go out and watch how God works. I'm now telling you there is no joy on this earth like the joy of watching God work!

166

There is a reason why Jesus needed to make this adjustment in my thinking. You see, by me giving Jenny the credit for tearing down the wall and opening the door, I was telling myself I need her. I was telling 'Jesus, I cannot do this work all by myself, I need Jenny!' I was getting my self-worth out from Jenny instead from God. I believe that was kind of like making Jenny god. So I repented and now I know to give all the credit to God! This also frees Jenny. You see, in a way, I was putting Jenny under attack from the enemy. If Jenny had a seizure, I could not do the work of the Father. I would just take care of Jenny, so the enemy knew the more seizures Jenny had, the less work I will do for the kingdom. So Jesus very gently corrected me. I love you Jesus!!!

Jesus has also revealed to me that He wants to be my Best Friend. The love of Jesus is unconditional. The time Jesus wants to spend with His best friend is unlimited. My Best Friend laid down His life for me. I must be worth a lot to my Best Friend for He wrote the Bible for me. My best friend keeps me from sinning. He justified me and wants to spend eternity with me He gave me life and gives me a reason to keep going. He defines my self-worth, and He protects me. I can literally ask him anything and get an answer. Having Jesus as my Best Friend has no limits! Jesus takes my pain and my sorrows away. He delivers me from evil. Most of all, Jesus works on this world for me. That is why I get up every morning and say 'Jesus, what are we going to do today?' Notice the word *we*, not me but we, that is Jesus and I make *we*!!!

Jesus has also showed me that loving others is a privilege. We love others because Jesus first loved us. If you try to love others to get your self-worth, you are going be disappointed. You love others because Jesus loved you first. We are to share the love of Jesus for Jesus commanded us to go to the ends of the earth and preach His divine Word. Freely you have received and freely you give is not an offering command, but a command to go and share the love of Jesus everywhere. As Pastor Dan said, "if you could show me one person who Jesus didn't die for then pass that one up."

For 39 and half years, I have had the privilege to love and be loved by Jenny. I have always called Jenny my biggest blessing from God. I have praised God for Jenny. I praised God for our children and grandchildren and for our time together. God blessed me with the knowledge to build our house and a business. I can tell you right now that if all that was taken away – our children and grandchildren, home and lively hood, and even Jenny – I know without any doubt that my relationship with God would still be perfect! I know all the other gifts are superficial; those gifts are momentary. The gift of God's love is forever. Nothing can take away God's love for you! The only way to lose His love is for you to give it away by an act of your own will. Jesus says He will never leave you or forsake you! And I believe in Jesus!

This morning I have been delivered of Fear. I did no battle, no warring, no casting out; I just stand firm on the Word of God and accept His love for me. Jesus delivered me. He showed me I was in fear of losing Jenny to death. Today, I came into agreement with God's Word that says we have life everlasting. Jenny will live forever so I don't have to be afraid of death. In my mind, I saw a picture like we are full of compartments. Jesus love overflowed into three compartments and filled them to the top with love. So Jesus removed the fear and replaced it with love. I will never be afraid of losing Jenny again. The other fears will be talked about later on in this chapter.

I know that the most important relationship you can possibly have in life is your relationship to God the Father, Jesus and the Holy Spirit! My relationship with God is in the gifts of knowledge, wisdom and understanding! The devil cannot take these gifts away! To lose them, I have to be willing to give them up! JESUS IS MY STRONGHOLD! The Joy of the Lord is my strength! There is a song that says, 'He gives and takes away', I believe Jesus gives but we give away. When I covet anything, like my love for Jenny, the devil realizes that he has control over me with fear of losing Jenny. Then the devil starts using that fear to bring on more fear. In my case, the fear of losing my kids and grandchildren, gave me fear on fear on fear. My wife and children are gifts from God; they are to be enjoyed not coveted.

The gift of loved ones should be enjoyed and a reason to praise God! Just as kids grow up and develop their own personality, we as parents need to guide them, and help them develop their personalities, yet still let them make decisions on their own. In order for us to make good Godly decisions, we must have our own relationship with God our Father! So the most important thing we can teach to our children is to have a relationship with God! Then we can rest and have no fear about the future because of their relationship with the Father. We teach this relationship by example, not just what we say. We show the world our relationship to the Father is our biggest priority. We are to manifest Jesus in our every word and action! For example, I don't call 911 in an emergency. I call on Jesus and get better results with no negative side effects.

Jesus said His perfect love cast out fear. He said He would never leave us or forsake us. If we believe in this truth and transfer that truth to our children, then they can live without the fear, knowing the truth and live in the truth of God's Word. I already know that Jenny and I and our children will perish from the earth someday. In my fear, I'm just trying to dictate to God when that passing will be ok with me. By trying to hang on in life I am losing life because I am living in fear.

I talk to God and tell Him that my relationship with Him is the most important relationship I can have. My self-worth comes from that relationship, not from my wife and children. Knowing I am in control of my relationship with the Father is really what sets us free of death and fear. I AM FREE to love the Father and Jesus and the Holy Spirit my best friends. I am to be the bride of Jesus, your bride knows you better than anyone and that gives me great joy! My wife and children will see that joy and freedom and want what I have! Fear of death and losing my wife or children no longer has a hold on me. My wife and children are free because the devil can no longer hold their health and wellbeing over my head.

Philippians 2:5 says 'let this mind be in you, which was also in Christ Jesus'. That is amazing! We can have the mind of Jesus Christ. I believe when we are born again we get all the gifts of the Holy Spirit. It seems to me when you start operating in those gifts you are getting the mind of Jesus. You start to focus on what God created us to be instead of what you are seeing in the physical. Also, the best part is you are no longer afraid of death. Having the mind of Jesus Christ is freeing and death can be something that we can all look forward to! Knowing who we are in Jesus is about the

169

best knowledge you can have. We can have the mind of Jesus Christ! We can have the love of Jesus! We can be like Jesus! We can live without fear, without worry, and literally without death. Jesus said to be absent from the body is to be present before the Lord. So be prepared and ready to do the work of the kingdom and when God calls you home, there will be no fear.

Jesus is love and so I am love. I am made in His image and likeness. So I live and love every day as if it is my last day! Tomorrow is promised to no one. So live everyday as if it is your last. Forgive everyone as if this was your last chance. Can you see the freedom in that? Jesus said not to worry, so a worry-free life is possible or Jesus would not have said it. Don't just live as if tomorrow might not come but live as if you might be called home in the next minute. Have a personal relationship with Jesus and fear, anger, hatred, and sin is a thing of the past because sin and Jesus cannot live in the same vessel. Put on the mind of Christ!

I pray every day to live the way I preach and we are all walking this life together. So if you see me stumble and fall pick me up and dust me off and I will try to do the same for you. Life is all about sharing what God has shared with us – His love! Freely you received so freely you give!

Jenny is healed! I know a lot of people think I am crazy to say that. God's Word says Jenny is healed. By His stripes, we were healed. It is pretty simple, but for some pretty hard to believe. But in my heart, I know Jesus cannot lie. I believe my coffee time with Jesus is the most wonderful time of the day. I literally cannot wait to get up and start talking to my Jesus. He is my Best Friend and I want to live my life through Him. I want the Mind of Jesus!!! To know that Jesus heals and forgives and gives us strengths and holds us with the righteousness of His right hand is so comforting! We walk by faith and not by sight. Faith is the substance of things hoped for and the evidence of things not seen. Thank you Jesus for faith to know you are working with Jenny and me.

If you were sick and bedridden and you had a friend who was so comforting and looking out for your every need, you would want to thank him and talk to him and praise him all the time. You would want to reward him for all the good he has done to you. Life would be centered on him, and you would miss him if he were late and or taken away. Your safety is in him.

I am not sick or bedridden but I do have a Best Friend who will never leave me or forsake me. My Best Friend is the best friend anyone can possibly have. I put my life, wife, and kids in His hands. He gives me rest and comfort and that is all I need. Jesus revealed to me there is no payback. Jesus just wants us to know that we are loved so we can be loved. So when Jenny is healed, I do not have to pay back His love for me – He just wants me to bask in His love for me, and enjoy his gifts He has for me. This is His revelation for me. You see, if Jenny was healed a week ago I would have tried to spend the rest of my life paying Jesus back for such an awesome gift. Jesus revealed to me that He wants me to love Jenny and bask in His gift of healing! That is true friendship. Jesus, I love you more every day. I want to fellowship with you every second of everyday!!!

Have you ever called Father God, Father God? I just found out what these two words mean. Father means to come forth from, and God means the source of life. So saying Father God means to come forth from the source of life!!! I just thought that was awesome!

Father God and Jesus, I want to thank you for all you do and have done. Life really is about our relationship to you God. Without relationship we are still like Adam after he ate the tree of good and evil. Thank You Jesus for restoring the relationship between You and I. I literally live to be in right relationship with You!!!

Thank You Jesus for your love flowing through us! Love always from Jenny and Ron.

Today I was walking Jenny through a campground, when I saw signs on a camper that said: BEER – the reason I get up every afternoon. I want to thank God for giving me purpose in life! My life is so full of joy and I purposely spread that joy. That is the joy of knowing and loving Jesus Christ! The real purpose of Jesus life was to show us our self-worth to Him. We must be worth a lot for the Father to send his Son to reveal our worth to us! GOD LOVES US!!! HE DIDN'T JUST FORGIVE OUR SINS!!!

HE WANTS RIGHT RELATIONSHIP WITH US!!!

It was September 14 and Jenny and I were sleeping. It was around 2:12 in the morning and Jenny's body started jumping around like someone was shocking her with an electrical defibrillator. I thanked God that He was with Jenny and me! Jesus said to enter His gates with praise. So I started singing His praise and thanking Him for His Word that says we are healed. I thanked Jesus that His Word says nothing can hurt us. Jenny's little body settled down and we went back to sleep. In my coffee time, I thanked Jesus again and I asked Him, "Jesus when am I going to see your signs? I know we are protected, I know I cannot add one breath to Jenny's life and my life, I know you are my everything and most of all I know that your love for us does surpass our understanding. I love you Jesus with all my heart and thank You with all my heart and because of Your heart of love for us I know I will see Jenny walking and talking again. Jesus, I'm tired of seizures in the middle of the night and the signs of them every night. These seizures and signs are from the devil."

"So I'm asking, is there anything else that I need to pray? I know I want to do Your will and to actually be Your will here on earth! Yet I believe I am missing something?" Jesus answered me, like He always does with a question? He said, "Shadrach, Meshach, and Abednego did not ask me to put out the fire." Jesus said, "You are still in bondage to these seizures Ron!" I repented for being in fear and thanked Jesus for being so patient with me. I promised not to let the seizures stop me from doing the work of the Kingdom. I thanked Jesus for all the good signs and encouragement He gives me every day. I thanked Jesus for loving me even while I'm in sin. I know the fire was hot, but Shadrach, Meshach, and Abednego did not fear the fire because Jesus dwells in them. I have Jesus dwelling me and I will not fear.

On September 21st, Jesus and I were having coffee and talking. Jesus told me I had not surrendered Jenny yet. I said, "I do not understand what else You want me to surrender." Jesus said, "You need to surrender Jenny's life!" Jesus said in order to live you must die to self. He who dies to self will surely live, but he who lives for self will surely die.

Matthew 10:39 He who finds his life will lose it, and he who loses his life for My sake will find it.

Jesus said, "Ron you are doing everything you can to keep Jenny alive, would you call her an idol?" I said, "I love you most and I put you first in my life, don't I Jesus?" Jesus answered, "Yes, you do, but you are torn between Jenny and I. That same day I went to a conference and I told my dear friend Will Riddle about what Jesus and I were talking about that morning. I told him that it is hard for me to understand. Will replied that it sounds like the story of Abraham. Thank you Jesus for loving me so much that you wrote the Bible for me. I am so blessed to know You, Jesus. I am so blessed to have the people you put in my life.

On October 2nd at 5:30 am Jenny had a seizure. I felt her body going crazy all night. Her breathing was so weird and yet I had peace in my heart knowing that God's Word says nothing by any means shall hurt you. I knew in my heart that Jesus was with us so I just relaxed. Then at 5:30 when Jenny went into seizure I did not even turn on the light. I knew this is a lie form the enemy and I don't have to look at it. I did roll Jenny on her side and as I did Jenny's little body started to relax and as I praised God for being with us and we both fell asleep. Jenny would normally spend the entire day in bed after a seizure. In the past, if I got Jenny up too soon she would go right into another seizure. This time I did get Jenny up and we got along with our day. We even went to the store and prayed for two people! I love Jesus and I believe Jenny and I are on our way up the mountain like Abraham was. I believe this journey will have a happy ending because of the Grace Jesus has for us, and the love Jesus has for all mankind. Shadrach, Meshach, and Abednego ask "What is your fire to us a king, My Jesus is with us and either way we have won the battle because Jesus loves us!!!" I ask what is your fire to me devil, I have Jesus living in me and I will walk and talk with Jesus all the days of my life. So no matter what the outcome is I know it is for the glory of my loving Savior Jesus Christ. Jenny and I both win because of the love of Jesus!

Jesus, I want to thank you again for trusting me with one of your most treasured possessions. I call Jenny my Jenny a lot but I know in my heart that Jenny is yours and I know how You love her and I am so blessed to be the one you choose to take care of her physical needs while here on earth. To some people I meet, this journey I'm on looks hard but when you know the love of Jesus and Jesus is walking with me every step of the way, the journey is not hard! I feel rewarded that Jesus thinks enough of me to let me hold and love one of Jesus' most precious possessions. Jesus is teaching me how to take care of Jenny's needs. I know in my heart that I am so blessed to have the love of Jesus and that is why when I see anyone on the street I tell them I am so blessed and I want to share the love of Jesus with everyone.

People ask me, "do you pray about where you are going or how do you know where to go? I answer them, "I never pray about where I'm going and I never put out a fleece." You see it takes no faith to put out a fleece or to ask God where should I go. Jesus said to walk by faith not by sight (fleece). I know that Jesus said without faith it is impossible to please Him. I know people that get so many details in their head, trying to figure out whether or not to do something. I just know Jesus told us to go preach the gospel to all nations, so I do. I can be going down the expressway and say, 'Jesus I'm tired please find us a campground'. The next exit says campground, so I go there and someone gets healed of cancer. It's a pretty cool way to travel. Thank you Jesus! I love to travel with Jesus! Jesus is my everything!!!

Ron, Jenny, and Jesus loves you all!

Heroes

Who are heroes? Can you prepare to be a hero? Are heroes born to be a hero, like it is predestined? Does Jesus like heroes? Do heroes have fear of anything? Let's look in the Book of Love and see if we can find some answers!

Who are heroes? I believe how you spend your time and what your motives are and what you believe in will determine if you are a hero or not.

First let us look in *time*. Yes, it all comes down to how we spend our time. Notice the word 'spend'. We all love to have money to spend especially in ourselves. If we do not have a lot of money, we sometimes become very stingy. I think we treat time the same way. When we are young, we tend to give up our time very easily. As we grow older we tend to let our own needs become our priority. For example, say your Grandma fell and hurt her leg. So she cannot cut her grass anymore. You think to yourself, "I can't fix her leg, but I can cut her grass!" So you cut your grandma's grass for free all summer and when she tries to pay you, you look at her and say, "I just wanted to do it for you, Grandma." You probably made Grandma realize that you are a hero and you love it when Grandma hugs you!

As you get older, other things might become more important to you than Grandma's grass. Like sports or dating or actually making money and so you say to your Grandma, "I want to cut your grass but I just don't have the time." You see how we spend our time can dictate whether or not we are a hero. How we spend our time depends with our priorities. Grandma has become second to sports or dating or making money or whatever you decide to spend your time on.

I believe that is what Jesus was talking about when Jesus said in Matthew 16:24-25:

> **Matthew 16:24-25** Then Jesus said to His disciples, "If anyone desires to come after Me, let him deny himself, and take up his cross, and follow Me. 25 For whoever desires to save his life will lose it, but whoever loses his life for My sake will find it.

I believe life is a gift from God and life is an allotted amount of time here on earth. What you do with your life can please God or make Him sad.

Jesus said "If any man will come after me." Notice the word *'if'*. It is up to you and it is your will to seek Jesus. We have a choice and we can choose to seek God with all our heart and mind and soul. Or seek notoriety and material things or even power which can be major distractions from seeking Jesus! So can seeking God make you a hero?

What does *'let him deny himself'* means? It could mean 'don't eat ice cream for a week' and that is denying self. But I believe Jesus was talking about giving away your time (your life). I think most people translate that part of Scripture into money, their tithes to the church and so they think they have denied themselves by giving up some of their money. I think God cares way more about how you sacrifice your time than your money because sacrificing your time is showing Grandma you love her. I believe giving up your time to cut Grandma's grass was a bigger gift to Jesus than anything you could put in the offering basket. So making the needs of others more important than your own needs can make you a hero. Giving away your love is very pleasing to God and can make you a hero in God's eyes. Your reward will be knowing that you pleased God with your time and your love! Grandma's hugs will be pretty cool also. Deny yourself and do God's will and you are a hero!

Jesus said to 'take up his cross and follow me'. What is 'take up your cross and follow me' means? I believe it means to ask God what He wants us to do with this life He has given us. We surrender to what God needs us to do for Him. If God came down and cut Grandma's grass we would say, "That is just God. I mean

He does things like that all the time!" God is good all the time, right? God is at eternity time, so He doesn't worry about time and He doesn't have to make money. So why would God want you to cut grandma's grass? To show your love for Grandma is showing you believe in God. That you love God and you are putting the need He showed you first in your life. God created us to be His love on the earth. Cutting Grandma's grass is doing what God would do, so if you cut her grass, people will see Jesus manifesting in you. When Jesus manifests in you, the hero in you is Jesus! It might seem simple to you but you are spreading the love of Jesus and I believe you are a Hero! You are taking up your cross and following Him.

If God wanted to play sports, He could and He could be the best without being at practice all the time. Nothing is impossible for God. God could do all those things and prove He is God and doing those things would show the world that He is God. But God created us to show the world who God is and to be His love on the earth. Yes being His love on the earth is more important than playing sports to God. God wants us to manifest his Love and God created us in His image and likeness. God wants His creation to be a reflection of their Creator. God wants people to see Jesus in us. In other words we bring Glory to God when we glorify our Creator. We call it being a hero but God calls it being Christ-like!

So why does God say for us to take up His cross and follow Him. Okay, just for a moment let's say you are god and you created the world and the human race. What would you want the human race to do? Would you want the human race to ignore you by watching television, playing sports or making money so they can have more toys that actually take them further from you? I don't think so! Would you want them to be dependent on themselves? Would you want them to look at their own knowledge to repair themselves? Isn't that making ourselves like god? It is like saying, "I don't need God." Is our knowledge bringing us closer to God or further away from God?

Do we just look to ourselves for the answer to everything? Are we our own god? When a man makes a mess out of this world, as god would you just walk away from them and say you guys made this mess so now you live in it? If you were god would you write down some rules for them to live by or some guidelines that explain right from wrong? As a god, would you want them to please you with the life you gave them? My God did give me rules to live by and He does clean up my messes and I love and respect Him. I will choose Him over all material things, I will pick up my cross and follow Him with all the days of my life!

If you are god and you made the human race, then what was your motive? As god, do you want to do everything for your creation or do you want them to look to you for an example in life? Do you want them to help each other and love each other? If you see someone hurt, do you want your creation to walk by and say, sorry about your luck or say I would help but I'm in a hurry helping others is God's job anyway. I believe God's motive for creating us was so He could do everything for us but for us to trust Him with our life, we need to have our faith in Him. God said He would provide food money and shelter for us. You know all the things we work so hard for are actually provided for us if we just trust God to provide them.

Make your first desire: your desire to see and meet Him. God gave us the perfect example to model our life after. Jesus just asks us to follow Him! God shows us He is love and love is never ending. Love is always looking to love more so when we love as Jesus loves we make our Creator very joyful. Jesus said He rejoices over us with singing. He said He delights in us. Parents get so excited when they see their children make good choices and good decisions. I believe Jesus delights in us when He sees us make good decisions. So all you need to be a hero is to be Christ-like! To love as Jesus loved!

If you were god, would you want your creation to freely give some of their time and by doing so love each other by saying, 'I can help you'. As god, would you want your creation to ask 'can I help you' or say 'I'm here and I will help you'. A hero is someone who knows he is not god but knows God and respects God and will take time to study Jesus who is the perfect example of life and model his life after Jesus. A hero will already know in his heart to help someone who is hurt and has decided in his heart what God needs him to do is the most important priority in life. That is a Christ-like hero!!!

178

How does a hero know what God wants for his life? One way is to check your motive. Okay, let us look at motive. Motives are very important because it will determine how serious you are. Let us say you find out Grandma has her hair done every Tuesday and then goes out to eat with the girls so you have this window of time to cut her grass, without Grandma knowing who is cutting her grass.

Grandma comes home from her day out every week and finds her grass cut and the yard manicured. Let us say you do not let anyone know at all who is cutting the grass. So grandma starts her own little investigation and decides it is the boy down the street. She gives him the credit for doing the grass. She tells everyone what a good boy he is and what a great job he is doing and she even gives him some money for cutting her grass.

How you react to this situation will tell a lot about yourself. If you get mad at the guy down the street for lying and take up the issue with him, your motive probably was not rooted in Love. You see, if you love Grandma and you cut her grass to make her happy who cares about the reward? Wasn't your goal to make Grandma happy and Grandma is happy! If your act of kindness is done out of love then God knows it and you'll get His reward and the boy down the street will have to repent to God for lying.

So if your motive was rooted in God's love and you know God loves you then your motive is pure and you really don't care who gets the earthly reward. You see how knowing that God loves you sets you free from what man thinks of you. What if some of your friends said 'we are going to Kings Island and we will pay your way so don't waste your time cutting the grass, Grandma thinks it is the boy down the street anyway so let him cut the grass'. You could agree with them and be mad at the boy down the street and take up the issue with him. You could say I'm going to Kings Island and I don't feel like cutting grass today and maybe never. You could spend your time fighting for the reward. So if your motive was to make yourself look good and be rewarded here on earth you were not very sincere about making Grandma happy, or sincerely doing the will of God and being Christ-like!

Let's talk about the boy down the street who takes the credit for cutting the grass. Maybe he is hurting. Maybe he has been beaten down all his life. Then along comes your Grandma and she sees a need in the boy and tries to fill it with love. Nothing ever justifies lying and I mean nothing! But if the boy lies for the attention and receives the reward, he will have to answer for those lies. You could be a bigger hero to God by just loving on him and by letting him have the reward. If you know God loves you and you get your self-worth from God, not cutting grass and not from Grandma. So this could be a chance to love the boy to Jesus. It would be a golden opportunity to lead the boy to God by telling him about the love of Jesus and you could demonstrate Jesus love to him by forgiving him. You could demonstrate God's love by being God's love! That is Christ-like!!! That makes you a real hero!!!

Motive can get you up in the morning with excitement on how to love others or a motive can say, "I'm so tired I think I'm going to sleep in and I'm only doing what I want to do today or I'm not doing anything today." Wow, that sure is a lot of I's. If everything is about you being the god in your own life, then you probably will wake up tired and probably depressed.

Let us talk about what happens if life is about you and your needs. Everyone that has an addiction is looking no further than themselves for happiness. Let us use pornography as an example. You get on the internet and watch until you give way to it. It felt good and in a little while you are looking at it again until you give way to it again. All addictions are the same in a way that they create momentary pleasure and a need for more pleasure. That need always escalates into you giving up more and more of your time until you gets consumed in it. The need for momentary pleasure will eventually rob you of your life. Addictions always start off innocently. You think to yourself, "This is great because I'm not hurting anybody. I'm not even hurting myself, like if I were on drugs or alcohol. The people in these movies look like they are having a good time and I am having a good time and so what can be wrong with this? It is free on the internet so it doesn't cost me anything."

The problem comes from how you spend your time. Yes, it is how you spend your time (or your life) when watching these movies. Since your life is all about you everyone else is secondary. That is the opposite of Christ-likeness. When someone calls and says, "Grandma hurt her leg. Can you go over and cut her grass?" Your answer will determine how much of your life is about you! If you're hooked on pornography or addicted to anything, I bet your answer will be *'maybe later'*. So watching those movies is taking you away from your love of God and the time you could spend with Him and helping Grandma. Pornography is killing a hero and you not being Christ-like! Can you imagine God calling Jesus and saying, "Come on, it's time to be crucified." and Jesus answered, "Let me finish this move first." It sounds funny doesn't it? I mean it sounds weird coming out of Jesus. It should sound weird if you say it!

Jesus in His word said 'freely you received so freely you give'.

Matthew 10:8 Heal the sick, cleanse the lepers, raise the dead, cast out demons. Freely you have received, freely give.

What did Jesus give us freely? I believe it is life and love. Life without love is useless! Life without love is meaningless! We talked about how addictions start. Let's look how addictions *(that is life without love)* can end. Some people are hooked on power. Some people take their addiction to power to the extreme. Just look at the life of Adolf Hitler or Karl Marx. They both changed the life of millions of people by spreading their hate and by killing anyone that did not agree with them. I don't know how their thirst for power started, but it could have started with them being given a simple task of watching over someone that had to obey them. The end of their addiction for power was not pretty.

Jesus changed the life of millions of people also by spreading His love freely and freely giving them life! Jesus changed the world without guns, without war and without killing anyone. I guess you could say Jesus started a war. The war Jesus started is against sin and unforgiveness. It is a war against hate and killing. The war Jesus started is against the devil. Jesus described love in Galatians 5:22-23 and putting off earthly desires in Galatians 5:24 and the fact we are spirit in Galatians 5:25 and our motivation in Galatians 5: 26.

Love:

Galatians 5:22-23 But the fruit of the Spirit is love, joy, peace, longsuffering, kindness, goodness, faithfulness, 23 gentleness, self-control. Against such there is no law.

Putting off Earthly Desires:

Galatians 5:24 And those who are Christ's have crucified the flesh with its passions and desires.

We Can Live in The Spirit of Love and Walk in The Spirit of Love:

Galatians 5:25 If we live in the Spirit, let us also walk in the Spirit.

Motivation:

Galatians 5:26 Let us not become conceited, provoking one another, envying one another.

What is love to Jesus? Galatians 5:22 and 23 describe it pretty well. Jesus also shows us what love looks like in Matthew 10:7-8:

Matthew 10:7-8 And as you go, preach, saying, 'The kingdom of heaven is at hand.' Heal the sick, cleanse the lepers, raise the dead, cast out demons. Freely you have received, freely give.

So for Jesus, love looks like healing the sick, cleansing the lepers and raising the dead and casting out devils and preaching His word boldly. You see, Jesus started a war against the devils. Jesus defeated the devil openly! In this war, Jesus gives us freedom and life. Jesus gives us control over the earth and the creatures of the earth and control over the weather but warns us to never control other human beings. Jesus gives life freely and He never takes it away. The only way to lose life is for us to give it away. How do you give life away? By letting yourself become addicted to anything that is just trying to please your own self. All of this is in the book I didn't make it up.

I mean I did not pay anything for my life! My parents were making love and loveable and huggable and then me came along for a ride! Even if that is not how your life started, those two people involved were trying to experience love at the time you were conceived. What happened after that was determined by how much of their time or life is willing to give you. You see, all addictions come down to putting your priority on yourself. Whether it is drinking, drugs, pornography, power or whatever, addiction is really about how you spend your time and making yourself the first priority!!! That would be a good definition for the word miserable! It is true that making your needs the first priority will make you miserable! And the devil happy!

So freely you received life from God and life is an allotted amount of time here on earth. So how you prioritize your time is very important. If you read the Word and start living the Word not just knowing the Word but living the Word you can become a hero every day to God. That's right! Every day! You still have life in you. I know because you are reading this. So you still have a chance to give your life away or become selfish and make your life miserable while only thinking about yourself. If you cut Grandma's grass and you never get the hug, and the boy down the street gets the reward and maybe some cash from Grandma, it's okay! You are learning what love is. Be God-centered not self-centered and trust God, not man to do the right thing.

Love is knowing who we are in Jesus Christ and that we have an all-knowing and loving God that will make everything right and we will experience His love every day. So don't care who gets the reward for good behavior. Say, "I know who I am in Jesus and He loves me!" Now that is a good attitude and the making of a hero!

If you cut Grandma's grass every week and she knows it and gives you a hug every week. You know you are putting expectation on her and if she forgets to hug you one week, you could be very upset about it. Again, put your expectation in God because when you put it in man someone will let you down and even worse you set them up to fail you. If you do put your expectation in the youth minister or the pastor or the church leaders you are setting them up to fail. You are putting an expectation on a human and we all know humans are not perfect and sooner or later they could let you down and when they do, it might not be pretty. That is why God said to put your trust (expectation) in Him.

Let us take being a hero up a notch. What if you are a scientist and developed a cure for cancer. Let us say you worked for 25 years and finally got this breakthrough. Then someone else steals your research and they receive the reward for all your hard work. Twenty-five years down the drain and the thief gets famous and rich! You could be very mad about it and want justice for you were wronged big time. So you hire a lawyer and go to court. The court case could go on for years but you know you deserve the reward so you fight on. People and Christians you know will encourage you, saying you are doing the right thing.

But if you know the Word and you are living the Word, you won't care who gets the reward because you will see people healed and cured from cancer. You will see people helped the rest of your life. Wasn't that the goal or was the reward the goal? If your goal was helping others you succeeded, so you and God is at peace and God's peace is worth more than any amount or notoriety. What if you proved in a court of law that your research was stolen and you received your notoriety and your riches here on earth but in your pursuit of them you lose your peace with God? I think you lost way more than you can ever gain.

1 Timothy 6:17 Command those who are rich in this present age not to be haughty, nor to trust in uncertain riches but in the living God, who gives us richly all things to enjoy.

You see you don't trust in uncertain riches but trust in the living God!!!

I believe the same Scriptures apply to the scientist and the boy cutting the grass. I know some people would say the same principles apply but I say the Scriptures because God gave us the scriptures and there are people who try to change them into principles and some people especially lawyers bend principles to fit into their agenda. I believe God's Word and I live by His Word so I don't need a principle to stand on. I stand on Scripture!

Here again, what was the motive for spending 25 years of your life to find a cure for cancer? If it was to heal people from cancer then he succeeded. He died to himself for 25 years and worked diligently to find this cure. Did his life sacrifice really about the notoriety and money? I know some would say it is the principle. The thief stole your life work and he received the reward. I put my trust in God and I bet God noticed. The Bible says we will all stand before Jesus someday for judgment. Truly, I believe notoriety and money are way overrated. I would much rather be a double hero in God's eyes than walk into a room full of doctors and receive a standing ovation. God wants to flow through us and He can if we make ourselves available.

God wants to flow through us all the time. We have to be willing to let His will be our will! Giving your time (life) and surrendering your time (life) is God's will. Your cross is simply being willing to do His will over your own. Make His priorities your priorities! I remember when I was young I loved watching Law and Order on television. I would make sure I was cleaned up and ready to watch it every Wednesday night. I even took the phone off the hook! I really liked that show. Now, I know I was not pleasing God! I know I was not available to Jesus for that hour a week. Now I realize my priority was me, myself and I and not Jesus and what He may have needed me to do during that time! I was not a hero!

If I make myself available to Jesus 24/7 then I have picked up my cross to follow Him. I have died to myself and I live to do his will on earth.

Matthew 16:25 'For whoever desires to save his life will lose it, but whoever loses his life for My sake will find it'.

You see, I was trying to please myself by watching Law and Order. I took the phone off the hook so anyone that called got a busy single, including God. I put my need in front of everything else! I know I was not a hero! You want to know how to lose your life for His sake.

For example, I could argue my case before Jesus and say "I was surrendered to you 167 hours a week and only thought of myself 1 hour a week." I could say to myself that it was not too bad. The Scriptures are the same if it is one hour a week or 100 hours a week. Jesus said to love the Lord thy God with all your heart and all your soul and all your mind. My sin wasn't watching Law and Order; it was making myself unavailable to Jesus in that hour. You see, you can play sports or whatever and still love God and live for God and be available to God. In fact, you can play sports and be a witness to your beliefs in God and that will make God very happy while doing something you love! What if my children and I were watching Law and Order and the phone rang and someone needed me. If I left to help that person right away, my children would see me put the needs of others over my desire to watch the show. That would have been a great witness and I would not have to say a word.

A hero is truly a hero when his actions are to bring glory to God and to manifest the love of God. A hero doesn't care about being a hero to mankind. A hero doesn't care for notoriety, and a hero doesn't want money! A hero will manifest the love of God 24/7 by just dying to yourself and putting God's needs in front of yours. Jesus in his Word says:

> **Matthew 6:1** Take heed that you do not do your charitable deeds before men, to be seen by them. Otherwise you have no reward from your Father in heaven.

Here, Jesus is talking about alms and I believe alms can be anything you do to bring Him glory. Like cutting Grandma's grass or finding a cure for cancer. Jesus also talks about no reward in heaven so there must be a reward in heaven if you do not seek one here on earth. Jesus will use you in all kinds of ways because you seek Him first, not glory here on earth.

What if Jesus had your mom go to Grandma and tell her the truth about you cutting her grass. You will not lose your reward in heaven because you did not seek one here on earth. Jesus gave you one here on earth through your mother so He can use your good deed to be an example to others as how to live. You see the difference? Because of your desire to do good (acts of kindness are God's will) and you did not care if anyone saw you or who got the glory (dying to self), then you were giving the glory to God. You are a hero to Jesus! If your mom steps in and tells Grandma the truth, you can accept the notoriety because you did not seek it. Your motives are still pure.

> **Matthew 6:2** Therefore, when you do a charitable deed, do not sound a trumpet before you as the hypocrites do in the synagogues and in the streets, that they may have glory from men. Assuredly, I say to you, they have their reward.

You see if you receive your reward here on earth like walking into a room full of doctors and receiving a standing ovation, you may lose your reward in heaven if your only motive was for that ovation. Even if someone else gets the reward here on earth don't fight for it and especially don't go to court over it. Going to court is like sounding the trumpet. God calls them hypocrites and not heroes.

> **Matthew 6:3** But when you do a charitable deed, do not let your left hand know what your right hand is doing

If at all possible do your act of kindness without acknowledgement from mankind. Jesus sees your act of kindness and He is the reward. I know of a restaurant manager that would put a piece of litter by the employee entrance door. From a hidden vantage point, he watched the employees walk in and if anyone picked up the litter, he promoted them. He knew they were not on the clock yet, but one person was willing to do the right thing and he rewarded them. God sees every good act of kindness (love) and He made us in His image (love) so sow some seeds of God today and every day! Life is simple! Just be LOVE!!! I know God is watching from His vantage point and He is promoting!

> **Matthew 6:4** That your charitable deed may be in secret; and your Father who sees in secret will Himself reward you openly.

While here on earth, God will sometimes reward you as a testimony to others. So if you are giving the love of Jesus and someone notices and makes it known to others, you were not seeking the reward so you did not lose your reward in heaven. Notice the clouds did not open and a voice from heaven say this is Bill in whom I am well pleased. God will flow through people to give you thanks. God's will is for us to be like Jesus! SO BE LOVE AS JESUS IS LOVE!!!

Matthew 6:5 And when you pray, you shall not be like the hypocrites. For they love to pray standing in the synagogues and on the corners of the streets, that they may be seen by men. Assuredly, I say to you, they have their reward.

Example: Mother Teresa did not do anything to bring glory to herself. Others brought her glory because of what she did with her life. She simply spread the love of Jesus everywhere she went and that was her pure motive. She never once said, "Look what I did!" But the world noticed because God wanted us to see it is possible to be the love of Jesus today. I believe Mother Teresa was a Godly Hero! I know in my heart that she is in heaven now with God and enjoying God to the max.

You see a hero can come in all shapes and sizes. You do not have to do things in secret all the time to be God's hero. Let us say you get a job at McDonald's and your boss tells you to clean the bathrooms. If you start to complain and say 'why me, I did it yesterday so let someone else do it today' or you could say 'okay' and you do the best job ever. What if you thought to yourself, "I will clean this bathroom as if Jesus himself was going to be the next person to use it?" Even if no one notices the great job you did, God noticed and to Him you are a hero! What I am trying to say is a hero could be someone that just goes a little beyond the call of duty.

Recently a lady called me her hero because about a year ago, I saw her in a restaurant. I noticed her hand was deformed and I walked over to her and prayed for her hand. A year later, she saw me in the same restaurant and showed me her hand was healed the morning after I prayed for it. All I said to her was to be healed in the name of my Savior, Jesus Christ. It only took five seconds of my life to pray for her and God used those five seconds to transform her life. Isn't God cool? As we talked, she told me how she and her husband came to eat there at least once a week for over a year, hoping to see Jenny and me again and to thank us for praying.

You might be thinking right now, "He is bragging after just quoting Scriptures about not bragging on yourself." I think the difference is I am actually bragging about what God did. I know by myself I cannot heal anyone but with God, all things are possible! I didn't give them the desire to look for me for a whole year; it was God who gave them that desire. You see, I know when I prayed that she was healed. I just stood on faith that His word is true. Evidently, God wanted me to know she was healed because He gave both of us the desire to be there at the exact same time a year later.

You see, it was God that wanted me to be rewarded openly. Never brag on yourself but always brag about what God is doing in your life. It gives others the faith to step out in their faith and you are giving them the how to step out in faith. If you need to see the miracle you probably have not died to yourself. If God wants you to see it, then it will happen right in front of your eyes. Plus my motive for telling you is to prove nothing is impossible for Jesus. If I told you this to make myself look good then I will pay by not being rewarded in heaven. That is a huge price to pay for a little notoriety now. In fact God could possibly say, "away from me! I never knew you!"

Matthew 7:22 Many will say to Me in that day, 'Lord, Lord, have we not prophesied in Your name, cast out demons in Your name, and done many wonders in Your name?'

I believe Jesus is talking about people that do these things to make themselves look good. They could care less about loving people or glorifying God. Example, you discover the cure for cancer and then go to court to prove it was you that found the cure. Truly you have lost your reward no matter what the outcome of court is.

Matthew 7:23 And then I will declare to them, 'I never knew you; depart from Me, you who practice lawlessness!'

Here Jesus makes it really clear that if we pray for people to be healed and cast out devils in the name of Jesus, He will honor His word and cast out devils and heal the sick because He gave us His word. So Jesus will flow through people and that doesn't mean they are gifted nor have a special anointing. He is just honoring His word. If you have iniquity in your life, like your motive is to make yourself look good, you might hear the words *I never knew you* on Judgment Day! We are working for Him and His glory because we really cannot add one second of life to our own life, let alone someone else. If you want fame and glory here and now, it will probably come but the cost is too high for you to bear.

Jesus said all things are possible! So when you pray it is impossible for nothing to happen! Just spread the love of Jesus everywhere you two go and let the love of Jesus flow. I said everywhere you (two) go because if you are born again then Jesus Holy Spirit dwells in you and is with you. You are never alone!

When a farmer plants a seed, let's say an apple tree, he doesn't go out the next day and say that the seed must be no good because I don't see an apple tree. He waits upon the Lord to turn that seed into an apple tree. No one on earth can literally turn a seed into anything without the miracle of life from God. Life is a miracle. God will not plant the seed for us; he wants us to plant the seed in faith. Like I said, God loves to work through us. Jesus said without faith it is impossible to please Him. Use your faith to move mountains and plant seeds. Someone planted a seed in you and you are slowly becoming a tree that can bear good fruit. Sometimes like the farmer, we have faith that the seed is growing even when we don't see anything happening on the surface.

I wonder how many people have ever heard the saying 'fear of death is actually the fear of the unknown'. I have heard that all my life. I believed in that all my life until recently when I realized it was another lie from the devil. It is really fear of death and we are trying to pass it off as fear of the unknown. If you know where you are going and that you have done the work of the kingdom for Jesus then we should welcome death, which is really moving on to be with Jesus. It is the passage to our reward of being in heaven with Jesus and it is our final act of faith.

If you have doubts about where you are going, then you will probably be in fear. If the doctor walks in and says you only have two weeks to live, so get your house in order. What would you do? For most people the answer is, "oh my God, what am I going to do?" At least they called on God and the good news is it is not too late! Jesus shows us how not to live in fear, in fact He calls living in fear a sin.

Let us look at Scripture and see what God says.

2 Corinthians 5:8 We are confident, yes, well pleased rather to be absent from the body and to be present with the Lord.

You see, to be absent from the body (death) is to be present with the Lord (real life)! The word says we are confident and willing. Do you believe it? Knowing Jesus will make you confident and willing. If you do not believe in the Scriptures then you have no moral compass that you can use as a guide in life. I can guarantee you anything else you use as your foundation for truth was written by a man and that man is in a grave somewhere, or he is on his way to one. I believe God has proven beyond any doubt that God is real and that God does exist and God will prove that He loves you! Please read on and just see if what God says about death makes any sense to you.

I believe the Scriptures to be truth and all the inspired word of God to be true. Yes, the Bible was written by men, and the authors of the Bible were inspired by God, but now can I prove it to be true to you. I simply act on what I read in the Bible and watch God perform on His word. No other book can prove itself true through positive action. I have yet to hear about Karl Marx for example healing the sick, or raising someone from the dead. Jesus said the things I do you will do also, and even bigger and better things than I do.

John 14:12 Most assuredly, I say to you, he who believes in Me, the works that I do he will do also; and greater works than these he will do, because I go to My Father.

Because I know and believe Jesus rose from the dead, we know He is with the Father. We have the same Father and Jesus is my brother. The works that Jesus did on earth are all possible for me too and greater works shall I do in His name. It is faith in the name of Jesus that gets the results. Not your faith but faith in the name of Jesus.

John 14:13 A And whatever you ask in My name, that I will do, that the Father may be glorified in the Son.

You can ask anything in the Name of Jesus and He will do it. We have His word on it, and it will be done. He will do it so our Father may be Glorified in the Son. Who gets the Glory? Our Father receives the glory through the Son. We are sons of the Father so bring your Father glory by how you live! DO NOT SEEK YOUR OWN GLORY!!! If you do, you might hear "depart from me, I never knew you!"

John 14:14 If you ask anything in My name, I will do *it*.

The only qualifier here is what you ask must bring Glory to your Father in Heaven. What if you had a girlfriend named Jenny and you ask God, "Please make Jenny love me. God you made her so cute and sweet and I just love her, so make Jenny love me. Would you, God?" The answer is in the Scriptures! God gave us all the right to make up our own mind. So in your prayer request you should ask God to help you become a man of God and the right girl will fall in love with you for sure! A man of God is irresistible to a woman of God and being a man of God is what you really want.

Show me promises like that in any other book and then back it up with living proof. You do not have to believe that at this moment but I hope this writing brings a desire for God who is the truth in your heart. First of all, I believe the Scriptures I quoted are true. I believe all the Scriptures are true! So you can see I believe we never die! I believe heroes have no fear of death. Jesus wrote the only Book that gives us power over death and you will receive this power through the love of Jesus. All other books about ways of life (like Marxism or Nazism) only give us power over other people and that power comes through the fear of death that you put on other people. You see the difference? We can live in the love of Jesus and love each other or live under some man's law that says, 'do what I say or I will kill you'. Try to find true love in any other book about life. There is no other book where the Author laid down His life for people to give us a truer look at or example of love than the life of my Jesus! Jesus said in John 15:12-13:

> **John 15:12-13** This is My commandment, that you love one another as I have loved you. Greater love has no one than this, than to lay down one's life for his friends.

I think that pretty much sums up the fear of death! God is asking us to lay down our life for his friends. Remember laying down your life might be as simple as leaving the phone on the hook during your favorite television show. Or it could be running into a burning building to rescue someone out.

We leave earth as a spirit and go before the Lord and stand in judgment for how we lived our life while here on earth. Jesus said death will have no hold on you. If you believe in Jesus, you should have no fear of death. Freedom is no fear of death and when the fear of death is removed we have a greater capacity for God's perfect love that takes away all fear! IT REALLY IS THAT SIMPLE unless you don't believe in God! Belief in God sets you free from the fear of death! No other belief system has the power to take away the fear of death. No other religion can promise freedom and life everlasting. My Jesus guarantees life everlasting! You get to choose if your life everlasting is with Him or in hell but it is everlasting life, so choose well! Heroes have no fear of death, and they love as Jesus loved UNCONDITIONALLY!!!

What does Jesus mean when He said my truth shall set you free.

John 8:32 And you shall know the truth, and the truth shall make you free."

I ask, free from what? Death is what you are set free from! We have all heard of someone that died while saving the life of another person and we call them heroes and they are! If you were suddenly faced with a situation like that, would you be willing to give up your life to save another person's life? Your answer will determine if you have fear of death or not. Death has a hold on you when the answer is no. You are set free from death and death has no hold on you when the answer is yes! So will you lay down your life for another? The answer is yes when you know Jesus!!!

If you know the love of Jesus and you let His love flow through you, your answer would be positively yes and with no doubts! You see how your belief in Jesus can set you free! Death is something we can look forward to because when you're in Jesus and you allow Him in your personal life. You know where you are going. That is true freedom!

Knowing where you are going is having peace of mind. Have you ever been going somewhere to meet someone and then got lost. Being lost makes you nervous. Being lost can upset your stomach. It will even make you uneasy and you may even start to sweat. Some people walk in these signs all the time. After a while, they think that an upset stomach as normal. Some say the golden years are the ache and pain years. These are actually signs that you do not have the peace of Jesus or the truth of Jesus and you need a revelation of the love of Jesus in your heart. That is why people will put off thinking about where they are going to spend eternity or they will just say I don't believe in that. I can almost guarantee you they would not lay down their life for another. Please understand I want to live as long as possible because I believe I have purposeful work for the kingdom of God to do! What I am trying to say is I am willing to die because I am looking forward to being present with my best friend Jesus.

What is present with the Lord mean? Who are absent from the Lord?

2 Corinthians 5:6 So *we are* always confident, knowing that while we are at home in the body we are absent from the Lord.

2 Corinthians 5:6 says that as long as we are at home in the body, we are absent from the Lord.

I believe what the Scripture is talking about is physically. I know that Jesus came and restored our relationship spiritually. So in the spirit, I can talk to Jesus anytime and all the time I want. I just cannot see Him physically or touch Him physically. I'm absent from the Lord because I'm still in my body which mean as humans we are limited to our senses and only granted spiritual eyes with limited vision.

2 Corinthians 5:7 For we walk by faith, not by sight.

Walking with the Lord by faith is the only way we can walk with Him and it is the only way to talk to Him. When we do as commanded, heal the sick or raise someone from the dead or cast out devils we sometimes see a leg grow where one was missing or a missing arm grows back or scars disappear. It is really cool but I have only heard of a couple cases where people say they personally saw Jesus.

2 Corinthians 5:8 We are confident, yes, well pleased rather to be absent from the body and to be present with the Lord.

I touched on this Scripture earlier so I will only add that I would like nothing more than to be present with the Lord right now. I know I can still be of use to Jesus so I really want to stay and be used by Jesus and I pray that before I go on I fulfill the work He raised me up for!

What will Jesus judge us on? I believe most people think we will be judged for our sins. Scripture says that our sins are forgiven and removed as far as the east is from the west. There are some conditions on forgiveness, and there are some sins that lead to death! I can think of some sins to death, unforgivness and although it is not a sin to death as you just read seeking notoriety here on earth may be something to look for or guard your heart for in your life.

How many of you have heard the scripture 'Without faith it is impossible to please Him'?

Hebrews 11:6 But without faith *it is* impossible to please *Him*, for he who comes to God must believe that He is, and *that* He is a rewarder of those who diligently seek Him.

Do you believe it? What is faith? I believe faith is love. Jesus said He came to show us the love of the Father. Why would Jesus want to show us the love of the Father? Because the Father has faith in us that if we see His love we will become love like Him and manifest the Love of Jesus and the Father all our life. Jesus showed us the love of the Father by showing us compassion, healing the sick, casting out devils, raising the dead. That is why Jesus commanded us to heal the sick and cast out devils and raise the dead.

You see when we meet a nonbeliever, we do not argue the love of Jesus or that He is real! We prove it by stepping out in faith and manifesting Love! Also, you must believe. For he that cometh must believe! That is strong languish "must believe" that God is a Rewarder of them that diligently seek Him. So what does God want so much that He sent His only Son to suffer and die for us? He wants us to believe Him, to love Him, and to diligently seek Him first in our life. That is to die to the things of this world and put aside our needs and lay down our life for others if need be! I think doing these things would make you a super Hero and your life would be pleasing to God, because your life would be an example of faith in God and a light to the world.

After all the two greatest commandments are:

Matthew 22:36-40 "Teacher, which is the great commandment in the law?" Jesus said to him, "'You shall love the Lord your God with all your heart, with all your soul, and with all your mind.' This is the first and great commandment. And the second is like it: 'You shall love your neighbor as yourself.' On these two commandments hang all the Law and the Prophets."

196

If you do these two commandments, I can guarantee you will be a Hero to God and to everyone you meet! For more information on being a Hero, just seek your Heavenly Father through your brother Jesus Christ, my Hero!!! A true hero will forgive as Jesus forgives. That is when they were nailing Him to the cross He said forgive them Father for they know not what they do! All Jesus ever did was good. He healed everyone, forgave everyone, taught everyone, and loved everyone unconditionally and even the top 12 left Him in His time of need.

Looking at the day Jesus died, you would say His ministry was a complete failure. Then Jesus rose from the dead and went to the apostles and breathed life a new into them just like when Jesus formed us out of dust and breathed life into Adam at the beginning! They received the new life of the Holy Spirit and His boldness. We receive the same Holy Spirit and the same boldness when we are born again. They are heroes because they went out and did as Jesus had empowered them to do! We have the same empowerment as the top 11 received. The top 11 could have stayed to themselves and never used these gifts from God. They had to choose to use them and so do we.

Read and study the life of Jesus! He is our example on how to live! Please don't just study the Bible to show everyone how much Scripture you can quote. Remember, knowledge puffs up but love edifies. The most important decision you will make in your lifetime is to have a relationship with your brother Jesus and your Father God. Remember fear is from the devil but love, perfect Love is Jesus and our perfect love of Jesus is our mission here on earth. Faith is believing Jesus and faith is loving as Jesus loved unconditionally! Start everyday with these simple words:

DEAR FATHER, in Jesus name I pray, as I walk down the street today I pray the people I see along the way, when they get home tonight and start to pray, will say, I think I saw Jesus today!

John 10:27-30 My sheep hear My voice, and I know them, and they follow Me. And I give them eternal life, and they shall never perish; neither shall anyone snatch them out of My hand. My Father, who has given them to Me, is greater than all; and no one is able to snatch them out of My Father's hand. I and My Father are one."

Relationship with Jesus and the Father through the Holy Spirit who dwells in us if we let Him, can make us in John 10:30 'I and my Father are one'! When you and your Father are one, you will go boldly as did Jesus and the apostles!

WHO IS YOUR BEST FRIEND AND HERO? SPEND SOME TIME WITH HIM AND KNOW HIS VOICE!!!

Remember: We do not live to be a hero. We are heroes because of the way we live for Jesus and not ourselves!!!

If you think, "I cannot go out and pray for people, because people might think I'm crazy", check who you are listening to: it is not God! He commanded us to love one another! Also you might have some pride issues. You know, putting your pride above the word of God! Just a thought!

Although they have nothing to do with this track, you should check out WWW.NECKMINISTRIES.COM. You will love Dan and Todd.

Let us summarize:

Who are heroes? Physically, a hero is someone who will run into a burning building to save another human being. In other words, he or she will die physically to save another person.

Who are heroes? Spiritually, a hero is someone who will die to himself or herself to give life for another. We have all heard the sayings time waits for no one, or time marches on, or his time was up so he is out of here. Spiritually, you can give life (which is time) to another by helping them with their homework or cutting their grass. You are dying to yourself because you make their needs more important than yours.

Can you prepare to be a hero? Yes! You actually start when you learn to obey your parents. For example, say you want to interrupt your dad while he is talking to someone. You are actually learning to give up your time until he is finished talking. Your parents may say 'be patient', and as you stand there, you are really learning to give up your time and your parents may reward you for being patient. The difference between being patient and a hero is, a hero will give up his time willingly and without reward.

Are heroes born to be a hero, like predestined? Yes! I believe we are all born to be heroes because Jesus asks us to die to ourselves. That can be as simple as waiting for your parents to stop talking so you don't interrupt them, or dying to self so completely that you will run into a burning building. The degrees of being a hero can start off small but grow into the ultimate dying to self. I can guarantee you the person that will run into a burning building started dying to self a long time before he or she ran into the burning building.

Does Jesus like heroes? Of course! I believe Jesus was the ultimate Hero. Jesus never lived for Himself. If you want to be a hero, just study the life of Jesus and you will see a Hero on every page of His life. So what makes Jesus the ultimate Hero? I believe, I know for a fact that the life of Jesus was the ultimate love story ever told. Jesus showed us how to die to self by never living for himself. When Jesus turned water into wine (his first miracle) He obviously knew He could do miracles and so did his Mom. Jesus told his mom 'no my hour has not yet come' yet He died to Himself and performed the miracle out of love for his mother. You see the motive and the reward is the same. The motive is love and the reward is love.

Jesus could have been the biggest show off this world has ever seen. He could just walk around saying, "Watch this" and done something spectacular every day. But Jesus never lived for himself. Jesus was just a man like us and so He had no power to turn water into wine. The Bible says He lived to show us His Father. He told his disciples 'you see me you see the Father'. We know Jesus was love so we know the Father is also love. We know love was the motive and love is the reward. Jesus is my hero and my example. I will live my life to love as Jesus loved.

Do heroes have fear of anything? No! A true hero will know Jesus and have surrendered his own life to do the will of God here on the earth. What is the will of God? God's will is for us to love each other as Jesus loves us. Unconditional love is never living for you alone! Unconditional love is perfect love and Jesus said my perfect love cast out all fear. Choose the perfect love of Jesus, and be set free!

Jesus said my truth (my love) will set you free and as always Jesus is right!!! So just be the love of Jesus and you are a Hero!

Love always Jenny, Ron and MY BEST FRIEND AND HERO JESUS!!!!!

THANK YOU JESUS! I LOVE YOU!!!

Hope or Carrots

The other day while attending a church, the pastor and his congregation came back to pray for Jenny. As they prayed, one girl put her hand on my shoulder and said, "I have a word for you from Jesus. Jesus said *don't give up hope*." Immediately, I started thanking God for that message. I hadn't realized I was losing hope already but I knew the last couple weeks I had a sadness in my heart that I couldn't figure out why and where this sadness was coming from. I had asked Jesus why I had sadness in my heart and didn't get an answer until I went to church that night.

I know for a couple weeks all the signs in Jenny's body were showing deterioration and after all these years you would think I should be able to just cast down these negative signs and continue to stand firm in my faith in God. I thought I was standing firm. I didn't realize how the devil was chipping away at my hope. I just couldn't figure out why I was so sad in my heart. Thank you Jesus for restoring my Hope in You!

Hope is so precious. The Word of Jesus says faith is the substance of things hoped for. If we lose our hope, we lose everything. You cannot have faith without hope. To me, hope is like the dream part of faith. I dream of walking with Jenny and holding hands. I dream of having coffee with Jesus and Jenny. I dream of Jenny being able to go to the bathroom on her own. Our friend Erin called the other day and said that she dreamed we were in a van going somewhere and she asks Jenny a question and Jenny started talking and answered the question. Erin said Ron you just started crying and you held Jenny. In a way you could say faith is the substance of things dreamed of. But I know we all have bad dreams and we hope our bad dreams never come true so I'll stick with the words of Jesus and say faith is the substance of things Hoped for. Even though dreams are not hope, I do want to thank you Jesus for the dreams of encouragement! What a delight to even have dreams of Jenny walking and talking. Thank you Jesus! Thank you Jesus for your words of hope and encouragement.

I remember when Jenny's condition first started. I took Jenny to the doctor and hoped they had some good news; that it will be a good report. When the doctors finally came up with the diagnosis of Picks disease, they told me that there's no hope and no medicine available for it. Upon learning that, I started praying for a miracle. At that same time, I went to the health food stores and bought all kinds of health foods, vitamins, minerals, drinks etc. Jenny and I had taken vitamins for years. We even had a juicer machine and Jenny had read a ton of books about vitamins and health. We even made our own formula for our children when they were babies.

At the very first conference we went to the teacher said how vitamins and health food could rob you of your faith in God because you were putting your faith in the vitamins. So I got rid of everything and put my faith, hope and love in God. The funny thing is that the very same people that taught me to put my faith in God are now selling vitamins for a living. It is a good thing my belief about faith in God is rooted from the Scripture and not what the conference teacher believed.

To this very day, I have stuck with my decision to put my faith in God. I believe my faith and hope in God is rooted in Scripture and in the Truth of His Word! I am glad to have made that decision because almost every day I meet someone that says, "Have you tried this or have you tried that?" I believe in God! I believe God will direct my path but if I will try everything else along the way, where is my faith and what is it in? Yes I hear the great stories about people that were healed by taking vitamins and I wonder if they are in bondage to vitamins now. That is, do they believe without their vitamins they will get sick again and maybe even die? If they miss a day or go somewhere and forget their vitamins what will happen to them? I believe vitamins are a form of bondage. I know people who have their beliefs in vitamins and think the vitamins have given them a lot better quality of life here on earth. For years, I believed in that also. Now all my belief is in Jesus and I can take Him everywhere, so I am never in bondage.

If I started giving Jenny vitamins and supplements etc. and Jenny was suddenly healed, where should I put or to whom shall I give glory and praise to? I have heard people talk about 'that doctor in New York, he said to do this and to eat that' and when people did what he said they were healed from cancer. The problem for me was as they told their testimony, they praised the doctor in New York and not God and I wonder what God thinks.

What if the doctor in New York told everyone to drink ten glasses of carrot juice every day and make sure the carrots are organic? The world would run out of carrots in no time at all and then what would we do? Maybe we should pray for God to send more organic carrots?

Are we to live in our own strength or let the joy of the Lord be our strength? I will not change my faith in God! God is my strength, God is my love, and my relationship to God is my Joy! I will eat carrots because God made them for us to enjoy but not to worship.

I know when I stand before Jesus at judgment I can say "All my faith is in You and You alone." I do pray for Jesus to bless the decisions I make and I know He does when my decisions line up with His teachings. Jesus turned water into fine wine instantly; He did miracle after miracle instantly. My faith, my Hope, my Love and my TRUST are in Jesus the Creator of us all, not in organic carrots. I'm sure organic carrots are good for me and if I had some I would eat them. But I just don't put my faith in them.

Jesus in His word talked about rest and peace:

Matthew 11:28-30 Come to Me, all you who labor and are heavy laden, and I will give you rest. Take My yoke upon you and learn from Me, for I am gentle and lowly in heart, and you will find rest for your souls. For My yoke is easy and My burden is light."

Are we resting in God if we have to drink four glasses of carrot juice every day? Are we resting in God if we have to read every ingredient in everything we eat? Jesus said not to worry about tomorrow and what to eat and how to clothe yourself! Are we going against His commandment when we worry about what we eat?

203

Matthew 6:31 "Therefore do not worry, saying, 'What shall we eat?' or 'What shall we drink?' or 'What shall we wear?'

I remember when everyone bought margarine instead of butter because we were told that butter was bad for us and margarine was good for us and now we are told the opposite.

Matthew 6:32 For after all these things the Gentiles seek. For your heavenly Father knows that you need all these things.

I believe Jesus is asking us to be an example to the world. Just because some scientist says something is good for us, should we follow the scientist down his path or believe God and walk down His path? God's path is one of trust in Him alone. If we worry about everything we eat, how do we show the world we believe in Jesus who tells us not to worry? The Word of God says 'your Heavenly Father knows we have need of these things. Trust Father God (Father means to come forth from and God means source of Life) so trust the SOURCE OF LIFE, and His Son Jesus)'. Jesus says trust in me and be free! Free of worry, free of doubt, and free of sickness!

Matthew 6:33 But seek first the kingdom of God and His righteousness, and all these things shall be added to you.

You see the big BUT there!!! 'But' seek you first the kingdom of God! If we are not studying our food labels, reading health books and chasing down organic carrots, we will have a lot of free time. If we spend that free time seeking earthly junk, we might be better off looking at the labels and health books. BUT if we spend our time seeking God and His righteousness (right standing with God) we can be free of worry and fear! We will not lack anything. Believe God when He says we will not lack any good thing.

I don't think God will have you running around in rags and eating out of dumpsters because you are seeking Him. How would that bring people to Him? On the contrary our rest in Him to provide for us will make people want the peace we have so we can lead people to Jesus Christ and His freedom!

The opposite of rest or resting in God is to hurry and be busy with the things of the world. To me, hurry is so close to worry. When I see people in a hurry all the time or so busy all the time and they worry all the time. Busy, hurry and worry has to be the work of the devil because the word of God says 'not to worry and to dwell with God for He will give you rest'. I hear people say "if I keep my kids real busy, I can keep them out of trouble." Guess what? It doesn't work. It will keep you exhausted to the point you are too tired to seek God. Then you might think "if I had some organic carrots I would have more energy to do the things of the world."

I pray for peace in their lives and thank God for the rest and peace He has provided for me. Jesus said He is no respecter of persons. So I know the peace and rest He has given me He will also give them. Thank you Jesus for the rest and peace of knowing You.

Matthew 6:34 Therefore do not worry about tomorrow, for tomorrow will worry about its own things. Sufficient for the day is its own trouble.

Again, don't worry about tomorrow. Trust God today for He knows what is coming tomorrow and has already taken care of it. If we get out the way and let God be God, tomorrow will be just great. Seek Father God and, 'seek you first the kingdom of heaven and all these things will be added to you'. If you go out and beat your brains out working two jobs and long hours providing for yourself and looking for organic food, you will be too tired to seek God and probably ask God, "where are You God and why am I sick?" Worse than that, you might ask, "God why did you let me get sick? God please help me! I'm out of carrots!" SMILE if you have the energy!

Just ask Jesus to bless everything you put in your mouth and ask Jesus to help you make healthy decisions. Jesus really wants to be that personal with you. So let Him! Jesus turned the water into fine wine and He will do the same thing for us. Ask Jesus to bless your food and He will bless it with what you need.

Jesus said to diligently seek Him with all your heart, your mind and your soul. Notice these things (heart, mind, and soul are yours) to do what you want with, they are gifts from God! Your health is a choice. You can believe in carrots or God. Believe in God and your heart, mind and soul will in the peace of God. You can rest in God and you will have time to seek Him, to love Him and to hear Him. Life is really about relationship. Relationship with Jesus is the most important relationship you will ever have. Relationship with Jesus will bring Joy that is beyond understanding and you will never backslide. You run right into His loving embrace! Jesus is waiting for you to choose Him! He really is everything!

> **Hebrews 11:6** But without faith *it is* impossible to please *Him*, for he who comes to God must believe that He is, and *that* He is a rewarder of those who diligently seek Him.

When we stand before Jesus for judgment, I believe Jesus will be more concerned about how much we trusted Him than how many carrots did you eat in trying to keep your body from decaying. After all Jesus said 'from dust you were made and to dust you shall return'. Jesus breathed life into the dust when He made Adam and He breathed life into our dust at the baptism of the Holy Spirit. Please accept the new life that Jesus breathed into you at baptism. For your new life in Jesus is a new beginning of understanding the freedom and with trust you now walk in if you accept His unconditional love. I see the word 'trust' in the Bible to be all inclusive, that is Faith Hope and Charity are all in one word: TRUST.

In Hebrews 11:6 you see 'without faith it is impossible to please Jesus'. To please God we must have faith in Him. God said we must believe Him and that is not a suggestion but a commandment! I do believe Jesus and I don't take His commandments lightly. I have faith in Jesus to provide for me. I know Jesus is always looking for someone to flow through. Just be a willing vessel for the love of Jesus to flow through and Jesus will flow his love to you and through you! Now that is faith working and pleasing to Jesus!

Jesus is a Rewarder of them that diligently seek Him. You diligently seek Jesus by getting the world out of the way. I mean when we put the junk of the world in front of Jesus like what I did for fifty some years. Yes, for fifty some years, I thought I needed to work to provide for Jenny and our children. I thought my reward from Jesus was my business, my job and being able to provide for my loved ones and in a way it was a reward from Jesus. My problem came when I put those things in front of Jesus. I would put off prayer time to work. I was seeking junk, like a newer car or a better whatever instead of seeking Jesus. I, too, read health books and was worried about bills. Actually I only sought after Jesus when I needed Him or when I was so exhausted and no amount of carrot juice would pick me up. I thank God for grace and leading me to His truth, to His love, to a whole new way of life! Peace and rest are just part of His love. He has the gifts of Joy and understanding and forgiveness, wisdom, freedom from the past and life more abundantly! Try to get that out of an organic carrot.

When I was younger I only talked to Jesus when I needed Him and only about what I needed from Him. I never talked to Him about why I was here on earth and if Jesus needed me to do anything for Him. Thank you Jesus for changing me! Thank you Jesus I now live for You and that is true freedom and Joyfulness! I will never again put momentary happiness in front of freedom and trust which brings the sustaining Joyfulness of knowing Jesus and Father God.

To diligently seek anything, you must set your mind on achieving the thing you seek. No one can learn anything without wanting to learn it. You must have the desire to know God if you are going to become friends with Him. When you fell in love with your wife, you were diligently seeking to know her, to please her and give yourself to make her happy. A relationship with Jesus is the same way! He wants us to fall in love with Him, to seek Him, to desire to please Him and to desire to spend time to know Him intimately. Jesus will be your Best Friend if you let Him. This is why Jesus said:

Matthew 6:24 "No one can serve two masters; for either he will hate the one and love the other, or else he will be loyal to the one and despise the other. You cannot serve God and mammon.

Serving earthy junk (a fleshly master) will rob you of peace and rest. By killing the desire for money and prestige you can have peace, rest and health by just seeking God with all your heart. If you seek God with all your heart, He will reward you in ways you never thought possible. Without Jesus there is no love, no peace and your heart will be attacked. The doctors are right when they call a heart attack a heart attack. The heart attack is brought on by stress, worry, and nonbelief! You can be free of all of that by trusting in God and making God the ruler over your life.

... or else he will be loyal to the one and despise the other. You cannot serve God and mammon.

I believe what Jesus is saying is if you will hold on to your junk and pass on the junk to your loved ones like it is good stuff and you think you are giving them a head start in life. In reality, you are showing how important junk is. Earthy, fleshly junk will make you despise God because God will ask you for some of your time. And people in love with junk will not want to be bothered with God.

Please don't try to change yourself. Ask God for help and then let God be God and get the junk out of His way. If you think you own any earthly thing, that thing actually owns you. Get rid of it now! Be free to enjoy great health and the stress free life Jesus talks about.

You will win souls to Jesus without saying a word because Joyfulness is contagious and Joyfulness is more than a bus ticket to heaven. It is more than 'if you died tonight where will you spend eternity'. Joyfulness is 'what if you live tonight how will you spend tomorrow'. Jesus said to bring heaven to earth. Bring Heaven to earth is totally possible. I thought freedom for me was to be free from earthly junk and earthly desires and it is. BUT true freedom is only found in resting in God and His power and might.

208

When you rest in the power and the might of God, you will have sweet sleep, you will have good health, you will be free of worry and most of all you will know that God loves you. The revelation of God's love is the biggest revelation of your life. Jesus never led anyone to freedom by asking them to recite a prayer. They saw the Joy in His heart, they saw the peace in His face, and they saw no lack. When Jesus wanted to feed the multitudes, He simply multiplied the loaves and fishes. Jesus just calmed the storm, He saw sick people and He healed the sick, raised the dead, and cast out devils. Jesus preached the word boldly. We can do all these things. But I think we will need more than carrot juice, more than health books, more than the world has to offer. We need a relationship with our Jesus! You will not hear Him and know his voice if you are too busy to listen. Jesus will not talk over the noise that we put in our life. Jesus is the still soft voice! Slow down and listen!

Please slow down and listen. When you hear His voice ask Him to show you the truth of what you are hearing in His word also. If what you are hearing doesn't line up with the word of God then you are not hearing from God. Discerning the voices in your head might seem hard at first because we need to be able to compare what we are hearing to His written word. Jesus will help you discern and learn His voice over other voices. Jesus gave us His Holy Spirit as a Helper, a Comforter and a Teacher. We have Jesus's Holy Spirit in us if we are born again. You are never alone and you will never be forsaken if you just trust in God!

I know when Paul taught about forgiveness for sin and freedom from the punishment of sin through the grace of God. People asked "Paul, are you saying should we sin more so grace abounds more?" Paul said, "No, I am preaching freedom from sin not a license to sin." We are free from sin and the bondage of sin (earthly desires) in the truth of Jesus Christ. The truth is we are free from the junk of the world, we are free from trying to live by the standards of others, and we are free to be the love of Jesus to the world.

I am asking, let God be God and let carrots be carrots. Please don't make carrots your God. Preach the Word of God, not carrots. I know I cannot eat ice cream all day or every day and expect God to make it nourishing to my body. Jesus in His word said we are not to tempt God with His word. I will not put my hand in a bucket full of poison snakes to see if no deadly thing will hurt me. I will not eat ice cream all day to tempt God to see if He will make it good for me. If a poison snake or spider through no fault of my own bites me, I believe and I know for a fact Jesus will take care of me. In the book of Acts, Paul got bit by a poison snake and just went on eating. He didn't panic and he just went back to what he was doing. Do you see the rest in that, the peace in that? The truth of God's Word was in Paul and Paul never doubted God's love.

I will eat good food and I do ask God to help me make healthy choices in food and drink. But I do not make food my God! I do not expect food to heal me! I put my faith in Jesus, the One who created the world. I know Jesus created carrots and good foods for us to eat and sustain our bodies, so I eat as best as I can and I don't eat junk food. I do ask Jesus to help me make healthy choices in the food I eat.

I'm saying I am free from the worry of what to eat to save my body because I trust God to be my provider, my health provider and my love provider. When you know you can trust God loves you, you can trust in His love. When you know God loves you, you will know God as your provider and you will rest knowing God is your Provider. I think God is pretty clear about whom to serve and who gets the praise.

Matthew 6:24 "No one can serve two masters; for either he will hate the one and love the other, or else he will be loyal to the one and despise the other. You cannot serve God and mammon.

I'm repeating this to make a point! Please, let me paraphrase: No man can serve both God and carrots, for either He will seek organic carrots (health foods and books) or he will seek God and truth. He will hate one and love the other. He will hold on to his carrots and despise God because he never believes in the love of Jesus. For you cannot serve God while seeking health through what you eat. Jesus said you cannot serve God and food. Health foods can be an addiction like gambling, drugs, sex, etc.

Jesus talks about a good report. Jesus asks us, "Whose report are you going to believe?" The scientist that said margarine is better than butter and that coconut is no good for you but now the scientist says butter is really good for you and margarine is now like eating plastic. For years, scientists said coconut is high in cholesterol so don't eat it for you will have a heart attack. But now they say coconut is good for you and it will help your brain.

We have had a Bible for over two thousand years. This book has lead people to the love of Jesus and truth on how to live a God pleasing life. I see the truth of God's inspired word do miracles. I see the love of God's Word led people to forgiveness and freedom. I know the inspired Word of God is life now and life eternal. I also see people in bondage to their organic food, going out of their way to try to save their own life. To me, this is sad because they could be free to help others and love others by just trusting in God the maker of the food instead of putting their faith in the food.

Matthew 16:25 For whoever desires to save his life will lose it, but whoever loses his life for My sake will find it.

It very well could have been the Bible that led a farmer to go back to the basics and start growing food organically. I am happy we have organic food. If somewhere along the line I found organic food on my plate, I would ask God to bless it and I would eat it. I would know God has blessed it and I know I am blessed by God not the food.

I want to thank everyone that has suggested ways to help Jenny be restored to health but I really know down deep in my heart that I believe it is God that will heal Jenny and not some diet change. I have all my belief in God and His love for us and it is His love more than anything I can do physically that will heal Jenny. Our battle is spiritual, Jesus said so! I do not remember any place in the bible where Jesus said go change your diet, you need to eat more carrots and then I will heal you.

Jesus does love us. Father God is the source of life and our source of life and they give us their Holy Spirit to be with us, to comfort us, and to lead us to His truth. So if you have a health problem, please go to the source of life and let God be God.

Doctors have their place in this world. Carrots have a place in this world. I wear shoes on my feet for comfort. I bless my food and ask God to make it good for what my body needs. I ask God to protect my loved ones and keep us out of harm's way. The more I talk to God, the more I know God and the more I know Him as my source of life! Don't confuse Him and His goodness with momentary health benefits of some food or something He gave us for comfort. Thank Him for these things but seek Him with all your heart and put your trust in the Creator of these things not the things itself.

Some people ask, "How do you trust in something that was written over two thousand years ago?" They ask, "How do you trust in someone you have never seen?" They ask these questions with an air about themselves as if to belittle me for my belief. Yet, these same people will trust in organic carrots or foods to have something in it which they have never seen. They really cannot see the difference in organic and non-organic food. So they have their trust in the person they are buying them from, or the certification sticker on the product. They trust in scientists and what their body tells them. They trust in what they can see, feel and touch. The very things that God tells us not to trust in, is what they believe in. I will put my trust in God and God alone will I trust.

Jenny and I trust in my Father and my brother Jesus forever! Hope is precious when Hope is in the Father of Fathers and the Brother of all Brothers. FATHER GOD AND JESUS WILL NEVER FORSAKE US!!!

Thank You and be blessed by the love on Jesus!

Jenny and Ron and Jesus bless you forever!

I want to add one more thing to the mix. All God really wants is *relationship* with us. Please realize all this talk about food and health is taking your thoughts away from your relationship with Jesus. Why do people study to look so intelligent? They can talk about nutrition, sports, the end of the world, etc. A while ago I watched part of a movie about the earth flooding, the axis of the earth is going to tilt and the earth is going to change drastically.

This very intelligent person sounded so sure of himself. He had a ton of evidence and talked about the Pope and how the church was preparing for this flood. I turned it off and sat quietly. I ask God what is this all about and God said all of these things are designed to take your mind off me.

PLEASE BLESS YOUR FOOD. COMMAND IT TO BE GOOD FOR YOUR BODY AND THANK GOD YOU HAVE THE POWER TO TURN A McDONALD'S HAMBURGER INTO THE NUTRITION OF ORGANIC CARROTS! THANK YOU JESUS FOR REVELATION, REVELATION AND MORE REVELATION!!!

MOST OF ALL THANK GOD FOR A RELATIONSHIP WHERE YOU CAN ASK HIM ANYTHING AND GET ANSWERED. JESUS IS YOUR BEST FRIEND AND YOUR TRUTH. TRUST JESUS AND YOU WILL NEVER NEED TO WORRY! I AM HIS BROTHER AND I TRUST HIM!!!

THANK YOU JESUS FOR RELATIONSHIP!

I'm Nuts?

It was March 11, 2013 and after observing Jenny, a fellow camper asked me, "How's do you contact the doctors while traveling fulltime?" I said, "I only have one doctor and He makes camper calls." She looked at me like I'm nuts. Then, I said Jenny is healed and she knew I was nuts.

I guess I need to talk about Jenny's condition for a few minutes so you will know what is going on in our life that is what the fellow camper was seeing in the physical. Jenny's physical condition seems to be getting worse. I am not pronouncing that on her, I am just trying to convey what is going on her physically. Smiling takes a lot of effort for Jenny. Her face muscles do not cooperate with her desire to smile. Swallowing takes a big effort to Jenny. It seems to be a really big discussion. Jenny even falls asleep while chewing her food.

Most of the time, it is very hard to tell if Jenny still can see. She will have her eyes open and looking at me but when I touch her, she jumps. I used to be able to get her to drink from a straw. Now she doesn't seem to recognize what it is in her mouth. Feeding her can take an hour and a half. For a while, Jenny seemed to like eating out where there was a lot going on to stimulate her. Now, that doesn't seem to make a difference. Foods that used to bring a smile on her face and a little excitement in her life just doesn't work anymore. I guess the worst part is how Jenny seems to get so frustrated and the blood veins in her face and arms looks like they are going to pop out of her skin. It is really ugly to see.

Jenny's body is starting to bend like the letter C. When I hold her on my lap she is bent into a C and now her body is staying in the C shape. Her arms are crossed on her chest. Her hands are fisted all time and her legs are crossed all the time. Showering her is a little difficult in the position she's in. I can see why people

214

who don't know God and only look at the physical would think I am nuts for saying Jenny is healed. Please read on and you will see I am not nuts! Jenny is healed. I have the word of Jesus Himself to believe in.

Traveling has become more difficult. I mean it is more difficult for me, not Jenny. It is more difficult for me because I miss her so much. When Jenny is awake, she seems to get fidgety and the only way to settle her down is to hold her on my lap and talk to her. When Jenny is sitting on my lap, she looks at me as I talk to her and she relaxes to where she falls asleep. I usually hold her until my legs go to sleep and start to hurt. As soon as I move her, she wakes up and starts getting fidgety again.

You might be thinking that I am spoiling her and I am! But I love it when I can just stop what I am doing and hold her on my lap. She relaxes in my arms to the point where she is like a wet washrag. I can move her arms and open her little fist, I can uncross her legs and I believe these are good things. I know it is difficult to dress her with her legs crossed and her arms crossed on her chest. When I do travel, I do not set goals. I just go as far as I can and let that be good enough.

Now for the good news about Jenny! Jenny and I are blessed to have a relationship with Jesus and Father God and through the Holy Spirit have the same life giving power, the healing power, the salvation power and power over the devil and his works. I have the same power and authority as Jesus gave the apostles. Thank you, Jesus!

Sometimes I wonder what people who don't know Jesus as their Savior do in times like these. Jesus says to walk by faith and not by sight. Jesus is life and life more abundantly. Jesus called the apostles and trained them and then sent them out to teach the kingdom of God has come upon you. Jesus also sent the apostles out to train others to heal the sick, raise the dead and cast out demons. The apostles preached the kingdom of God and then they passed their relationship to God on to the church. We are His church. We are God's chosen people if we chose to be. We are ambassadors for Jesus! I'm a son of the living God and because I know God loves me. I can look at Jenny and know she is healed! If you think I am nuts or crazy for saying Jenny is healed, go ahead think I'm nuts. That is okay. God calls me his SON!!!

I would rather be walking by faith with my Jesus and be thought of as nuts than to be smart in your eyes! You say, "I need to look at reality, Jenny is getting worse." You say, "Don't get your hopes up too high Ron, you will only be disappointed." Why would I believe you or men that tell me 'protect your heart, Ron and don't be a fool for Jenny is dying right in front of you"? People think I am living in denial. People say I'm living in some kind of finesse world because I believe in God. In God there is no such thing as having your hopes too high! "All things are possible. In God there is no disappointment! All of God's promises are true" The people that say I am crazy or a nutcase need to know God is real, God is truth, God loves me. And those people need to experience the love of God! I'm not nuts, I'm just peculiar and I love it!

> **Deuteronomy 14:2** For you are a holy people to the LORD your God, and the LORD has chosen you to be a people for Himself, a special treasure above all the peoples who are on the face of the earth.

Yes, I am a peculiar person to you, but I am beautiful to my Father in heaven and He has chosen me to take to himself. If I am nuts, I want to stay that way for eternity.

The people that say I'm nuts need to have a relationship with Jesus. I remember when I went to mass every Sunday and Holiday and received Jesus into my heart through communion. It was so wonderful to know Jesus was in me until the host dissolved. I could talk to Him for a few seconds. Yes, I had the body and blood of Jesus Christ in me for a few seconds.

When you really start to seek a relationship with Jesus and you put Him first in your life, you will come to the truth that Jesus wants to be with us and with us, to talk to us and His plan is for us is to manifest Jesus 24/7. Communion was not just at the last supper and every time you reenact the last supper. Communion is for every second of your life! Along with that revelation, I realized Jesus loves me and the two of us can talk, laugh, walk and cry together. In fact, we live together as one. I am one with Jesus and I know the life giving power of Jesus flows through me as did the life giving power of God the Father flowed through Jesus the man while He was on the earth.

I want to put to rest the words I used in the last paragraph, 'reenact the last supper'. Reenact is a poor choice of words, it sounds like we are acting. Jesus said in Luke 22:19:

> **Luke 22:19** And He took bread, gave thanks and broke *it*, and gave *it* to them, saying, "This is My body which is given for you; do this in remembrance of Me."

THIS DO IN REMEMBRANCE OF ME! Jesus said 'this is my body and blood as he took bread and wine and blessed it into His body and blood'. I think people have been arguing ever since whether or not this is symbolism or did Jesus really change bread and wine into the body and blood of Jesus?

To me, the answer is so simple because Jesus came to show us life is really in your spirit. In the beginning, Jesus breathed Spirit life into dust to make mankind in his image.

> **Genesis 2:7** And the LORD God formed man of the dust of the ground, and breathed into his nostrils the breath of life; and man became a living being.

Isn't that cool? Jesus breathed life into the dust! I believe it because God said it! I don't need any other proof. Life is in your spirit. Jesus loves us all and He proves His love by dying for us all. I believe it! Do you?

I believe the whole Bible is true and I can't figure out why is it so hard for some people who claim to be believers to believe that Jesus changed bread and wine into the body and blood of Himself? Again, Jesus said it so and I believe it. For me, it is easy to say Jenny is healed because Jesus said so in His word. If you cut your finger, you expect it to heal. It is easy to believe the little cut will heal because you have seen it so many times. I ask you, "Who made the blood that has to flow through your body to sustain life and then suddenly become a clogging agent when you cut yourself?" If you said only a genius could do such a thing, then you're right. God is my God, God is my genius, God is my healer and God is my Best Friend. You can say that I'm crazy but God says I'm His Son!

I just believe what Jesus said in His Word and there is really no arguing the point in my mind. Jesus said that He created the world and I believe it! What is there to argue about? Jesus came and changed keeping the law from physical to spiritual. Jesus said to renew your mind, to be baptized in the Spirit, to live in the spirit and your battles are spiritual. Jesus said without faith it is impossible to please Him. Faith is your heart belief or better put it is your spiritual belief.

I can tell you this: By FAITH I receive Jesus into my heart 24/7 and by FAITH I live with Jesus in renewing my mind to live the word of God made flesh by turning my fleshly desires into Spiritual desires of being like Jesus. THANK YOU, JESUS!!!

I also believe that with God all things are possible so why would I not believe Jesus when He said 'THIS IS my body and my blood'? To me that settles it and there should be no argument! It is His body and blood. Jesus didn't say that this symbolizes my body and blood. Jesus said THIS IS!!!

Matthew 26:26-28 And as they were eating, Jesus took bread, blessed and broke it, and gave it to the disciples and said, "Take, eat; this is My body." Then He took the cup, and gave thanks, and gave it to them, saying, "Drink from it, all of you. For this is My blood of the new covenant, which is shed for many for the remission of sins.

I have the Word of God to believe in! The words 'THIS IS' are so simple to believe. What I don't understand is where all the unbelief comes from? Jesus is in my heart 24/7 and we will live together forever! When people tell me I need to protect my heart, I tell them Jesus is my Protector. You see, my heart is protected by the love of Jesus! Jesus said to bring heaven to earth. To do that, ask Jesus into your heart and start living in heaven now. Heaven is not the destination – heaven is Jesus living in you NOW!!!

Doctors study for years and years to become a doctor and then they have to read the updated materials all their life to stay up-to-date with the changes in medicine. My Doctor wrote one book and it has stood the test of time for thousands of years and with no updates. I believe my Doctor and when I go to my Doctor I don't have waiting lines to see Him. I don't have deductibles and I don't have insurance contracts. I have FAITH, I have TRUST, and that gives me HOPE and most of all I have God's Word for life more abundantly!

If you listen to people talking about doctors, long enough you will hear stories about doctor's mistakes and doctors not caring! I'm tired of hearing about side effects of man-made medicine! I'm tired of hearing these words "sometimes you have to get worse before you get better or what alternative do you have?" Where is that in the Bible? I don't watch television but I hear people talk about all the new diseases that are being promoted on television. I really don't understand how people can think I'm the one who is nuts.

I don't have any of their diseases and I thank God for His Word that says disease is captivity from the devil. The devil said he came to steal, kill and destroy our life. I cannot think of a better way to describe sickness than killing, stealing and destroying your life. You don't have to be sick too long to realize the truth. Your sickness is (stealing) your life, sickness can (kill) you and sickness is (destroying) your life. Jesus was very clear about who came to kill steal and destroy you. Jesus said I am life and the truth will set us free!!! THANK YOU JESUS FOR TRUTH, LIFE AND LOVE!!!

How can people put their faith in doctors that advertise on television? For example, Doctors advertise, "if you have these signs then you have Restless Leg Syndrome and we have a pill for you." The day before they started advertising, almost no one had even heard of Restless Leg Syndrome. Then, they tell you the side effects of the medicine will probably kill you but your legs won't hurt and we will be rich so come see us now. Now that is a side effect your doctors can live with. It is really hard to understand how people can say that I'm the one who is nuts.

I don't want to put all your doctors down because there are some really good ones out there. Truthfully, I might not be here if not for doctors. Before my faith was this strong for God, the doctors were all I had to keep me alive, and I thank God for them.

Now I thank God for faith. Through God's truth, my faith in Jesus has grown over the years to let me be so in love with Jesus and trust in Jesus that I put my life in His hands. If your faith in God is not that strong then by all means go to the doctor so you can live to have another day to seek Jesus and trust in Jesus. Jesus will meet you where your faith is! Actually that is another way God shows He loves us. God is extremely patient and will work through doctors if we ask him to until our faith grows to be in Him alone. Thank you Jesus for truth and faith and grace and letting us live until we understand your love for us enough to TRUST IN YOU ALONE!!!

Is a person a nut if they love and trust Jesus? I live to hear from Jesus. I live to be with Jesus and walk with Jesus, and talk to Jesus. I live to be like Jesus – that is to preach His word boldly, to heal the sick, to raise the dead and to cast out devils. To set the captives free is my desire and with Jesus living in me, nothing is impossible for me. Trusting in God is like breathing to me. Knowing God is all powerful is wonderful to me, but knowing the Creator of the universe loves me is life and life more abundantly to me. He knows me personally. He hears me! And Jesus is so real I can talk to Him like you talk to your doctors. The only difference is with Jesus, there are no evil side effects! The best knowledge you can gain in life is: God wants to call you His son! Yes, God wants you to be so close to Him that He knows you by name!

With Jesus I get love! It is real love and not sympathy that creates a desire for more sympathy. I do not have bills that add to the tress and I don't live in captivity of medicine and doctor appointments. I live in freedom of asking God 'what are WE going to do today?' I love my Jesus and His freedom from all sickness. Jesus is freedom form diseases and freedom from death! I'm not nuts the way you think of nuts because I am free and I don't live in fear or in need of sanitizer to keep the germs away. *I'm in love with Jesus* and the side effect for loving Jesus is everlasting life! *I believe in Jesus* and the side effect of *believing Jesus* is Joy, Peace, Faith, Hope, freedom from fear, perfect health and knowing the perfect love of Jesus is for us 24/7! Don't forget you can be a Son of God too!

I see people get healed instantly when they hear the Word of God preached! I see the lame walk. I see the Joy in the hearts of people that hear the Word of Hope from Jesus and that is what Jesus came to do, give us Hope! Trusting in Jesus is SETTING THE CAPTAVIES FREE. Forgiveness is freedom, health is freedom, a life of Joy is freedom and life starts with an intimate relationship with Jesus. I simply put my trust in God and his words of truth! The word of God has not changed for thousands of years and I believe God is the final word! I know God's love is all I need and I know God loves me so I am being purified daily. Ask God for the truth and seek God for relationship and I guarantee Jesus will hear your prayer and answer your prayer and with the truth that sets you free!

John 8:32 And you shall know the truth, and the truth shall make you free.

The truth in the Bible is setting Jenny and I free from all sickness and all infirmities! Jesus is purifying us, watching over us and most of all JESUS IS LOVING US. I no longer pray for the sick and downtrodden because nowhere in the Bible did Jesus say I will pray for you. Jesus just commanded sickness to go. Jesus is our example. I follow Jesus and I just command the sickness to go and it has to go! If your faith is not there, then go to the elders and their prayer of faith will save the sick. Notice that it is the prayer of faith, not the prayer of fear! THANK YOU JESUS for making your love so clear! Yes, thank you Jesus for making Jenny and I peculiar! We are so blessed to know Jesus love us! I could write a book a thousand pages long and still not thank God for everything He has done. I love being peculiar!

Jesus and Jenny and I love you and we pray for you to be peculiar too! Are you a Son of God? Does God know your name? Is your name written in the Book of Life? The answers to these questions can all be YES if you just ask God for intimacy with Him and trust Him in a real relationship.

It is my desire for everyone to know God so well that you will proclaim His Word boldly and bask in the perfect love of God that frees us from all fear and sends the devil packing back to Hell! Life is easy when you trust God!!!

Judgment Day

"What will judgment day be like?"

"What will Jesus judge us on?"

"Will sin be a big deal on Judgment day?"

"When will Judgment day comes?"

"Will we stay in the grave until the Judgment day?"

"Will Jesus Judge us or Father God?"

"Was being saved an automatic entry pass?"

These are some questions I have asked my Jesus in what I call Coffee Time With Jesus.

What will Judgment day be like?

In my travels, I have asked people what they think Judgment day will be like. Most people seem to have a view of Judgment day where Jesus is filled with compassion and they are secure knowing Jesus knows their heart and Jesus will know they are good people and so they believe they will be in heaven someday.

Jesus talked to me a while back about good people. When I talked to Jesus about the retired people in the campgrounds, I was meeting I was totally surprised by His answer. You see in the last couple months of Jenny's life, I sat on the couch holding her on my lap for days. During this quiet time, I witness a lot of good people who by earthly standards are really good people. They didn't hurt anyone, they didn't cause any trouble, they pay taxes and they recycled plastic and aluminum cans. They even used the right kind of laundry detergent. In their quest to be good, they have set their own standards of right and wrong or may I say they go by the worldly standards for good and evil. Jesus said the devil has us doing all these things to make us think we are good. Most of them retires and had some pet dogs to love, so in their hearts they think they are caring people. It seems that even in sharing the love they choose who or what will receive their love. I wonder how that stacks up on Judgment day… I hope that doesn't sound judgmental. I am just wondering out loud.

Do you realize that Jesus said there will be a time when people think they are doing right but the end is death?

Proverbs 14:12 There is a way *that seems* right to a man, but its end *is* the way of death.

I'm not sure if what I have described in the paragraph above would bring death, but listen to what else Jesus said and decide for your own self. Please consider these words because eternity can be in the balance and Judgment day is on the way.

Proverbs 14:13 Even in laughter the heart may sorrow, and the end of mirth *may* be grief.

A while back, I was at a party at a campground and I witnessed the crude jokes and the laughter of drunken people. They were laughing out loud, but on the inside, I believe their hearts were sorrowful. I perceive this because on Sunday they were packing up their camper and had to be sober for the drive home. They were screaming at each other and fighting. Jesus in His word has said *from the Heart a man speaks*. From what I heard that Sunday morning, I would think their hearts were sorrowful. I know their words and actions sounded so miserable towards each other.

I thanked God I could witness to their 12 year old son even if it was just for the weekend. I pray for them to receive the love of Jesus into their hearts and for them to come to know the true Joy of the Lord. Some of the sadness I felt for them came from the knowledge they shared with me as I tried to speak to them about Jesus. I was rejected. No, I was not rejected but the message I wanted to share with them was rejected. They told me they already knew Jesus and that they are already saved.

Why are there so many backsliders in the church today?

Proverbs 14:14 The backslider in heart will be filled with his own ways, but a good man *will be satisfied* from above.

I believe the backsliders of today have gotten an empty message of 'get baptized today and you will have a bus ticket to heaven right now'. I call that message empty because it does not change your life. It does not give you any hope or desire for a transformed life and it does not change the way we live our everyday life. It is just a false sense of security.

It is like trying a 20 year old to save for retirement. Yes, you can puff him up about retirement and he may see the wisdom in saving money now. But afterwards, his earthly desires and priorities will take over and he will lose interest in his savings account and he will be spending every cent he makes now!

In other words, the pleasures of today will take over the desire to save for retirement just like the pleasures of today will take away your desire to live a God pleasing life if all you have is a bus ticket to heaven. In fact, the bus ticket to heaven message is so empty that it encourages one to feel saved and not even think about a relationship with Jesus or glorifying the Father through the Son.

There is nothing in that message about bringing Heaven to earth. Bringing heaven to earth is bringing Joy to the earth; and Joy is the encouragement that will keep us from backsliding. Total Joy is what we will experience when we stand before Jesus and hear the words *well done my faithful son or daughter.* Joy is a gift from God and we can experience joy everyday of our life. Unlike saving for retirement that gets boring, Jesus gives us the Joy right now and every day. Joy is our encouragement from God so we can experience heaven right now and not backslide into the world.

If all God wanted is for us to be saved then He didn't need to send His Son and have Him go through all what He did for us. God could have left us in the Old Testament and said just try to not sin! If you try to live a good life which is only based on what will happen in eternity and you don't have the encouragement of Joy, you will probably backslide. The draw of the world we live in is so strong we will be sucked away from God and drawn into the flesh and momentary pleasures of the world. That is why Jesus tells the Joy of the Lord is our strength. Did you know that backsliding is only mentioned in the Old Testament? I believe it is only in the Old Testament because God realized people need more than law and the promises for eternal life to keep us on the path to Heaven. Jesus came to be our example of how we can have Heaven on earth and to show us the difference between the momentary happiness of today versus the Joy of living from the strength and having a relationship with Jesus. We can walk in the same knowledge and revelations as Jesus the man by simply believing in Jesus the Son of God and our Father God. Walking in knowledge and revelations sure beats the empty message of I'm baptized and saved.

What is the Joy of living from strength as Jesus did?

It is living to give of yourself that is to love as Jesus loved. The Joy of the Lord comes from watching the transformation of life from our earthly desires to knowing Jesus loves us. And through that relationship with Jesus and with revelations of Jesus, your spirit will come alive. It is this new life that will enable you to be the Joy of the Lord to everyone you meet. Life is all about helping others to understand Jesus and why He came. Follow Jesus, love Jesus, and you will have understanding of the ways of Jesus so you too can give the Joy of the Lord. That is how we live to help others.

Joy comes from knowing Jesus loves you to a point that the circumstances of life cannot take away that Joy. When you know in your heart that Jesus dwells in you, walks with you, talks to you, guides you and Jesus is proud of you and Jesus loves you, you will have the Joy of the Lord in your heart 24/7! And that is a good Joy of the Lord and a good Judgment day.

The Joy of the Lord is a Joy that no man can take from you. Unlike the momentary happiness of this world which is here one second and gone the next. The Joy of the Lord is sustainable through life because you live in the Joy of having Jesus lives in you right now! Yes, Heaven is the ultimate goal but you cannot save up good deeds to go to heaven and you cannot deserve it or earn it. But you can live in Heaven right now and that is when you let Jesus be Jesus and let Him be your source of self-worth.

What does it mean to let Jesus be Jesus? Jesus wants to be intimate with us. He is not just some distant God we pray to and wonder if He even cares. He is not just for the big problems in life, like sickness or accidents. Jesus wants to be there when we stub our toe, when I ask Jesus where my car keys are and He says they are in the trunk lid where you left them. I just marvel at how Jesus wants to be in my everyday life every minute of the day. That is how we send the devil and sin packing. We simply let Jesus into our lives and get so intimate with Him and we become one with Him. You let Jesus be Jesus by seeking Him or making Him the most important person in your life. When you do, He will give you revelations of how much He loves you and that the two of you can become as one. Did you ever ask Jesus, "Jesus what are your dreams? Jesus what makes You and Father get up and shout to the rooftop for Joy?" Yes, the answer is Joy. Jesus created us to be Joy and we become Joy by our intimate relationship with our Creator.

Have you ever met a married couple that when she speaks he can finish her sentence? That is an intimate relationship that comes from years of loving each other. Jesus said we can have the mind and the eyes and the heart of Jesus Christ. Go for it! Have a relationship by simply asking God. I want to manifest you Jesus every day in every way possible. I have Jesus living in me and so can you. Simply ask God for this relationship and start thinking and talking to God every day and every minute. Jesus will bring Joy into your hearts which you cannot explain. And people will see Him in you and want what you have! Heaven on earth!!!

With an intimate relationship with Jesus, we can have Jesus as our Brother and our Savior. Jesus is our Advocate to the Father who is Love and Joy beyond any measure. No man could do what Jesus did except if He has the revelation in His heart of how much the Father loves us. I know my Father God loves me but I still respect His Judgment!

How do you get a relationship with Jesus like that?

First, we need to ask Jesus for a personal relationship. Second is to believe a Joy of knowing Him does exist. Trusting in Jesus is the hardest part for most people. Jesus made following Him so rewarding that it is almost too easy for most people. Jesus said the simple will believe and follow Him but the learned will spend their time trying to figure Him out. I pray the learned backsliders will run into a simple-minded frontslider that is taking the Word of Jesus seriously and has allowed the true love of Jesus to penetrate their hearts and dwell there. I pray this simple-minded frontsliders will be able to demonstrate the Joy of the Lord so well that the learned backslider will 'leave his own ways' and find a way to seek Jesus with all their heart.

Proverbs 14:15 The simple believes every word, but the prudent considers well his steps.

I feel so honored to be simple! I must be simple because I believe every word spoken by Jesus. I simply believe the Word of God and I don't even need any scientific proof to support my beliefs. It is called faith! Pretty simple isn't it? If you read about the apostles and how Jesus walked up to them and said, "Come, follow Me" and they did follow Him. There is no prep work needed to follow Jesus. We simply put off what we believe to be our priorities and let His priorities become our priorities. By this, I mean I still go to the grocery and I go about my day. The only difference is I am in constant communication with Jesus and if I see a need like someone is hurting or I sense the heaviness from someone, I ask God what He wants to say to that person and I do it. Sometimes I just tell them Jesus loves them and sometimes I pray for healing. Whatever I hear from God is what I do. It is simply listens and being obedient.

I believe Jesus is calling us all and we just simply answer yes or no. Jesus proves that there really is a simple way of life for us. I title the simple life in one word, BELIEVE. For me, believing is receiving the love of God and the Joy of the Lord right now. Believing is trusting in God to talk to you. Believing is discerning who is talking to us. Choose to believe and have a good Judgment day decision right now!

If you listen to the stories that Jesus told while He was here on earth on how the wisdom from these stories reach across thousands of years and touch our lives still today. That seems impossible and yet it is real and His words are right in front of us every day. There is life in the words of Jesus. There is Joy for us who choose to live in the life of Jesus. And yes, there is salvation in His life recorded thousands of years ago. I simply believe and Jesus does the rest. My belief has given me such Joy and such peace and most of all love. A love so real that I will lay down my life for my Jesus and in doing so I probably confound the wise. My Jesus is simply my Best Friend and I simply love Him! If you love someone and believe in someone then you can lay down your life for that person and never look back. The stories in the Old Testament and the New Testament paint a picture of love so rich in mercy that one cannot help but see the true Joy of a Loving God!

Proverbs 14:16 A wise *man* fears and departs from evil, but a fool rages and is self-confident.

Because I believe, I fear and that makes me wise. Sounds like I contradict myself. I mean, I said I feel honored to be simple minded and here I say I am wise. To accept the word of God without any proof makes some people think I am stupid or simple-minded yet in God's eyes I am wise because I trust not in my own understanding but I trust in my God and that is simple to me. Jesus proves his love for me!

Personally, I simply trust God's opinions that say I am made in His image and likeness. Personally, I trust in the knowledge of knowing Jesus and Father God loves me for no other reason than they said so. You see how simple that is! You see how that makes me wise in my Father's eyes! Father God and Jesus do not have to prove their love for me because I trust in them and look at the sacrifice in the Cross and know in my heart that they think I am worth it! That is some big self-worth, isn't it?

I must clarify something. I said I fear and yet most of the time I describe fear as faith in the devil. Fear is believing that God cannot handle the circumstances in your life and fear is believing the devil has power over God and our circumstances. Fear is being afraid something bad will happen and not trusting in the power of God to overcome our circumstances. In Proverbs 4:16, I believe we are told it is a wise man that fears the wrath of God for unrepented sin. The Fear of God is a very healthy fear for it comes from respect for our Judgment day. It is like fearing the just punishment of your earthly father because you are doing something wrong versus being in fear that the devil can do something bad to you and God cannot protect you. I have complete trust in my Heavenly Father and my Jesus. I have a healthy respect for their power and I have no fear of death because my Jesus through His love for us conquered death and prove we have life everlasting. You see, I have no fear of the devil because I simply live in the Love of my Jesus and my Father but I respect and obey them and fear their just punishment should I be so *wise in my own eyes* to start following my own path or the paths of the world.

Proverbs 16:25 There is a way *that seems* right to a man, but its end *is* the way of death.

Today, the *'way that seems right to a man'* is defined as the ways of the world. We have been taught the ways of the world from television and our peers. They say it is politically wrong to say or being told we cannot pray in schools etc. are just some of the ways that seem right to a man and yet we see their ways bring death to our children and our country. I hear people say, "Look what has happened to our children since they took prayer (Jesus) out of school!" Then the usual conclusion is but what can I do about it? The answer is simple! *You can change the world one heart at a time!* The person that wanted prayer out of school was just one person at some point in time. He changed hearts one heart at a time. So can you! Start operating in the gifts of the Holy Spirit just like what the apostles did. You know it all started with Jesus the man, and we have the same gifts as Jesus.

I have departed from evil not because I try not to sin but because I live in the revelation of the love of Jesus Christ. That is, I focus on Jesus and what He needs to be done instead of focusing on the devil and trying not to sin. I don't focus on Jesus not being in school. I focus on Jesus and the power I have to change one heart at a time. This is the peace that Jesus promised and you receive peace by simply trusting and believing in God. Jesus said in Proverbs 23:7:

Proverbs 23:7 For as he thinks in his heart, so is he.

If we think or focus our thoughts all day about not sinning, we will probably sin because sin is all we are thinking about. If I think about all the bad side effects of not having Jesus in school then I am defeated before I even have coffee with my Jesus. Instead, I literally get up every day and ask Jesus, *"What are WE going to do today?"* I know Jesus the Leader of the universe came to earth to show us the love of the Father and to show us how much Jesus and Father God want to spend time loving me!!! I have a purpose and my Coffee Time With Jesus is fruitful and I know I am one day closer to having Jesus in school again. Thank You, Jesus! I love you too!!!

Now that Jesus the man has left the earth, He wants us to be His representatives here on the earth. Jesus wants me to show someone His love today and I have just made myself available! Pretty simple isn't it? Am I simple and wise? I'm sure I am! That sure beats being a fool and relying on my own skills so I will be happy, even for just a moment. "But the fool rage and is confident in himself," says the Lord! To be confident in your own abilities is foolish and unwise. I choose to focus on my Jesus and I will be wise and simple-minded! I choose to have the Joy of the Lord in my heart and not momentary happiness in my head.

The people I talked about earlier gets up every day and do whatever they desire to make themselves happy. Most had raised families and now their only goal is to do whatever they think will bring them happiness and it seems they are confident God knows their heart! It seems they are confident they are good people and they are confident they are on the right path to pleasing God. In fact they are so confident they don't want to spend any of their time with my Jesus. It seems they are confidently turning away from the joy of having a relationship with Jesus the King of Love and they miss the Joy of heaven here on earth. They are confident and God knows their hearts and I believe they are wise and confident in their own understanding. And most of all, the devil is confident that they are not going to do anything to further the Kingdom of God today.

When I asked them, "What did you do exciting today?" their reply went something like this: "Well, we went to that little antique

231

town down the road and looked around at the shops. Then we ate out and we had a nice lunch. You know, it was just something to do and a nice way to fill up some time. The weather was nice and so we had a nice day." I would truly hate my life if having a nice day is controlled by the weather and just doing whatever I thought would give me momentary happiness.

I thought, "where did this notion that we are on the earth to please ourselves come from and where on earth did the notion come from to just pass away your time?" I just cannot find that in my Bible, can you? I do find the opposite though. Here Jesus asked Adam:

> Genesis 3:10 So he (Adam) said, "I heard Your voice in the garden, and I was afraid because I was naked; and I hid myself."

Can you image if Jesus suddenly walked up and said, "why are you spending this life I gave you just trying to please yourself?" Would you run and hide because the naked truth is not so pretty?

> **Genesis 3:11** And He said, "Who told you that you were naked? Have you eaten from the tree of which I commanded you that you should not eat?"

You see in the first story of the Bible we see how important it is to discern our thoughts. Look how the world could be different if Adam just used discernment. If we discern our thoughts then we will realize that wasting time trying to please ourselves is not wise.

> Hebrews 5:14 But solid food belongs to those who are of full age, *that is,* those who by reason of use have their senses exercised to discern both good and evil.

Here Jesus is talking about discerning our thoughts to figure out which are from God (good) and which are from the devil (evil). Who is telling you one person cannot make a difference (the devil) if you have thought you cannot make a difference. I believe you have heard from the devil. I love hearing from God and He tells me to change the world one heart at a time. I know you are hearing from God or you would not be reading this. Jesus says we have to have our senses exercised to discern. So exercise your senses and hear from my Jesus today.

John 10:27 My sheep hear My voice, and I know them, and they follow Me.

We can hear the voice of Jesus every day and we need to hear the voice of Jesus every day. How can we follow Him without hearing from Him? Jesus is alive and real and He is talking to anyone that will listen! Does one heart at a time seem simple to you? Think about the car for example. From one man's dream came the car. Then came jobs making cars, then roads, tires, batteries, lights, heaters, air conditioning, rest stops, expressways, repair shops, gas and oil refineries, trucks and oil rigs, etc.! You get the picture. One heart at a time works!

John 10:28 And I give them eternal life, and they shall never perish; neither shall anyone snatch them out of My hand.

Isn't that cool? Jesus will give to us eternal life and we will never perish, neither shall any man pluck us out of His hand! I don't know about you but I want that promise in my heart and I will take time out every day to listen for the voice of my Jesus for the rest of my life. I can tell you this: hearing the voice of Jesus and spending time with my Jesus is the absolute best time of my life. I love my Coffee Time with Jesus and talking to Him all day long.

Maybe we should change our saying from *have a nice day* to *have a nice eternity*. That might wake us up to the fact there is an eternity. Maybe we should talk about eternity more than the pleasures of this earth. After all, there is a Judgment day coming.

So I asked Jesus, "What is it about these people that makes me kind of sick to my stomach?" The answer from Jesus surprised me big time. Jesus gave me a scripture and His answer was a giant wake up call for me!

Revelations 3:16 So then, because you are lukewarm, and neither cold nor hot, I will vomit you out of My mouth.

I think the people I talked to might have been what Jesus was calling lukewarm and yet they were so sure they were on the right track to heaven. It was really alarming to me! Being spewed or vomited out of the mouth of Jesus doesn't sound very comforting to me. Then Jesus added these people are worse than murderers and adulterers and thieves. I asked Jesus, "How can that be? I mean they are good people and they just don't seem to have a purpose." Jesus answered saying *'murderers, adulterers and thieves'* at least know they are sinning and have a chance to repent. The sins of murderers, adulterers and thieves are blatantly open so there are people of God who see their sin and will help or lead them to repentance.

"Ron, the good people you are talking about don't even think they are sinning. They are proud and think only of themselves." I said to my Jesus, "That is so sad. How will they know to repent?" Jesus replied, "They not only don't know to repent but they are complacent. They are unavailable to me and they only live to satisfy their own needs. They walk through the world without compassion for life and their sole purpose is to make their selves happy." Then Jesus added, "Being complacent and unavailable to me is foolish and very unwise."

Jesus went on to say, "It is easier for a murder, an adulterer and a thief see a need to repent for their sins than for a wise man to see a need to repent for his sins. A wise man, being complacent and confidently walking his own road of satisfying himself will make himself unavailable to me and will not have a desire for a relationship with me!"

I thought how sad that is and I believe I felt the sadness in the heart of God also. I praise my God for bringing this situation to my attention and for showing me there is still hope. The hope is that we (Jesus and I) can change one heart at a time. That's right! My Jesus has told me to change the world one heart at a time, so that is what I do. I simply do not worry. I do not have a big master plan and I do not have an agenda. I will simply hear the voice of my Jesus and I simply obey. Pretty simple isn't it? To change one

234

heart at a time is so simple and yet Jesus has showed me His plan works! I don't need corporate sponsorship or a big staff. I don't even need bricks and mortar. I simply follow Jesus and give His love to everyone I meet! Pretty simple isn't it? *One heart at a time works for me!*

I know when I tried to talk to the lost people I met in the campground about God some of them brushed me off. They said we know God and we have a good relationship with Him. Most of them didn't even go to church because they didn't want to be preached to and because it makes them feel guilty. They had excuses like 'the people in churches are hypocrites'. They gave me a lot of excuses and some sarcastically asked me, "If Jesus came today, what church would he choose?"

I answered, "We are His church, we are His people and we are His representatives here on earth." The real temple of Jesus Christ is allowing Jesus to live and manifest inside you. You are His representative and as such you are to represent His love to the world. Yes, you will make a difference when you simply demonstrate the love of Jesus. Simply invite Jesus into your heart and ask Him to reveal Himself to you and you will be the difference the world needs! I don't know how many of them listened but I am sure one heart was changed.

Notice also how they said the people in churches are hypocrites. Almost like they think the church building is the church. The church building is just bricks and mortar and cannot change your heart. It is the people inside the church who are the real heart of Jesus. If they choose to know Jesus and choose to be His representatives here on earth, then they will have the power to change things here on earth. We are to live the life Jesus showed us. We are to help people see Jesus and when we choose to be His representative and focus only on Him, we can help others to see Jesus in us and they will want the Jesus they see in us. That is how Jesus can use us to change the hearts of people on this earth and we change them one heart at a time. So simple isn't it? Thank you Jesus for being my Best Friend.

When we see Christians as hypocrites, maybe it is not so much the church's problem but a problem inside ourselves. Maybe we need to look inside ourselves and see the emptiness. You know the place where Jesus should be. As Christians, our hearts should be full of love for others. I believe our heart is crying out for a purpose and that is why we feel so empty and why we try to fill the day up with things we want to do and yet we are not experiencing the joy of the Lord. Jesus said, "We can have the eyes of Jesus, the heart of Jesus and the love of Jesus" and I want it all.

I know Judgment day is close for me and I want to use every tool that Jesus has given me to please Him. I don't want to miss a minute or a chance to manifest Jesus to the world. I want to bring glory to my Heavenly Father and my Jesus and I do bring glory by emulating them and loving people the way Jesus did. I will never try to attain heaven through works but I will prove I believe and I will prove I know Jesus loves me by the works I do in His name! To do the works of my Father and my Jesus proves that I know they love me and flow through me. I will never try to gain my self-worth by what I do. I have my self-worth because I know Jesus loves me and He is proud of me! That is better than money in the bank.

Jesus said to bring Heaven to earth and so having Heaven while on earth must be possible. I believe when we stand before Jesus for Judgment, if we hear the words 'well done my faithful son' we will be so full of Joy and the world would not be able to contain it! So to me Heaven is Joy and we can experience heavenly joy right here on earth. The Joy of the Lord is our strength and His joy is contagious. Today, go give some contagious Joy of the Lord to everyone you meet. In fact go have some fun and infect everyone!!! Tell them it is Jesus season!

I know my Jesus loves me, do you? That's a good eternity!

Love you always Jenny, Ron and especially my Jesus!!!

Mad

Today, I have become so angry. It came upon me so fast that I didn't have the time to take every thought captive. I just got so mad and wanted to break something or hurt someone. So I cussed at God. And immediately, I realized that I had gone too far with this madness so I took a shower to cool down and then apologized to the Lord. I asked Jesus, "What happened? I haven't had this kind of anger for a long time." So Jesus explained to me what brings on anger.

Mad? What is it? Have you ever gone to bed at night and decided to be mad in the morning? Have you ever broken something so it could make you mad? Have you ever wish your car not to start so it could make you mad? This sure sound stupid doesn't it? If we don't make plans to make us mad, then how does it happen so easily? What is mad? Some people think it is the opposite of happiness. I think sad is the opposite of happiness and mad is the manifestation of sad. Sad is always about me and putting myself first.

Happiness? What is it? We have all made plans to make us happy like, "I'm going to Kings Island tomorrow." We tell jokes to make us smile. We eat to make us happy. We even have happy food like ice cream! Happiness is usually momentary. The sad fact is, happiness is always about me and what I'm doing. Happiness is something that has to be achieved. Happiness almost always involves someone else doing something right for you. Like getting your hair done or your nails done, or when you order right at McDonald's. You see something has to be right for you to be happy. Your car has to start, life has to go your way, and life is about you and what you can get out of it. It's expensive but I'm worth it, attitude. You can be happy one second and sad the next.

Joy? What is joy? Is joy different than happy? Yes, we can be joyful for extended periods of time. Joy is always about others and doing something for them. Joy is getting up in the morning and being excited about life because you can and will give someone that day the gift of love. You see, the joy of life is giving your life away. Joy is putting yourself second and others first. Joy is a lifestyle of giving unconditionally. Joy is not what can I get but what I can give. Joy in a word is Love! Joy is the manifestation of love.

Who sets the standard for love? The answer is Jesus! How is Joy love? The Bible tells us love is a spirit. So is sad a spirit? Yes, sad is a spirit. Galatians 5:22-23 says:

Galatians 5:22-23 But the fruit of the Spirit is love, joy, peace, longsuffering, kindness, goodness, faithfulness, gentleness, self-control. Against such there is no law.

Love is a spirit! I need to read that again: *'the fruit of the spirit is love, joy, peace, longsuffering, gentleness, goodness, faith, meekness, and temperance; against such there is no law'.* Notice all these fruits are to be given away. They are no good to us if we try to hoard them for ourselves. These fruits are to flow through you not just for you. Jesus said freely you received so freely you give. What good are the fruits of the spirit if we never shared them? Yes, we are to live the fruits of the spirit not just have them. For example smiling at someone you pass on the street will almost always bring a smile on his or her face.

The end of Galatians 5:23 says *'against such there is no law'.* So is love lawless? The cool thing is the spirit of love needs no law! You see if you love yourself and others, your love manifests as joy, peace, longsuffering gentleness, goodness, faith, meekness, and temperance. All these manifestations are for others. Love is all about doing for others. If everyone lived in these gifts, then we really would need no law. Love is the truth that sets us free. Law is all about limiting others, controlling others, and keeping us in bondage!

The devil is the author of fear. You fear the consequence of the law. Law only regulates things; law can't make me love you. Law has no reward for obeying it and law is empty of all the fruits

238

of love. Law only takes away! Law punishes. If you break a law then you are a criminal so law also labels. Law breaks down your spirit. If you break enough law you can become discouraged enough to give up and say I'm just going to live this way. Law is discouragement, law cannot edify us, and law confines us. Law tells us we have limits. Law sets boundaries and law is the opposite of love. Law sets standards that limit freedom. Law hardens your heart and takes away your hope. Law condemns and breaks down your spirit to despair and so you will give up. Law can make you want to commit suicide. Law has no mercy. Law makes you pay, (for example taxes, fines, penalties). Law is never fair like the law of taxes will never be fair. Law makes you have a license and permits.

Law brings in sadness and law is where the devil has all his power. Law is always breaking our spirit and demanding our time. Law can kill your spirit, steal your heart and destroy your life. That sounds like the work of the devil to me! (kill, steal and destroy) Jesus came to expose the law of sin and death for what it really is! The work of the devil! Jesus shows us how to live in the fruits of love. Jesus showed us how to keep all the laws of the Old Testament in one word, love! The devil turned the laws into guilt, shame and condemnation.

In fact everywhere you see the word law in the paragraph above you should put in the words *the devil!* Jesus made the law so how can it be as bad as I made it out to be. The laws in the Old Testament are to show us how to live a pleasing life for the Lord while we are still flesh. God wrote the laws so we know they are good. What happened to the laws of God? Law defines sin for us and sin causes death. The devil changes our focus from how to live right in the law in the fear of sin and death. The devil keeps us focused on the spirit of fear (sin and death), instead of the Holy Spirit, the spirit of love for Jesus (freedom and life). I believe Jesus came to fulfill the law so we could be free of the bondage of the law and be who He created us to be. Jesus even broke some laws to show us how the law had been corrupted. For example, Jesus healed on the Sabbath and that infuriated the Pharisees so much that they wanted to kill Jesus. Why? Because Jesus was taking away the power they had over the people. Jesus wanted to take away the fear of man, fear of death, and a lifetime of bondage.

> **Hebrews 2:14-15** Inasmuch then as the children have partaken of flesh and blood, He Himself likewise shared in the same, that through death He might destroy him who had the power of death, that is, the devil, and release those who through fear of death were all their lifetime subject to bondage.

So Jesus came to deliver us from the spirit of fear. Jesus saw His people in the Old Testament were subjected to the bondage of sin and death through the power the devil had in the law!!! Jesus also came to deliver us from the bondage that the devil had over us, namely sin and death as defined in the law of flesh and blood. I call it the law of flesh and blood because Jesus calls it that and to make the distinction of the old law (fear) and new spirit of the law (love) that we now live in. Jesus came to set us free from sin and death. To be free of sin and death just read and study the life of Jesus because He is OUR EXAMPLE OF HOW TO LIVE!

Jesus came to fulfill the law and not to destroy the law. So what does fulfill mean? In life, if you fulfill any contract or agreement or covenant, then it is finished. You do not continue to pay for something when the terms of the contract are fulfilled or paid for! Jesus paid the price!

Jesus made the laws of the Old Testament to tell us how to live in the flesh, to tell us how to respect one another in the flesh, and to tell us right from wrong in the flesh. Man, while living in the flesh has fleshly desires. With the fall of man, the devil showed us that in the flesh we are an easy target for him to tempt us. He proves it every day. Maybe I should say we prove it every day. The devil even gets us men to help him. Please read all Chapter 23 of Matthew. Jesus was talking to the Pharisees. For example, verse 4 says:

> **Matthew 23:4** For they *(the Pharisees)* bind heavy burdens, hard to bear, and lay them on men's shoulders; but they themselves will not move them with one of their fingers.

240

In the hands of man, laws can become heavy burdens and grievous burdens to be carried upon our shoulders. Jesus healed on the Sabbath, in the face of the Pharisees! Jesus said in Matthew 11:28-30:

Matthew 11:28-30 Come to Me, all you who labor and are heavy laden, and I will give you rest. Take My yoke upon you and learn from Me, for I am gentle and lowly in heart, and you will find rest for your souls. For My yoke is easy and My burden is light."

You see we are concentrating on fulfilling the law and Jesus wants us concentrating on God! When we have communion with God, our burden is light and God gives us rest! You can never rest in performing the law. In the law, we were commanded to rest on certain days. But even on the day of rest we had to do or not do certain things. Jesus changed rest from a commandment to a gift. Jesus said, "I will give you rest."

Jesus proved the law needed to be changed from sin and death in the flesh to life eternal in the spirit. When Jesus said in Matthew 5:17:

Matthew 5:17 "Do not think that I came to destroy the Law or the Prophets. I did not come to destroy but to fulfill.

If the law was good as is, then why did Jesus need to fulfill it? Jesus needed to fulfill the law so we could enter into the new covenant. When Jesus said, 'I did not come to destroy the law or the prophets but to fulfill.' Notice law is tied in with prophets. Everyone will all agree that Jesus did fulfill all the prophecies of the prophets. So Jesus fulfills all the prophecies, but some people don't think the law was fulfilled. Yet Jesus said so in the same verse you cannot separate the two. If one is fulfilled then both are fulfilled.

Matthew 5:21-22a "You have heard that it was said to those of old, 'You shall not murder, and whoever murders will be in danger of the judgment.' But I say to you that whoever is angry with his brother without a cause shall be in danger of the judgment.

You see how Jesus changed the law of flesh and blood: to the spirit of the law! Notice how before you had to actually kill someone to be judged for murder. But now, if you have anger towards your brother, anger is enough to be judged for murder. There is a spirit of anger and if we let it manifest in us we are guilty of murder in our heart.

Ephesians 6:12 For we do not wrestle against flesh and blood, but against principalities, against powers, against the rulers of the darkness of this age, against spiritual hosts of wickedness in the heavenly places.

I hope you see how Jesus changed the law from physical manifesting to spiritual manifesting. The war Jesus is talking about is literally in the spirit world, the stakes are for eternity. The war is in our mind and we need discernment. The Pharisees were not listening to God when they hollered for Jesus to be crucified! The war is not just 'did you eat pork or not', it is for our very soul, our spirit. The greatest gift from God is we now have communion with Him!

Old Testament	New Testament
God was a distant being only visited once a year and only after great preparation and only in the Holy of Holies. Or God would speak to His people through a representative like Moses.	We now have communion with God 24/7 and no preparation needed except to ask God into your heart by repenting.
Blessing and curses handed down 4 generations or more	Born again of the Holy Spirit and your first generation with God the father. So you have no curses, just blessings.
Sin and death, penalties and blood sacrifices for sin atonement	Sins are forgiven and removed. Death removed and no more blood sacrifices. Jesus is the atonement and our Advocate.

Sins had to be paid for by repenting and with atonement sacrifice by your first-born livestock. It had to be spotless and no broken bones. You paid for sin all the time and because you sin all the time the atonement was never over.	Atonement for sin is moved into the spirit world. You repent in your spirit and you are forgiven by faith. If you do not repent, you actually pay a bigger price for unrepented, habitual sin. You pay with a loss of personal relationship to God.

I thank God we now live with the spirit of love and by being loved as Jesus is love so are we. We are to manifest the spirit of love 24/7. I hope to show how the spirit of love can triumph over all the evil spirits talked about in the paragraphs above.

Galatians 5:16-18 I say then: Walk in the Spirit, and you shall not fulfill the lust of the flesh. For the flesh lusts against the Spirit, and the Spirit against the flesh; and these are contrary to one another, so that you do not do the things that you wish. But if you are led by the Spirit, you are not under the law.

You see we must discern which spirit we are listing to!

Love is the opposite of law! Love removes fear! Jesus said, "My perfect love cast out fear."

1 John 4:18 There is no fear in love; but perfect love casts out fear, because fear involves torment. But he who fears has not been made perfect in love.

Love sets us free from boundaries, torment and fear. Jesus said all things are possible.

Matthew 19:26 But Jesus looked at them and said to them, "With men this is impossible, but with God all things are possible."

Mark 9:23 Jesus said to him, "If you can believe, all things are possible to him who believes."

We are to believe Jesus came to set us free from sin and death! We are to believe in the truth that Jesus is love so we are to be loved and that sets us free. We are to believe in the perfect love of God that cast out fear!

Mark 10:27 But Jesus looked at them and said, "With men it is impossible, but not with God; for with God all things are possible."

Freedom from sin and death is possible. I believe all things are possible with God and with God dwelling in me nothing is impossible for me!

Love encourages us, love rewards us, love makes us saints, and it was the love of Jesus Christ that made Him shed His blood for us to be sanctified. Love builds up our spirit to love and be kind to others. Love is charity and love gives us hope. And Jesus said He is our Provider, our Health Provider, our Protector Provider and our Love Provider! With God as our provider, how can we worry and have fear?

Love never has to build prisons with guards to keep us in. Love is limitless love has no boundaries! Love is hope and edifies us. Love softens our heart and gives us a desire and a freedom to help others. Love tells you to give out of your heart. Love does not demand like taxes with fines and penalties. Love rewards us with Joy unspeakable. In a word, love is God! God is always freeing our spirit to new heights of love and we are in eternity time so love is now and forever. Jesus came to build your spirit, to redeem your heart and rebuild your life so love can flow through us like mercy and grace that is new every day! It is so easy to love God because God is love and we have God dwelling in us so our nature is to love naturally! Jesus said that He made us in His image and likeness. God is love so we must be love. The consequence of love is more love! We have all seen people that are so in love and we say they glow. Jesus said we are to be the light of the world. Love glows and fear goes!!

So could a world exist without law? I believe a world does exist without law and we all know its name, HEAVEN! Jesus in His word said 'bring heaven to earth'. In other words, live by the spirit of love and manifest the fruits of love by giving heaven to all you meet. Is that possible? How do we bring heaven to earth?

To bring heaven to earth we must first die to self. To die to self we must be born again and invite Jesus Christ into our lives!

2 Corinthians 5:17 Therefore, if anyone is in Christ, he is a new creation; old things have passed away; behold, all things have become new.

When you become a new creature in Christ, you will live for others. You will love them and not live for yourself! The most valuable thing on earth to most people is there is time. We have all heard someone say, "I don't have time for this right now." What they are really saying is, "I don't want to give up my time for you right now." So when you are giving away your time to help others you are dying to yourself. If you see a broken down car alongside the road and stop to help, you are giving them your time. You will say that their needs are way more important than yours. That is dying to yourself. Putting the needs of others ahead of our own needs is bringing Heaven to them. I can guarantee that when you help others, you will be joyful! Jesus said the joy of the Lord in my strength. Think about that for a moment. When you are strong, you feel invincible. You can conquer anything and nothing in life is too big a problem for you. What can take your strength away? The law will take your strength (joy) so fast and discourage you to the point of quitting! Law can make you mad!

I want to go back to mad and sad for a moment. I don't recall hearing of anyone ever going out of their way to make themselves mad. So where does mad come from? It must have a source. I think sad comes from a feeling of helplessness and despair. When we feel there is nothing we can do about a situation, we get sad. When we feel powerless to stop something, we get mad. So mad is the second stage of sad. Even when we have the power to stop something and don't use that power, we get mad. For example, if our car runs out of gas, we get mad and tell ourselves we should have checked the gas gauge. We might even call ourselves stupid for forgetting to gas up the car. We get mad and think now we will be late for whatever. We are mad because we have to wait on someone to bring us gas. Mad is always about time. There is never enough time.

So getting mad is really about how we spend our time. Mad is a decision we make. For example, you're excited because you decided to buy yourself some new clothes and you can spend a lot of time picking out just the right outfit. And then you became happy because you found the perfect outfit for you. Then you go to the check out and get delayed for some reason. You can lose all the excitement and happiness in a moment because of the delay. You can walk out of the store mad because you were inconvenienced. How many times have you been really mad at someone and in the middle of you telling them of, your phone rings and you answered hello in a happy voice. Mad is a spirit we choose to be in agreement with.

Jesus said 'the joy of the Lord is our strength'. I believe there is a spirit of joy in us and a spirit of mad near us. I believe we make choices to listen to the spirit of joy or the spirit of mad all our life. So mad must be the strength of the devil. I know the devil can get me so mad that I blame God for my madness and I have even cussed God when I was mad. If mad was not a spirit of the devil, why would we want to blame God for our madness? We all know that God is the source of life, and life here on earth is an allotted amount of time. So when something we don't want to do requires some of our precious time, the devil of mad kicks out joy until we make a conscious decision to have joy kick out mad again. So joyfulness or madness is a decision that we make. In the shopping example, we had a choice to make: to be mad at the checkout clerk or to bless the clerk! If we chose to bless the clerk we could of walked out joyful, instead of being mad.

So how do we kick out the spirit of mad? Again, die to self. If we are living for God and loving God our time is His time. We have God's power in us. We have God's authority in us. We can take authority over the spirit of mad and use our God-given power to kick it out. You see, when we kick out a bad spirit, it can be near us but not in us unless we invite him in again. Then the spirit of mad is kicked out and mad becomes something we don't have to deal with except as a temptation! When temptation comes, say *I recognize you and I choose to resist you devil by thinking about Jesus* and the devil will flee! It really is that simple! The devil hates it when you know the power and authority you have in Jesus.

When we are living for others and when we are living to please others, peace is the normal result of giving to others. When we have peace, we have gentleness. When we have gentleness, we have meekness. You see how all the gifts come into play when we take every thought captive and kick out everything that is not of love! Jesus is love and He came to earth to show us what love looks like here on earth. We are to manifest love 24/7. Love triumphs over the law and mad all the time.

You see, if we have love we will keep all the laws automatically. Jesus said in Matthew 22:37-40:

> **Matthew 22:37-40** Jesus said to him, "'You shall love the Lord your God with all your heart, with all your soul, and with all your mind.' This is the first and great commandment. And the second is like it: 'You shall love your neighbor as yourself.' On these two commandments hang all the Law and the Prophets."

If you love others, it would be impossible to kill someone, or to steal from someone, or to just hurt anyone. You can keep all the law of the Old Testament in two commandments: 'love God with all your heart and mind and soul and love your neighbor as yourself'. You could be right to all the laws you want and you cannot make me love you. But you can show me love and I will love you forever. Jesus said we are made in His image and likeness. Jesus is love. Jesus was love on earth and His love will reign forever. Jesus showed us love and I will love Him forever. So don't rule your life with law that makes you mad, rule with love and be loved and let the Joy of the Lord be your strength!

In closing, I want to add one more idea: I talked about being made in the image and likeness of God. I'm having coffee with Jesus right now and we are talking about babies.

I think the closest example of the love of God is how good parents taking care of their baby.

It might seem that when the baby cries, something is wrong. So mom or dad will pick up the baby and hold it. When you pick up the baby and hold him, you pat him on the back and he burps. You automatically say he had a gas pain. So we parents assume something is wrong when the baby cries such as *'he is hungry'* or *'he has gas'* or 'he gift wrapped a package in his diaper'. What if the baby has nothing wrong and then we think he is spoiled. We have all these ideas about why the baby cries. We know he was made in the image and likeness of God. And since God is love he is love

247

and maybe he just wants to be loved! Yes, I believe even at this very early age he wants to give love or be loved.

When a baby coos at you or smiles at you, he is giving you love unconditionally. He is saying, "Mommy you did everything right today! I love you mommy!" We respond with unconditional love by holding him close and kissing him and wrapping him up in our arms. This is unconditional love like God's love for us!

If the baby spits up all over our new outfit, we have unconditional forgiveness for him. We don't write that on the calendar to bring it up at a later date. The baby keeps no record of wrongs either. He doesn't understand forgiveness but he gives it unconditionally. Our unconditional forgiveness is the basis for unconditional love. The love and care we give to a baby is really teaching us to die to self. We are showing him his importance to us and that we really care by putting his needs above our needs.

If the baby was crying and we walked by and said, 'I love you', but didn't tend to his needs then we did not love him. What if we said, "I love you. Just call me if there is anything I can do." Did we show love to the baby? With care like that, the baby would surely die. So die to self, so others might live.

Love for a baby is easy because we see the innocence. When the baby spits on us, forgiveness is easy because we know the baby meant no harm. The baby had no agenda and he had no motive, just innocence. What I am trying to say is if we all looked at each other this way with mercy and grace of God, the world would be a loving, forgiving, God-pleasing place to live. Kind of like a place I have heard of called HEAVEN. Jesus said to bring heaven to earth. Just believe in your Brother Jesus and all things are possible.

God is our Father so we are his children and Jesus is our brother so we are family! And in our family we live with only one law, LOVE!!!

Loving unconditionally leads us to forgive unconditionally. It causes us to die to ourselves unconditionally it to keep no records of wrong. So stay in communion with the Holy Spirit continually, against such living there is no law!!! There is no mad, there is no sad, just the JOY OF THE LORD AND THE STRENGTH OF THE

LORD IN OUR HEARTS!!! THE DEVIL WILL FLEE AND WE ARE SET FREE!!!

As Paul said to the Corinthians:

2 Corinthians 13:14 The grace of the Lord Jesus Christ, and the love of God, and the communion of the Holy Spirit be with you all. Amen.

To keep love alive you must stay in constant communion with God 24/7 and have some real time set aside for Jesus every day! Die to yourself and live to please God!

Love you always, Jenny, Ron and Jesus.

Ron's Prayer

Thank you Jesus and Father for creating me. I come into agreement with your Word that says, you designed me to be in the image and likeness of you. I will never again let the devil tell me who I am. I will never again let people dictate who I am. I am free to bask in Your love, to walk in Your protection, and to be who You created me to be! I am created to do the work of Your kingdom! I die to myself, and I live for YOU alone! I agree with You that my life is special and I am special because I am in You and You are in me! I have the mind of Christ. I have the love of Jesus flowing through me and I have picked up my cross to follow You! I pray for a never ending flow of knowledge, wisdom, and understanding of You, Jesus!!! ✗

Fellow men cannot hurt me! The devil cannot hurt me! Life is amazing. God you are amazing! YOU LOVE ME!!! I don't need others to praise me! I don't need the approval of others! I am free to love everyone just the way Jesus did. Jesus loved everyone freely! Jesus is our example of how to love! Now I can be an example of the love of Jesus Christ! I can love others freely because I was created to be loved! Being loved by others no longer defines my self-worth! Jesus, Your love defines me! Your love carries me. Your love is my self-worth. You see me at my worst and love me so I can be my best! My best is You in me and You are in me so I am my best in You! Jesus, I love you because You loved me first! You created me and chose to love me! ALLELUIA!

You called me like you called the apostles. They were sinners like me but You said, 'Come follow Me'. They did follow You and I will follow You. When I think of sinning and going back to my selfish desires, You were there to pick me up! You said temptation is not a sin. The only way to let a devil in is to be in agreement with him! So I fall out agreement with him and come into agreement with you Jesus! I will never be alone. I will never be forgotten. I will never again be ashamed of whom I am!

I am in agreement with you Jesus! You said I am born in the image and likeness of You, God! We are one because I am in agreement with Your Word that says You gave me life that is precious and full of joy! I will honor You with every word from my mouth!!! I live to praise You, Jesus and praise You, Father and praise You, Holy Spirit for Your love for me! Your love is like a fire giving warmth and light, and consuming darkness!!!

In the name of Jesus I will set the captives free, I will heal the sick, I will raise the dead, and I will preach Your Word boldly! I will praise you with my whole heart!!! I don't need other people's approval of me. I need them loving you Jesus!!! What better way to teach Your love than to be transparent and let them see Your love in me. Let them see Your love coming out of me! We are to be a river of You, Jesus just as You are a river of life so am I! Jesus, Your love is never ending and so is my love for You!

For years now I have been saying that when Jenny and I approach people on the street Jenny can tear down the wall and open the door to let me talk to them about Jesus. Now I know that it is Jesus that opened the door and tore down the walls! I have Jesus, so I cannot be defeated! Jesus opens the doors, unlocks their hearts and Jesus flows in like a river through me! Jesus uses me to manifest His love! Jesus is love, so I am Love! ALLELUIA!!!

You want to see Jesus, come see me! I know who I am! Jesus said to Moses, "Tell him the 'I am' sent you." Guess who I am? Jesus sent me so I must be the 'I am' that Jesus sent! He sent me so I send you said Jesus! The labors are few but harvest is plentiful. Get out and do some harvesting! Don't just tell them about Jesus, give them Jesus! Show them Jesus! BE JESUS!!! The kingdom is at hand! I AM the kingdom! Jesus dwells in me and I dwell in Him! Jesus said 'bring heaven to earth'. Freely I received and freely I give! That is heaven.

Jesus said, "Love your neighbor as yourself." We should love ourselves because we have Jesus living in us. Love your neighbor? If that seems impossible, give them Jesus! I know you can love them when they have Jesus in them. In fact it is impossible not to love them when the Jesus you gave them manifest in them!

You see, I died to myself. I now live to manifest Jesus. I love life. I love who Jesus made me to be. I am one of those who Jesus sent! When Jesus sent His apostles out, they had no fear because Jesus' perfect love casts out fear. Jesus sent me, So I fear not!

I have heard a lot of songs and poems that are trying to describe love. No one can describe love perfectly. Unless they know the PERFECT LOVE OF JESUS and then you don't just describe love, you manifest it!

MAY GOD BLESS YOU WITH HIS PERFECT LOVE!!!

Ron, Jenny and my Best Friend, Jesus!

Sickness and Faith

First, I want to thank Pastor Don for being such a good friend and a very good Pastor! Coming back to Carrabelle and the good people of his congregation is like coming home to a good home for me and Jenny. The warm hearts of everyone here have given us light and warmth. It is true the special people of Don's congregation are good people and a true blessing to be around.

You might wonder why I used the word 'good' to describe Pastor Don and the people in the congregation. I could have very easily used the word great or greatest or excellent or superior to describe all of you. I chose the word 'good' because when Jesus spoke the world into existence He said "It is good." And when Jesus was finished He called His creation, "Very good." In my pursuit to be like Jesus, I am trying to use His words in my vocabulary. Plus I think when we try to describe people in better terms than good, it is like putting down good and maybe elevating us to a higher standard. I remember in Mark 10:18:

Mark 10:18 So Jesus said to him, "Why do you call Me good? No one is good but One, that is, God.

So calling you good is putting you in some very good company!

Most of the people know Jenny and I have been coming to Carrabelle Beach for four years now. Probably everyone has lost a loved one. Most people would say losing a loved one is never easy. I lost my mom last December 22, 2012 and she was 93 years old and really she was ready to go. In my heart I felt as though Jesus sent her an angel and ask her if she wanted to spend Christmas on earth or in heaven and mom chose heaven. I can tell you this that 5 days before mom died, Jenny and I were sitting with her having coffee and mom talked and walked to the bathroom. She was alert and her only complaint was that her body hurts. Two days later, I received a phone call from my sister saying mom had taken a turn for the worse. Mom died two days later in her own bed with her loved ones being around her and we were all in peace knowing it was the right timing of the Lord Jesus Christ calling her home. I don't feel as though I lost my mom. I feel like she decided to go home to her final reward.

I believe that is how death should be. I can tell from watching people's reactions that most people in the last eight or nine months have looked at Jenny like she should be in a home or better yet, I should release her spirit to go be with the Lord. I believe sickness is from the devil. The devil's mission is to kill, steal and destroy our lives. One look at Jenny and most people would say the devil is succeeding in his mission.

If you go by the outward signs or the circumstances, you then would be right. I guess that is why Jesus told us not to look with our eyes or be carnally minded. As soon as you look at the problem, you will take your mind off Jesus and the fact you have His Holy Spirit living in you and you will start feeling weak and helpless to solve the problem. You run to the doctor who only has the knowledge to practice medicine. You are falling right into the hands of the devil.

Jesus said it is the prayer of faith that will heal the sick, not the prayer of fear. We are to have the mind of Christ and the eyes of Christ and the love of Christ in us and flowing through us. We are to be like Jesus looking down on our problems and not like helpless humans looking up through our problems. From God's vantage point which is our vantage point, when we have the eyes of Jesus even mountains seem small. We are to speak to the problem and command it to change. Don't talk to God about the problem; He already gave us the answer. Jesus gave us the same power over the devil that He has. Just believe and use your power!

A lot of people who pray for someone will talk to God about the person they are praying for almost as though God does not know the sick person. They talk to God about the problem or when we talk God about ourselves and we talk to God about our

254

problems. Don't pray the problem. It takes no faith to pray the problem or to ask God for help. Jesus said it takes a prayer of faith to save the sick. A prayer of faith is praying the answer God gave us for the problems. Jesus showed us compassion by commanding devils to leave. Jesus commanded sickness to leave. Jesus forgave us all our sins and Jesus showed compassion by raising the dead for us the living.✗

Jesus did all these things by having a relationship with His Father; a loving spiritual relationship! Jesus said our battle is spiritual and our armor is spiritual! We accept the fight physically and we do an exceptional job physically and physically we are very compassionate. Jesus commands us to be compassionate physically, so taking care of the physical needs of others is very God-like and is very pleasing to God. God just wants us to be compassionate in the spiritual battle also. Jesus wants us to have a relationship with Him so when the battle comes we are ready both spiritually and physically to do His will on earth. Jesus would never command us to do something without giving us the tools to do it with. We have the command and the tools. Let us put them to use and have some fun. Just believe in God's Word!

Jesus said when He comes back we should have the devil under our feet. Jesus gave us the same Holy Spirit that raised Him from the dead. I have the Holy Spirit of Father God and Jesus living in me! There is nothing that can get in His way except my unbelief. Fear is of the devil and fear is faith in the devil. Fear is unbelief and fear will rob you of faith. Don't give way to it. Just believe in God!

We are to know the will of the Father and do His will! To know His will, look to the Words of Jesus who said He came to reveal the Father to us. Jesus was perfect love so the Father is perfect love and we can be perfect love if we are surrendered to the Father and have relationship 24/7. Jesus is perfect love. Jesus is the perfect love that casts out fear (devil). Look to the Bible and read how Jesus took charge over every situation. Don't read the Bible and trying to figure out if this is true. Just believe the one who said 'He cannot lie' and accept the Bible as truth. Accepting the Bible as true is the childlike faith Jesus talks about. The more you believe the more you are set free. Jesus said, "My truth will set you free." I know that the more of the truth of Jesus you have in your heart the harder it will be for the devil to talk you into sinning. Just believe in the Word of Jesus and you are set free of the devil and you are free of his sinning nature! We do not have a sinning nature. We are made in the image of God so we have to accept a sinning nature of the devil to have one. Just cast it off and accept the gift of being a Son of God and a brother to Jesus. If you are born again then receive your sonship into the family of God. You know Jesus never had a sinning nature and so neither do you!

Jesus was a man while on the earth and was as human as we are. Yet I never read anything about fear being in Him. He is our example to follow and look up to. Let the love of Jesus in your heart and watch fear flee. Just believe and let Jesus in Your heart and be free. Begin the new life Jesus came to give you. Begin by asking Jesus everyday these words: 'Jesus what are WE going to do today?' Read His commands and thank God for the power and authority to do them!

Circumstances do not dictate the outcome of sickness, YOU DO!!! With Jesus and Father God dwelling in you, you BETTER dictate the outcome. Jesus did not die just to be the atonement for sin! Jesus came to show us we have power over DEATH and so death does not exist. We just leave for Judgment and we should only leave when Jesus calls us home; not from sickness that we have God's power over. Jesus describes sickness as captivity and bondage which is how we should describe sickness. Sickness is not Picks disease; sickness is not cancer or any other name we give it! Sickness is captivity and bondage. Jesus said He came to set the captives free and He did and so can we! Just believe!

Jesus also told us to take every thought captive to the obedience of His word. If you're watching television, I can guarantee that you are not taking every thought captive. And I can guarantee you that the Lord that sent His only Son to teach us and be our example in life will not talk over the noise of the television. Be still and hear His voice. You want the truth that sets you free? Just be still and hear His Voice! Get up in the morning and ask yourself, "What does Jesus want to do today?" For some reasons, we think life in God is all about God helping us to have a nice day. Again, that is the reverse of what our life should be. We are here to

256

do the work of the kingdom! Ask the Lord every morning, "What are we going to do today?" Ask Jesus, "Who do you want to set free today?" and He will lead you to someone that He wants to set free! Watching someone set free is joy beyond our understanding! I want that every day!

Kingdom work is listening for our marching orders and then doing them. Jesus said over and over 'I only do what I have seen My Father do'. What did Jesus do? He healed, forgave, cast out devils to set people free, raised people from the dead and preached the Word boldly. So we can say 'I only do what I have seen my Father do!' Jesus gave you and I the same set of orders and by faith we can complete them. Just believe! Jesus would not ask you to do anything without giving you the power to do it. Jesus said you were given the measure of faith, so what is holding you back? Maybe you don't believe Him. That would be a tragedy. Jesus died for me and I will not waste my time trying not to sin when I can spend my time glorifying God by believing Jesus lives in me. That is taking the tragedy of nonbelief and turning it into the MAJESTY OF BELIEF!!! I'm set free and I thank you Jesus!

Don't wait for someone else to do it you will be missing out on all the fun! You will miss the joy and the love of Jesus. You only have one life to give so make the best of it for Jesus. You are the best Jesus has and Jesus is okay with that. The devil is the one that makes you feel insignificant! I hear Christians say "Oh, Lord! Bring the rapture. I want out of here." I think to myself, "That sounds REALLY self-centered!" Not all my loved ones are saved so I know I need more time. I pray for God to put off the rapture! Please don't think for one second you don't have a mission to accomplish because you do! Please don't say I can't because with Jesus in you, failure doesn't exist. Just believe and nothing will hold you back!

Don't read the Bible to see if it is true. Don't argue with it! JUST BELIEVE IT!!! CHILDLIKE FAITH IS NOT AN OPTION!!! Childlike faith is praiseworthy! Power and authority are yours for just believing! If you need proof or have an argument in your mind about anything you read in the Bible you are in doubt and lessoning to the devil! Just believe what you read in God's Word. When I read the Bible I put myself in the place of Jesus. The Bible

257

says Jesus raised Lazarus from the dead then I read Ron raised Lazarus from the dead. It is simple Jesus said for us to raise people from the dead and so we can. Just believe.

If I look at the circumstances of my life, I see the deterioration of Jenny's condition. The circumstances will make me think death is coming real soon. The circumstances make me look like I'm crazy for saying I believe the Word of God. Am I crazy to declare Jenny is not going to die of this disease? Am I crazy to declare Jenny will live, Jenny will walk, Jenny will talk and Jenny will be totally normal again right now? You see I have the Word of Jesus that Jenny will be totally normal! I have the Word of Jesus that says by His stripes Jenny was healed. I believe and I declare it to be and so it is, I have the word of Jesus on it!

Two different women over the years have delivered two words of knowledge from God to me. The first came about three years ago when I came across the Scriptures about a sin to death.

1 John 5:16 If anyone sees his brother sinning a sin which does not lead to death, he will ask, and He will give him life for those who commit sin not leading to death. There is sin leading to death. I do not say that he should pray about that.

After reading this Scripture, I ask God to reveal the sin I needed to repent for. I waited and when I never heard from the Lord, I pleaded, "Please God! You know I choose You. Only You have life!" I knew God knew I would change and turn away from all wickedness if I just knew what I was doing wrong. After a couple days of asking the Lord about this Scripture, Jesus sent me a messenger.

The next morning, a girl came to my camper and said, "I have never done this before but I believe I have a Word from the Lord for you." She said, "I have no idea what this means to you but the Word I keep hearing to tell you is *not to death*." I thanked her for being obedient to Jesus and for telling me the word God had for me. I immediately had the peace that surpasses all understanding in my heart. I continue to this day to speak those words over Jenny, "Jesus said *not to death*." Now I pray in thanksgiving for I know that

Jenny is healed and I know that Jenny will not die of this disease. Thank You, Jesus for coming into my life and renewing my mind!

About a year and a half later, Jenny and I were in a campground in Tennessee. They had a little church service in the campground so Jenny and I went there. It was a bright sunny morning and the service was under a pavilion with no walls. Jenny and I arrived late and as we approached the pavilion we were very quiet because we were on grass. The wheelchair made no noise but still somehow a lot of people turned around to see who came up behind them. I was kind of startled by them turning around because we made no noise and the preacher did not say anything or even look at us. Anyway after the service, I was walking Jenny back to our camper and some women stopped me to say why they turned around in the church service. They said even though it was a sunny day they felt the whole pavilion light up when we came. One woman said, "You glow with the love of Jesus in you!" Then they walked away.

As Jenny and I continued to walk to our camper I had tears running down my face. I was crying so hard because I ask God to let me manifest His presence everywhere I go. I had my head down because I didn't want everyone to see me crying. There was another younger girl walking in front of us that suddenly turned around and ask if she could pray for Jenny and I replied, "sure." But before she started to pray, her two sons and husband that was behind us came walking up. As we talked for a moment I had reached my hand down and picked up Jenny's hand to hold it and with my other hand I was rubbing Jenny's face. This girl, the mother of the two boys said to her sons, "do you see why I said every time I see this man with his wife, I tell you boys I see Jesus?" She continued to tell them, "You see when you don't feel good. Jesus is there with you holding your hand. Jesus will rub your head to comfort you and if you cannot walk, Jesus will pick you up and carry you into your camper."

Then she started to pray for Jenny. In the middle of her prayer she stopped and said, "Wow, I just received a Word for you." She went on to say, "This one is to manifest the glory of God." After she finished her prayer I went to the camper and looked it up.

John 9:1-5 Now as Jesus passed by, He saw a man who was blind from birth. And His disciples asked Him, saying, "Rabbi, who sinned, this man or his parents, that he was born blind?" Jesus answered, "Neither this man nor his parents sinned, but that the works of God should be revealed in him. I must work the works of Him who sent Me while it is day; the night is coming when no one can work. As long as I am in the world, I am the light of the world."

As I read the Scriptures I knew God was talking to me through His messengers again. Isn't it amazing that the Creator of the universe has time to talk to me? We are all this special to God and if you're going through anything tough right now, ask the Creator to talk to you and He will comfort you also. This is why I tell everyone that me and Jenny are so blessed! Jesus wants a relationship!

So when people look at me like I am crazy, I let them look because I know the truth of Jesus sets us free and the truth is God loves me and I will stand on these Scriptures and I will see Jenny walking and talking. I know Jenny and I will have coffee with my Brother, Jesus! What a glorious day that will be! I command it to happen and it will happen because Jesus gave me His Word on it. Jesus said that anything I ask in faith I will receive that the Son may bring glory to the Father. Do you know the meaning of the words Father God? Father means to come forth from and God means the source of life. So when I go to MY FATHER GOD, I am going to the one from which we all come forth from and is the source of life. I mean I might as well go right to the source and I go to Him through my Brother Jesus. I call that being blessed!

I know Jesus loves Jenny and I so much. He came to restore the relationship Adam lost by eating the fruit of the tree of Good and evil. Jesus came and restored that relationship so we walk and talk together 24/7. I have a relationship with Jesus and my Father 24/7 and there is no better place to be in the company of my Jesus and Father. If people want to say I am crazy, I don't care. I know who I am and I know who loves me. Jesus said we will be peculiar and I love being what Jesus said I would be! I know Jesus said we can bring Heaven to earth and I know I am already in Heaven because I know Jesus and my Father loves me! Father God calls me His Son! Believing as a child in the Word of God is rest and it is the only blessing I need! So to be blessed, I rest in God!

Yes I want Jenny healed and yes I am seeking her healing like I should because Jesus said by His stripes we were healed, done deal! I also know that some people have said look how much closer you are to God because of this sickness in Jenny. I do not and will not ever believe that God puts sickness on people to bring them closer to Him. If you believe it is the will of God to put sickness on people to bring you closer to Him, you should never go to a doctor because you are asking the doctor to sin by going against the will of God! Also if sickness is the will of God, then we should never fight it and we should just accept it. We should pray for more sickness so we can be in His will! You see how contrary to the Word of God sickness is! JESUS SAID HEAL SICKNESS, DON'T ACCEPT SICKNESS!!! More especially, don't expect it!

No one comes to God unless He calls us first. I don't see anywhere in the Bible where Jesus called anyone and said if you do not come I will make you or your wife sick to get your attention. He might let a donkey talk to you but He never put sickness on any one. Sickness is the work of the devil, not God. If you believe God put sickness on you, you will not or should not fight to get better. I mean after all you think it is the will of God, right? Look at what Jesus calls sickness: captivity, spirit of infirmity, bondage. And Jesus said that He came to set the captives free, to free us from the bondage of sin and the spirit of infirmity.

We in America have doctors that have a name for every kind of sickness. But I believe all sickness is a spirit of infirmity and if you cast out an evil spirit of infirmity the sickness is gone, the pain is gone and health with life is back. Your health is renewed like the eagles. We can and should live in divine health every day. Divine health is ours for just believing!

I believe the first line of defense in sickness and diseases is the church and not a hospital. If your faith is in doctors then by all means go to the doctor and live another day to have time to learn what a relationship with Jesus looks like. Learn what divine health is all about. The love of Jesus is so strong and it is His will to heal all! Jesus will meet you at your faith level and even heal you through a doctor but when you get to heaven, wouldn't it be cool for Jesus to honor your faith like He did the men in Hebrews 11. I know when I get there I want to hear the words, "Well done my GOOD AND FAITHFUL SON. RON YOU BELIEVED ME!"

Faith is a substance like Jesus said but I believe the substance of faith is how much of your life did you live by the spirit of faith, the spirit of love, the spirit of truth, and how much did you believe in Jesus. Yes, sin will be an issue for some but only for those that did not believe enough to repent. I really believe when you are standing before Jesus for Judgment, how much you believed in his coming and dying for us to have a relationship with Him is going to be a bigger factor than how much you repented for sin. I mean when you have a relationship with Jesus the devil flees and takes sin with him. Then if you do fall short of the glory of God you have an advocate and your advocate is JESUS AND JESUS LOVES YOU AND WILL FIGHT FOR YOU!!! When I sin, I go to Jesus and thank Him for removing it and thank Him for restoring me back to Himself right away. I do not dwell on that failure. I dwell on Jesus and in His forgiveness for it is the truth of God that sets us free from sin. Just believe and watch the Word of Jesus come true for you too! It is the truth that sets us free and Jesus is the truth!

Sin is so overrated in church today. I know it is a big deal. Sin can put me in hell for eternity so sin is a big deal! I said that it is overrated because I have been told to overcome sin I have to fight the devil all the time. When I am fighting the devil, I am actually giving him power and that makes him some big guy I have to power up to fight. If you meet someone that says they are fighting the devil, please tell them the Word of Jesus said stand firm in His Word and Jesus does the battle for us. In other words, I don't get up trying not to sin every day. Being sin concusses is setting yourself up to sin because that is where your mind is. Trying not to sin every day brings us to a place where that is all you think about and after a while you will give in. If all you think about is sin, you will grow tired of fighting sin and you will backslide. Jesus said 'I am the truth that sets you free!' Freedom is life more abundant and fighting the devil is bondage, captivity, death and despair.

I don't get up and try not to sin. I get up to do the work of the kingdom by keeping my mind on Jesus so I don't have to fight the devil because he is already defeated by Jesus. Jesus never fought the devil. He just ran over the devil because Jesus is like a speeding freight train on its way to Heaven. Jesus laid down some big tracks for us to follow! Let us all be a speeding freight train that destroys the works of the devil and full of the love of Jesus. And by manifesting the Love of Jesus, we will fill all our passenger cars to overflowing! Kingdom work is rewarding and uplifting. It is Joy beyond our understanding. Kingdom work is full of purpose so you don't grow weary and you won't backslide. In fact, Jesus said He will give you rest. You will *frontslide* right into the loving arms of Jesus for the biggest bear hug possible. It is a bear hug with a big 'well done my faithful Son who serves'. Jesus is alive and well and He wants to flow through you and for you to manifest Him 24/7! MANIFESTING JESUS IS HOW NOT TO SIN!!! JESUS LOVES ME AND I KNOW IT SO I WIN!!!

If you are a man, do you remember when you fell in love with your girlfriend? You hope with all your hope that she would fall in love with you. Your mind was on her 24/7. When she did fall in love with you, you relaxed and her love gave you peace in your heart to where you Joy was so full. You'll say, "I will marry you and take care of you the rest of your life." When you seek a relationship with Jesus as diligently as you seek a spouse, you will have the love of Jesus that surpasses all understanding and it adds new meaning to the words *'take care of you'*. The Joy of God's love surpasses all our understanding! I believe in the loving joy of Jesus so I receive the loving joy of Jesus and I know Jesus loves me! That is truly the everlasting Joy of the Lord! I don't understand it but I sure enjoy it!

Most people are taught that receiving Jesus into your heart and being saved is a bus ticket to heaven. I hear preachers asking, "If you died tonight, where would you spend eternity?" These preachers are only selling people life insurances but instead of paying the premium with money you pay with good deeds. Then after a while you get tired of paying the premium because the policy is just words on paper and maybe you hear about the joy of the Lord but wonder what that is? Being Christian becomes a bunch of works. They hear of a life more abundant here on earth but wonder where that is? We really need to teach relationship with Jesus comes first. When you were seeking a wife, did you go to all her friends and do nice things for them hoping that somehow that would win her heart? No! You went right to her and pursued her to win her heart.

A relationship with Jesus is pursuing Jesus first. You cannot have the Joy of the Lord without knowing Him. Jesus said bring heaven to earth. I tell you living with Jesus in you is bringing heaven to earth and then you can spread heaven around. Freely you received the Joy of knowing Jesus so freely you can spread the heavenly Joy of knowing Jesus around. Jesus is the ultimate motivator. His call to action was given to the 12 and then to the 70 and then the 120 and now to you! Turn off the television and the computer and anything that distracts you from Jesus. Jesus told me to get the world out of the way and then you will hear what I have to say! Remember, Jesus will not talk over the noise of the world – you have to set time aside to lesson and just believe.

The world says 'don't get your hopes too high or you will be disappointed'. Yet my Bible tells me nothing is impossible for me with Jesus Christ living in me. I believe the Word of God! My hopes are Jesus high!

The world says to a new Christian, "You're on fire now but don't worry you will cool down," and some people calls it backsliding. To some degree in church today, it is almost expected for a new Christian to backslide. In the church today, we pray to have new converts and yet Paul prayed unceasingly for the established church. The real attacks from the devil comes after you are baptized and on fire. The devil wants to steal those new seeds before they root into your heart, and with us saying don't worry he will cool down is like pronouncing that on them. Encourage as Jesus encouraged! Be light as Jesus was light. Love as Jesus loved. Live as Jesus lived. Do the things you see Your Father do and you too will have the Joy of the Lord. You will have converts that come to you because they will see the Jesus in you, the Joy in you, the Love in you and you will be contagious. People will want what you have! Just give them Jesus and be the contagiously contagious Jesus! It's a good to be loved!

The world tells us to do this or to buy that and you will be happy. Jesus told me that happiness is the opposite of Joy. Happiness always comes from getting something for you or having something done for yourself and happiness is always momentary. Happiness is always about being you. Joy is doing for others and Joy is sustainable forever!

The world says for us to do nice things for others and God will love you. That's backwards! Jesus didn't come to reap servants that are trying to please Him by works. Jesus came to reap sons and daughters who are in a faith relationship with Him! You serve others because of your intimate relationship with God! You do not serve others to have a relationship with God! When you truly have a relationship with Jesus and Father God, the Joy of the Lord glows in you and flows out from you and people will want what you have. You bring people to God because of your relationship to God. You don't bring people to God to have a relationship with God! God is the light that people always go to! Let your relationship shine the love of Jesus to everyone you meet. Jesus told us to preach the gospel to the entire world so it must be possible for each one of us. You are in this world so preach right where you are. Jesus will use your light to be His light right where you are. Just believe with God all things are possible and they are! You too can be light because you have Jesus in you!

Life and light are called the Joy of the Lord! Read the life of Jesus and you will see the ultimate Giver! Read His life and you will see Jesus gave Himself to show people the love of His Father but you cannot give the love of the Father until you have a relationship with Your Father! It is really hard to give away something you do not have. Life more abundant, life full of Joy, life of peace, and life of rest is impossible without knowing the one that makes all things possible. Please read about the possibilities and start a relationship with the one that makes all things possible! You cannot earn one and you cannot deserve one but I can guarantee you Jesus want you to receive His relationship free of charge. Then Jesus said freely you received and freely you give. Give His love, give His peace, give His hope, give His trust, and you will light up the world. Most of all, tell people how to have a relationship with Jesus.

Get the worldly out of the way and then you will hear what I have to say: Thank You from God! It is worth repeating! Get the impossible out of the way by having a relationship with the one that makes all things possible! Imagine the possibilities, imagine the Joy when you walk through life knowing Jesus the Son of God is your Brother and Father God is your FATHER!!! Yes, being a Christian is more than a bus ticket to heaven!

I'm going to close with this story form Jesus. Suppose you're married and you have a young son and he was being bullied in school. Every night he asks his dad to talk to the teacher and so his dad does. The teacher said he will look out for Billy but he cannot be everywhere Billy is. So the three bullies knock Billy's books out of his hands while in the hallway. They still kick him around on the playground. So you decide to enroll Billy in Karate class, Boxing class and in a Martial Arts class. You want Billy to learn how to defend himself. In 6 months, Billy has won all kinds of awards and is great in every class. In the fall when school starts again you are excited and you tell your wife this year will be different for Billy will show those three bullies a thing or two.

But Billy still comes home every night and complains about the bullies beating him up. Dad asks "son why don't you kick their tails, you know you can," Billy says, "Dad, I don't want to make them mad at me, they might go and get more bullies."

In our new covenant with Jesus we have all the weapons we need to kick the devil back to hell. Jesus came and demonstrated these weapons. Jesus wrote down the instructions for us to pass on to future generations so the bullies will know they cannot mess with us who are in the Lord. We have the best defense system mankind has ever seen. Jesus is more than a bus ticket to heaven, He gives us power and authority and life without fear of bullies. Kicking out bullies in the name of Jesus is bringing heaven to earth.

Jesus said the only two requirements are to believe you received the power and authority and then use them. "I will show you my faith by my works" We should walk in power and authority! So when a bully called cancer comes on you and you are walking in power and authority; you will just command it to leave in the name of Jesus and believe by faith it is dead and gone. We give the bullies names like cancer or the flu but there are really only three big bullies:

1. *Kill*

2. *Steal*

3. *Destroy*

Jesus called them devils and spirits of infirmity and He ran right over them. He put them under His feet. Are you getting the picture? We have power and authority and we are commanded to put the devil under our feet. So power up and use that God-given authority. Give the devil some hell because he will give you a big dose of it if you let him!

Jesus, Jenny and I love all of you!

The Comforter

John 14:26 But the Comforter, *which is* the Holy Ghost, whom the Father will send in my name, he shall teach you all things, and bring all things to your remembrance, whatsoever I have said to you.

Read John 14:26 again. Do you see the words, '*He* shall teach you all things'? That is the Holy Ghost. It will teach you all things. Yes, you can read your Bible and learn about God and that is good. I bet you know some people that have read the whole Bible and quote a lot of it and when they walk away, you think to yourself if they only lived what they know. There is a knowledge that no book can give you. There is a knowledge that no preacher or teacher on earth can give you.

Who will teach us?

"But the Comforter, which is the Holy Ghost, whom the Father will send in my name, he shall teach you all things"

Jesus himself taught the disciples for years. Jesus tried for years to disciple his apostles and Jesus, as a man, could not get His disciples to understand Him. There are numerous Scriptures that prove the disciples did not understand Jesus as He spoke to them. Jesus the man could not give his disciples courage. They were huddled in a room, fearing for their life, with locked doors as if that would help. As Jesus was crucified the apostles thought they lost everything and in one moment of time, Jesus the Son of God came and in the form of the Holy Ghost give them His Holy Spirit and gave them the Comforter from the Father, and from the Comforter came boldness, courage, knowledge, understanding, and wisdom to have a whole new life. Jesus said we will recognize them by their fruits.

Matthew 7:20 Therefore by their fruits you will know them.

Physically no one could see anything different in the apostles until they stepped out into the world and proclaimed the truth of Jesus and proved their acceptance of the Holy Spirit. This stepping out is the fruit of the Holy Spirit being manifested in courage, boldness, knowledge, understanding and in the wisdom of their new life. That's right! You don't have to wait. You just step into this new life. You cannot earn it and you don't have to wait for it. You literally step out in Faith and the gifts will manifest!

It was not until the Holy Ghost came into the room and filled them with the Holy Spirit and Jesus breathed His very own Spirit life into them like He breathed life into Adam after He formed him from the dust. Notice Adam did not wait for his life – he just started manifesting life as Jesus watched His creation come into existence. Do you see the similarities? Jesus as God formed Adam from dust and breathed life into him and Jesus as a man taught the disciples but He could not give them His Spirit until He left the earth and ascended into heaven. Then and only then could Jesus as the Son of God give His Holy Spirit to His disciples and to all that would believe and receive. I believe and I receive!!! So if you are born again start manifesting the gifts!

The Holy Spirit of Jesus came so they received boldness and courage, knowledge, and understanding and life that is the new life that Jesus said would come after His death. That is the comforter we welcome into our lives! Do you see that even the greatest teacher in the world Jesus the man could not make his own disciples to understand Him until they were filled with the Holy Spirit of Jesus.

Reading your Bible is not enough. Studying your Bible is not enough. You must invite the Holy Spirit into your life. You must seek a relationship with Jesus above all! Can you imagine trying to learn enough about your prospective spouse so you could get married and your only source of information about him or her was hearsay from others that read about him or her? That sounds pretty difficult doesn't it? It is not very intimate is it? Please ask God to be your best friend and then listen for His voice. Ask Jesus to send His Comforter to you and expect all the gifts of the Holy

269

Spirit to be yours right now! How will you know if you have them? Step out in faith and start talking about God and your relationship to God and tell everyone you meet God is alive and well in your life. Better yet let the new you manifest to everyone you meet.

Nothing was impossible for Jesus the man, because He believed, like nothing is impossible for us that believe.

Mark 9:23 'Jesus said to him, "If you can believe, all things are possible to him who believes."

So why did Jesus have to wait to give His Holy Spirit to the apostles until after He died? I believe if Jesus the man gave His Holy Spirit to his apostles before He died, they would have their Faith in Jesus the man and not Jesus the Son of God. We can give the Holy Spirit of Jesus to others as men of Christ because Jesus said we can, but we only give the Holy Spirit by our Faith in Jesus Christ the Son of God.

Why did Jesus call His Holy Spirit the Comforter?

Think about life in terms of comfort. Maybe you are a race car driver and you can drive 200 mph on a race track and be totally comfortable being in control of the car. Then someone says, "Come with me in my little plane that will take you flying at 200 mph and you're definitely will be very afraid big time." In the car, you have no fear but in the plane you have fear because you are out of your comfort zone. You see the apostles were in their comfort zone being with Jesus the man. When Jesus the man got crucified and died, the apostles hid because they lost their comforter; their faith was in Jesus the man. Father God wanted us to have our faith in Jesus the Son of God because Jesus the man could not be with each and every one of us 24/7 but the Holy Spirit can and is with us 24/7. THANK YOU FATHER GOD AND JESUS!!!

Why do we need a Comforter?

I believe reading your Bible is a good thing to do but to understand the wisdom therein and to let it transform your life takes a willingness to sit quietly and listen to Jesus the Comforter. Jesus is my best friend and I receive all my self-worth from Him personally. Jesus is my personal Comforter. I need Him for understanding, courage, wisdom and life. I receive all my self-worth from my Jesus and our relationship to each other.

I will not give others power over my life. You cannot hurt me. I will not give you power to hurt me. You can call me anything, you can reject me, you can hold my past against me but you cannot destroy my relationship with my Jesus. Jesus said I will never leave you or forsake you. I believe my Jesus!

Hebrews 13:5-6 Let your conduct be without covetousness; be content with such things as you have. For He Himself has said, "I will never leave you nor forsake you." So we may boldly say: "The Lord is my helper; I will not fear. What can man do to me?"

I am a child of God and I love being His child! I am forgiven and I love being forgiven! I put all my self-worth in what my Father says about me!! Jesus said I love you Ron with every drop of his blood and Jesus in His Bible gave me a personal guided tour of how to live. Jesus knew that knowledge was not enough so He gave me His Holy Spirit the Comforter! I simply believe Jesus thinks I am worth it all and I receive it all! THANK YOU JESUS I LOVE YOU TOO!!!

A woman in a campground told me I was nuts because I told her the only doctor I would go to is Jesus. She actually made her comment more derogatory than that but I cleaned it up a little. As she walked away I told her "you can call me nuts or whatever you want," Jesus calls me His brother and Father God calls me His son and I am secure in the love of my Father and Brother. I get my self-worth from there (Jesus and Father God) relationship with me not what others say about me. I also forgave that lady immediately!

I received the knowledge about sonship from reading the Bible but I received the power to live it out from my relationship with My Jesus. Do you see the disciples learned and walked with Jesus the man for years but as soon as He died their faith died with Him? Never put your faith in a man, for we are just men and if you put your faith in me for example, you have just set me up to disappoint you. Somewhere down the line I might not live up to

271

your expectation and boom your broken hearted and hurt. Jesus would not let His disciples put their Faith in Him as a man, and He was the greatest man to walk the earth! So never put your faith in a man. Your faith and your trust should be in God and nothing else.

Can you imagine what Jesus would have done if He got His self-worth from His apostles and His ministry. When they deserted Him in those last days, by our standards, He should have been broken. I'm sure He felt all the emotions, depression, rejection, unforgiveness, bitterness, self-pity, and being all alone. I mean He even saw His disciple deny Him three times. It was one of His closes friends that betrayed Him. Was Jesus broken? No? He went on and finished what His Father had for Him to do and in the end Jesus won the victory over death and made an open show of the devil so we could know the devil is defeated. How did Jesus the man overcome all that rejection, simple, the same way we can! Put your faith in God and let God be God. Ask God to be your best friend and then let Him be your best friend.

Listen for His voice. When Jesus the man was in His trial I am positive he focused on His relationship with His Father and I am sure Jesus heard the voice of His Father to see Him through His trial. If Jesus was getting His self-worth from His ministry and the miracles His Father did through Him, He would have been broken and never would have made it to the cross. Remember the apostles deserted Him and His ministry at that point looked like a complete failure. Jesus was not defeated because He looked to His Father for His self-worth not His earthly accomplishments. If we focus on Jesus and our relationship with Him we cannot be defeated either! Focus on Jesus for all the promises in Him are yea and amen!!!

2 Corinthians 1:20 For all the promises of God in Him are Yes, and in Him Amen, to the glory of God through us.

Jesus is our example of how to live and Jesus said forgive them.

Father for they know not what they do! Right in the middle of His trial.

Then Jesus our Giver of life, came back to life and gave His Holy Spirit the Comforter to each and every one of us. Jesus is the ultimate Giver and gave us the ultimate example of how to live and then Jesus gave us His unconditional love through His unconditional forgiveness.

I don't know about you but I will receive these free gifts and I will be an example of the love of Jesus every day for eternity. When you receive the baptism of the Holy Spirit with fire you receive power to stand on your own two feet and proclaim the word boldly. You receive it all! So do it all!!!

What was Jesus talking about when He said we will do better works and bigger works then He did?

John 14:12 "Most assuredly, I say to you, he who believes in Me, the works that I do he will do also; and greater works than these he will do, because I go to My Father.

Some people think Jesus was talking about preaching because we have mass media now like radio and television and internet. To them greater works would be to reach the masses at the same time. Yet, others have said we will do greater miracles but didn't Jesus do the greatest miracles, and the greatest deliverances, and raise people from the dead. So how could ours be better? Who would determine which was better?

Maybe the greater works are having children. I mean, I don't think Jesus fathered any children when he walked the earth. Jesus never married. I truly think the bigger and better works are the baptism of the Holy Spirit and fire. Jesus never did this as a man and yet He gave us human's power to baptize in His name! Isn't it amazing to think baptism of the Holy Spirit was never performed by Jesus until after Jesus rose from the dead? Jesus gave us this power because He knew how important it is to our understanding of His word. Without the death of Jesus, we could not receive the comforter. Yet because of His life we have a desire to know Him as the comforter. We understand when we receive the Comforter as the Holy Spirit into our hearts.

John 16:7 Nevertheless I tell you the truth; It is expedient for you that I go away: for if I go not away, the Comforter will not come to you; but if I depart, I will send him to you.

Here, Jesus is telling the apostles it is expedient for them that He goes away. You see it was expedient because they had all their faith in Jesus the man. This is true because when the trial came they ran and huddled together in a locked room. It sounds like Jesus is excited to go away doesn't it? I think the excitement in Jesus was knowing the apostles would have understanding, boldness and faith in Jesus the Son of God; not Jesus the man. Jesus was able to send the Comforter to them and ultimately to us but not until after he rose from the dead.

Think for a minute how uncomforting it is not to know something. For example, if you are in a lot of pain and you go to a doctor and you pray please God don't let this be cancer. When the doctor walks in and says the test came back negative for cancer, you are immediately comforted. You received comfort form knowledge and now you can proudly and boldly have a new lease on life and now you are ready to take on the problems of the world. Can you imagine the apostles when Jesus came in the room and proved He was still alive? The Joy of the Lord was their strength and they proved it to everyone. Please accept this precious gift of the Joy of the Lord and your heart will sing to the mountain tops.

How long will the Comforter be with us?

John 14:16 And I will pray the Father, and He will give you another Helper, that He may abide with you forever

Thank you Jesus, for your loving us so much you sent your Holy Spirit and he shall abide with us forever.

I believe we are to be the love of Jesus and to give the love of Jesus to others and in doing so we give them the desire to know Jesus! Like Jesus the man, we have to wait until the timing is right to baptize. Jesus gives the increase through the Holy Spirit for courage and boldness. In other words don't be in a hurry to see increase because we cannot give increase only Jesus can. If we are in a hurry we may become discouraged by trying to make things happen on our own timing. We must let God be God and let God give the increase. We see the need to wait in scripture also! I'm sure Jesus wanted to give the apostles all this power and knowledge but Jesus new to wait on His Father's timing. When Jesus said it is expedient that I go, I believe He said this because He was in constant contact with His Father and from His relationship with His Father He could let His Father's timing be His timing and Jesus was not being discouraged.

I am talking about the baptism of the Holy Spirit not the baptism of water.

We sometimes get in such a hurry to see someone baptized that maybe we are playing Holy Spirit in our lives instead of waiting for the Holy Spirit to come when He knows the timing is right. When we baptize prematurely, we sometimes see the people backslide and then we think to ourselves, they just did not get it. Jesus did not need to boast about the number of people He baptized to have a successful ministry.

When the timing is right we can receive it as did the apostles who got it right away and didn't backslide, I believe we can receive and not backslide, when we wait on the Lord. Please don't put God in a box, and say we have to wait on the Lord, if you feel led to baptize someone then by all means do so because that must be the right timing of the Lord. All I am trying to say is if you have any doubt, you might want to wait until you hear more clearly and if you are baptized so you can count heads for a testimony next week, please check your motive. My friend Dan said "don't just lead them to the Lord, GIVE THEM THE LORD" to which I added; watch Jesus brings the increase!

Now that's my Jesus!

Love always Jenny, Ron and Jesus!

Who Is In Control?

It was January 29 and I was at a heated pool at the campground when Jenny had a seizure. It just came to her. And on our way back to the camper, Jenny had another one. So I got her cleaned up and placed on the couch. This time it took a long time for her to come back to baseline. It is amazing to me how I can write and talk about how great God is and how much He loves me but this is where the rubber meets the road and I will see if the teaching from God have traction and is His love really in my heart?

I have talked about before or asked the question, "In an emergency, do you call on God or call on man such as the 911 hotline?" The answer is very clear for me in this situation and that is to call on God. Not necessarily because of great faith but because I know the doctors don't have any answers for Jenny's condition. So I just stayed alongside her and prayed which is the best thing I could do. The problem this time was Jenny isn't coming out of the seizure and getting back to baseline. As I prayed, I kept hearing the words of the doctor saying it will be a big seizure that will take Jenny away. I asked God, "How does a doctor have the right to speak these curses over Jenny and then I have to stand in faith and break those words of death off her." I just know to lean not on my own understanding but to draw my strength from the One who made strength. I also know I was hearing from the voice of the devil saying she is dying and I was lessoning. At the same time I was hearing Matthew 7:11 says:

Matthew 7:11 If you then, being evil, know how to give good gifts to your children, how much more will your Father who is in heaven give good things to those who ask Him!

In my mind I kept asking God, "I know I have asked, and I know I have asked in faith and I could not do this to a dog or cat so when am I going to see your love manifest in Jenny? I know Jenny is healed but what is taking so long for the healing to manifest in her? Father Your Word says, how much more that your Father in Heaven shall give good things to them that ask. I am asking for Jenny's healing to manifest in her now." Jenny's condition seemed to be getting worse so I propped her back and head up to help her breath. I finally when to bed with Jenny on the couch, trying to sleep was horrible without Jenny next to me. I kept getting up to check on her.

The next morning, I made Jesus and me some coffee. I asked Jesus what was going on with that Scripture. Matthew 7:11 seems very clear to me but I could not figure out the timing of it. It seemed as though I was losing faith over it instead of building my faith with it. Jesus said, "How did the devil tempt me in the desert?" I said, "By misquoting the Scriptures when you were very weak from fasting for 40 days." Jesus said, "You didn't hear that Scripture from me yesterday." Here I was upset all day yesterday because I could not figure what Jesus was trying to tell me in Matthew 7:11 and now I found out the voice I was listening to was not from the Holy Spirit!

Discerning voices can sometimes be difficult. I usually discern by telling if the voice I am hearing is taking me to new heights of God's love or away from God's love. Yesterday, I didn't discern very well because I was dwelling on Jenny and the circumstances not the truth in the word of Scriptures. I know the devil has some very creative ways to tempt me but this was the first time he used a Scripture to deceive me. Jesus said, "I am the rock and upon this rock I will build my house." In Matthew, Jesus said:

Matthew 16:15-18 He said to them, "But who do you say that I am?" Simon Peter answered and said, "You are the Christ, the Son of the living God." Jesus answered and said to him, "Blessed are you, Simon Bar-Jonah, for flesh and blood has not revealed this to you, but My Father who is in heaven. And I also say to you that you are Peter, and on this rock I will build My church, and the gates of Hades shall not prevail against it.

I believe Jesus was saying that the knowledge Peter received from Father God is the rock upon which the church is built. Peter said, "Thou art Christ the Son of the living God." Jesus said, "Blessed are you Peter for flesh has not reveled this knowledge to you but My Father in Heaven gave you this knowledge." So upon the knowledge of Jesus being the Christ Son of the living God is the rock that we stand on! All the Scripture and all the truth in the world has to have Jesus as the foundation or it will fall. If I had stopped questioning God yesterday and started lessoning to God like I did today I could have walked in the Joy of the Lord and been rejoicing knowing Jenny was just fine and in the hands of the greatest doctor in the world.

> **Matthew 16:19** And I will give you the keys of the kingdom of heaven, and whatever you bind on earth will be bound in heaven, and whatever you loose on earth will be loosed in heaven."

I believe the keys of the kingdom of heaven are Joy, Peace and Love of Jesus in your heart and knowing that Jesus is the rock we build our beliefs on! I separated myself from those beliefs for a couple hours but thank you Jesus for my safe return. I will bind Your truth in my heart and in heaven my soul shall rejoice with You and I will lose all the earth or fleshly desires to free myself so I am free to do Your will here on earth and in heaven. Jesus, You are so special to me and I want to be just like You here on the earth. I pray for your wisdom not to display smartness to others but to pray for others and to have Your wisdom and together for us to set others free! I thank You Jesus for setting Jenny and I free of the bondage of the world. My life is Your life Father and in You will I live forever.

I know some people will say that Jesus told Peter is the rock upon which Jesus built His church. I just ask you to read what follows in the next four scriptures:

> **Matthew 16:20-23** Then He commanded His disciples that they should tell no one that He was Jesus the Christ. From that time Jesus began to show to His disciples that He must go to Jerusalem, and suffer many things from the elders and chief priests and scribes,

and be killed, and be raised the third day. Then Peter took Him aside and began to rebuke Him, saying, "Far be it from You, Lord; this shall not happen to You!" But He turned and said to Peter, "Get behind Me, Satan! You are an offense to Me, for you are not mindful of the things of God, but the things of men."

Peter was letting the voice of the devil speak through him and Jesus rebuked the devil at once just minutes before Jesus heard the voice of the Father coming through Peter. You see how we must take every thought captive and discern whom we are listening to. I believe that Jesus was talking about the knowledge of Jesus being the Christ, Son of the Living God is our ROCK to build our beliefs on, our future on and our whole life, family, and extended family on.

Jesus said, "my people are destroyed for lack of knowledge."

Hosea 4:6 My people are destroyed for lack of knowledge. Because you have rejected knowledge, I also will reject you from being priest for Me; because you have forgotten the law of your God, I also will forget your children.

What knowledge is Jesus talking about? First and for most it is the knowledge of Jesus being the Son of the living God. I believe Jesus has taken me to the very foundation of His church so He can build me on solid Rock and now He wants to show me more truth in discerning so I can be solid in my belief of Him. Being on solid Rock will make me bold to proclaim His word. Second is discerning our thoughts even to the discerning of who the Antichrists are! Yes, Jesus in His word said there are many antichrists. If we cannot recognize the antichrist, we are going to be torn and sifted like wheat. I believe Jesus used wheat in this illustration because even the smallest wind can control the direction of the wheat. That is why Jesus gave us a rock to stand on.

1 John 2:18 Little children, it is the last hour; and as you have heard that the Antichrist is coming, even now many antichrists have come, by which we know that it is the last hour.

I have heard people say we are in the last times. Some even say that when the antichrist comes it will be in the last days. I think John was really clear saying is even now are there many antichrists. I haven't been led by the Spirit to concern myself about the last times. I believe all that talk about the last times has been going on for over two thousand years and Jesus said no one will know the hour or the day, so it is not important to me. What is important is for us to know the truth of God's Word and to set others free. To do that, we must be able to recognize the antichrist as the enemy and win them over to becoming Christlike by pouring the love of God all over them.

1 John 2:15-17 Do not love the world or the things in the world. If anyone loves the world, the love of the Father is not in him. 16 For all that is in the world — the lust of the flesh, the lust of the eyes, and the pride of life — is not of the Father but is of the world. 17 And the world is passing away, and the lust of it; but he who does the will of God abides forever.

In these three passages, John is telling us how to recognize the antichrist in ourselves and others. Here, he is also showing us that all the things of the world will pass away. Whatever is your desire right now, like a better job or more of anything in the world, it will just pass away. Stop for a moment and think back to what was your biggest concern four years ago, two years ago or even two days ago. John tells us, "He that doeth the will of God abides forever." The will of God is so simple and it is to love as Jesus loved, to forgive as Jesus forgave. Read your Bible to see the example Jesus was for us. Don't study it to show how many Scriptures you can memorize. Just be Jesus on the earth. The best form of worship is to become who we are worshiping, worship Jesus by being Christlike!!!

1 John 2:19-21 They went out from us, but they were not of us; for if they had been of us, they would have continued with us; but they went out that they might be made manifest, that none of them were of us. But you have an anointing from the Holy One, and you know all things. I have not written to you because you do not know the truth, but because you know it, and that no lie is of the truth.

280

1 John 4:3 And every spirit that does not confess that[a] Jesus Christ has come in the flesh is not of God. And this is the spirit of the Antichrist, which you have heard was coming, and is now already in the world.

I don't see how John or anyone can make it any clearer that the antichrist is in the world now and how to determine who the antichrist is.

2 John 1:7 For many deceivers have gone out into the world who do not confess Jesus Christ as coming in the flesh. This is a deceiver and an antichrist.

I have heard people call President Obama an antichrist. He will not acknowledge Jesus as the Christ Son of the living God! He is one of the antichrist! So pray for him to be transformed by the blood and truth of Jesus Christ. Jesus came for everyone, even the antichrists of the world. We can live in a great country again and we will manifest the love of Jesus Christ to the world. We shouldn't pray to have President Obama impeached. Impeachment would only change the flesh. We should pray for President Obama and his followers to become Christ-like. We should pray for America to become Christ-like!

So now we know how to discern who the antichrists are. Jesus talks about discerning our thoughts. Let's bring the Scriptures into modern day living. I really do not see how anyone can watch television and discern their thoughts. The actions and words come at you so fast there is no way we can discern our thoughts. If what I am saying about television is not true then why would advertisers pay over a million dollars to advertise for 10 seconds during the game on Super Bowl Sunday? As we walk through life we have thousands of ten second intervals to demon straight the love of Jesus and the difference between Christian living and living non-Christian. As Christians, we have to make Godly decisions all the time and that can be really hard when we allow ourselves to be distracted by something that is so easily turned off. I bet there are people reading this right now that will say television is not that bad. I bet they can tell me about the commercials on television where they saw a little kid and yet they cannot tell me what the preacher talked about last Sunday at church service. Television has a lasting impact on our lives and it is not always a good impact.

Jesus was so in tune to discerning that He recognized the devil coming through Peter immediately. Peter had traveled with Jesus for three years and still did not discern who he let talk through himself. Remember, Peter was not filled with the Holy Spirit yet for Jesus had not died and arose again.

I found out yesterday I have a long way to go in discerning my thoughts. I have a Great Teacher and a Best Friend to guide me. Thank You Jesus for being my Best Friend and Teacher. The examples Jesus just gave me in the Bible are good ones and I will learn from them. Jesus has revealed to me the best way to hear His Voice is to listen. Yes, listening to and for the voice of Jesus is the best way to have a relationship with Him. Yes you have to read your bible to know Jesus. Pastor Dan Mohler once said, "When you squeeze a Christian you should get a big squirt of Jesus out." Those are probably not his exact words but they are close. Dan is saying when you are truly filled with the Holy Spirit and you are put to the test of life, when life doesn't go the way you want it to don't let the circumstances of life take away your Joy of knowing God. Sometimes, when we get squeezed in your life, everything but Jesus comes out. If you study the life of Jesus, you see every time Jesus got squeezed more love and forgiveness came out. To Jesus, every squeeze was an opportunity to demonstrate who He was in the world. For you and me, every squeeze should be an opportunity to demonstrate the love of Jesus also.

For example, I have a friend who was complaining because life was very upsetting. He and his wife were both out of a job for a while. Finally she got a job and a week later he got a good job also. The day he was to start his job, his wife's car has a blowout in a bad neighbor. He got so upset and was screaming at God 'you finally get me a job and now I'm going to be late on the first day. I will probably get fired'. He said he went on and on. He finally got her tire changed and on to work. When he explained to his new boss what happened, his boss said, "Settle down. You made the right choice. I would not let my wife stranded in that neighbor either."

282

The point I am trying to make is we can take matters into our own hands or we can surrender to God. What if the man upon hearing his wife had a flat tire just stopped and prayed for God to send a Christian to change the tire for her. What if he prayed for his boss to understand? He could have been in peace knowing he asks the only one that can make good out of this situation. Our problem is we just try to solve our own problems in our own strength and then when God makes your boss an understanding boss we don't even know to give the credit to God because we had never asked God into the situation. If we do see God's hand in our situation, we might even beat ourselves up saying how could I be so stupid not to trust you God!

God is so much more in our life's than we know. We can work our lives through God and have peace and rest or we can be in panic mode all the time. When the storm came at sea Jesus was sleeping on the boat and the disciples were going crazy in fear. They woke Jesus up and said 'don't you care, we are going to drown and you are sleeping'. Jesus got up and told the sea to be calm!

Mark 4:35-41 On the same day, when evening had come, He said to them, "Let us cross over to the other side." Now when they had left the multitude, they took Him along in the boat as He was. And other little boats were also with Him. And a great windstorm arose, and the waves beat into the boat, so that it was already filling. But He was in the stern, asleep on a pillow. And they awoke Him and said to Him, "Teacher, do You not care that we are perishing?" Then He arose and rebuked the wind, and said to the sea, "Peace, be still!" And the wind ceased and there was a great calm. But He said to them, "Why are you so fearful? How is it that you have no faith?" And they feared exceedingly, and said to one another, "Who can this be, that even the wind and the sea obey Him!"

I ask my dear Jesus to bring that story to my mind any time I start to panic about anything. If I have doubt or fear of anything, I pray for a remembrance of the disciples in the boat. I also know we have the same power and authority Jesus has and He said we will do bigger miracles than Jesus did.

Look what Jesus said "why are you so fearful? How is it that you have no faith?" Jesus will ask us those same questions someday. I know you can say but they lived with Jesus and He was right there on the boat with them so why were they so fearful? Actually Jesus is right here with us also. We have His Holy Spirit living in us so why are we so fearful? Why are we without faith? Jesus dwells in us, we can be in continual commutation 24/7. We have better commutation than the apostles did. Jesus is actually living in us! I believe that is the Good News that sets us free of worry and unrest. "Father, I want to thank you and your Son Jesus for being here with me and for living in me and for your word in my heart that sets me free to be in love with You!"

Jenny and I are doing just fine thanks to my Jesus coming to set us free of worry. Sometimes I think about how much I love my Jenny and how that love for her grows more everyday which seems impossible but I know it is true. Then I look to my relationship with Jesus and Father and the Holy Spirit and I know love grows through knowledge, truth, forgiveness, and most of all seeking each other with all our heart and all our beings. Jesus, I give you my soul and all that I am and all that I will ever be! I live to glorify you Jesus and Father God and the Holy Spirit that lives in us.

Remember, Jesus never prayed for something to happen; He just commanded it to and it happened! So never pray for peace or healing or for someone to be set free from the devil. Command it to happen just like our example Jesus did.

The title of this chapter is 'WHO IS IN CONTROL?' The answer is You when you know you have a relationship with Jesus Christ the Son of the Living GOD!!!

With promises like these, you know you are in control when you use faith in the name above all names: Jesus Christ.

Mark 16:17 And these signs will follow those who believe: In My name they will cast out demons; they will speak with new tongues

Remember: signs follow a believer not led a believer.

Mark 16:18 They will take up serpents; and if they drink anything deadly, it will by no means hurt them; they will lay hands on the sick, and they will recover."

Matthew 28:18-19 And Jesus came and spoke to them, saying, "All authority has been given to Me in heaven and on earth. Go therefore and make disciples of all the nations, baptizing them in the name of the Father and of the Son and of the Holy Spirit,

Jesus, Jenny and I love you always!

Take control and be in control for the same Holy Spirit that raised Jesus from the grave resides in you!

Your Inheritance

The day after my mom's death and while I was having coffee time with Jesus, He started talking about comfort zones. How stepping out of a comfort zone will make you grow in the Lord. Leaving a comfort zone is like stepping into the unknown. Like the first day of school for a child. He is leaving the comforts of home and going into the unknown. This transition will be a lot easier for him if his mom removes the fear by guiding him and assuring him it will be okay. After a short amount of time, his fear leaves and he will be comfortable there also. The reward for facing the fear is new knowledge and a bigger world.

For mom, her comfort zone was her family and her familiar surroundings. Fear will hold you in a comfort zone until someone helps you remove the fear. It is like crossing a bridge only we never know how long the bridge is or what awaits us on the other side. I believe Jesus sent a Comforter for mom and took her to the final reward of being with Jesus and Father God and a new world without fear.

I believe life is about preparing and helping others prepare to meet our Creator. It was Friday, 21st December 2012 at exactly 9:30 P.M. when mom crossed her last bridge. I thank Jesus for allowing mom to be in her comfort zone right up to her entrance into her eternal life. Mom was truly blessed to have almost all her loved ones alongside her. I believe mom had the peace of mind, knowing her loved ones were at peace, with her going to be with Jesus. When we cross the bridge in faith, Jesus brings us to a new level of comfort. Jesus through His example is preparing us for the big bridges in life and Jesus comforts us with His love. Thank You Jesus for loving Mom and for being her loving guide in this transition. I like to think of mom's passing this way: Jesus just gave mom an invitation to spend Christmas in heaven with Him and all His loved ones and mom said yes!

The life of Jesus is our example of how to live and how to love. Jesus uses the Bible as a tool to teach us and we have a free will to decide if we want to follow Jesus on the narrow path or walk the path of destruction while thinking it is our own path. Either way we all get to cross the bridge and stand before Jesus for Judgment. If we prepare for our judgment the Judgment seat will be sweet and we will be in the loving arms of Jesus.

I know mom has crossed the bridge and is in heaven with Jesus. Today, I pray for everyone reading this to be on the narrow path that Jesus talks about and for all of us to see the narrow gate and that it is open wide for us. I know on that Friday night, my mom stood before Jesus and was judged. I believe her judgment was sweet and she is in the loving arms of Jesus and the Father! Actually I kind of envy her when I think of the Joy in her spirit! Mom is finally able to be with Jesus and Father God.

Jesus said in Matthew 7:13-14:

Matthew 7:13-14 "Enter by the narrow gate; for wide is the gate and broad is the way that leads to destruction, and there are many who go in by it. Because narrow is the gate and difficult is the way which leads to life, and there are few who find it.

So we see by God's Word that strait is the gate and narrow is the way that leads to life and only a few will find it. I believe mom and dad walked the narrow path and went through that gate. How do you find the narrow path? Simply put you have childlike faith in God. I believe mom had that childlike faith. I believe mom never gave up on God. Even when her prayers were not answered as fast as she would have liked, mom stood steadfast in her belief that Jesus would answer them.

In other words, we choose the path. The wide path is full of earthly goods and some happiness. Contrast that with the narrow path: little earthly goods, but full of Joyfulness. In my quiet time with Jesus, He explained to me the difference between happiness and Joyfulness. Jesus said happiness is the devil's counterfeit of

Joyfulness. Jesus showed me happiness is living for yourself, and Joyfulness is denying yourself and living for others.

Happiness comes from someone doing something for you and it is momentary. It can come and go within seconds. We actually make plans to be happy. We can plan to go to Kings Island and on that day have perfect weather, no long lines, great food... And when we go to our car to leave, if the car doesn't start we lose all our happiness in one second!

Contrast the happiness of living for yourself with the joy of living for others. Joyfulness is you doing something for others. It is forever and stays with you even in your times of need. Choosing to help others is choosing the narrow path and in doing so receiving the Joyfulness that will surpass our understanding. It is bringing Heaven to earth as Jesus spoke about in the prayer we call the "Our Father".

Jesus commanded us to die to self. I know mom died to herself all her life. Mom would give of her time to anyone that asks!

Luke 9:23 Then He said to them all, "If anyone desires to come after Me, let him deny himself, and take up his cross daily, and follow Me.

I know there is a spiritual war going in your spirit 24/7. The only way to win this war is to recognize you are in it.

First you must recognize that our battle is in the spirit world and our battle is for our eternal life and this spiritual battle will determine where you will spend eternity.

Ephesians 6:12 For we do not wrestle against flesh and blood, but against principalities, against powers, against the rulers of the darkness of this age, against spiritual hosts of wickedness in the heavenly *places*.

For we wrestle not against flesh and blood – flesh is material that can and will rot away. Blood is trying to pass on these material things on to loved ones. I believe material treasures are the curses of

288

modern day. I have seen people work so hard to have something to hand down to their children when they die. People write wills so the children will not fight over their inheritance. I believe this is the *worrying about tomorrow* that the Bible talks about not doing. I met a couple that thought they simplified their lives by only having one child only to see her go into drugs and an alternative life style. Then the parents had no one to leave their junk to.

My parents left us an inheritance of material things. I believe their motives were pure and they just saw these things as keepsakes. I can tell you this: Jesus gave me the best inheritance anyone can ask for. The day before mom died, when Jenny and I went to see her, as I entered her bedroom the hospital nurse said, "Your mom has not recognized anyone today." I thought to myself, "Mom doesn't have her hearing aid in and she doesn't have her glasses on, so maybe she cannot hear us or see us and it may be hard for mom to talk."

I leaned over her bed and said, "It is Jenny and Ron. We're here to see you, mom." There was no response. Then I looked at mom and leaned over her again and said I'm Ronnie the one that shocked your china closet and mom smiled and tried to laugh. The nurses came to their feet as they were really surprised by mom's reaction. I know the next day I called to see how mom was doing and my sister Pat answered the phone. She said, "I heard you got mom smiling yesterday. I didn't realize it then, but I think it might have been her last smile." Thank you Jesus for the best inheritance anyone could ask for!

I am so blessed to find the truth. Jesus said our fight is against principalities, against powers, against the rulers of the darkness of this world, against spiritual wickedness in high *places*. Principalities are devils, rulers of darkness are devils, and spiritual wickedness is listening to devils and doing what they say. Today, we could say our fight is against the principality of business. Notice the word sin in the middle of bu-*sin*-ess. Our fight is always against time and against the sucking power of material things. Material things do suck the life right out of you. We work hard to get them, to keep them nice, to preserve them, to keep them clean and we worry about who gets our junk when we leave this world. Sounds like false idols to me! As I walk closer to the Lord I realize anything that takes my mind off Jesus can be a false idol.

Look how hard we will work to have something nice. Look how many hours and days we will give up our loved ones to supply them with the right clothes and material things. While we are out working so hard for our children, the *Rulers of darkness* – which are the evil spirits, come in to steal our loved ones. When these evil spirits stole our loved ones, we say we worked so hard for our children and they say all we wanted was for you to spend time with us, dad. I know now I would have loved more than any material thing on earth to have more time with mom and dad. I kept thinking tomorrow or next week I'll have time and that tomorrow and next week never came. New cars, second home, season pass to see the bangles, all fall short of just having time to be with and talk to my mom and dad. Most people know you can talk to God anytime so they put off talking to God also. I have learned that intimacy with Jesus brings more Joy than anything material could ever could. I used to like movies but now to watch a two hour movie is wasting 120 minutes I could be spending with my best friend Jesus!

So how did mom and dad overcome all the material things of the world? They found the truth of God's Word.

John 8:32 And you shall know the truth, and the truth shall make you free.

The truth is we should have our hearts seeking God. We should be telling our children to seek God and His joyfulness, by putting the needs of God first in life you are *dying to self*. The inheritance we can pass on to our children is the truth of God's Word. We can do this without involving lawyers, wills and government regulations. We are free from all that. The inheritance should be such that no one can steal, kill and destroy it.

The inheritance we should pass along is the truth of knowing Jesus loves us and we are the sons and daughters of Father God. The Freedom and truth Jesus is talking about is knowing material things no longer hold us in bondage. It is knowing we will never die! Our spirit is alive in us now and forever. While here on earth, we can choose to follow Jesus and walk in the love of Jesus and have Heaven as a reward. That is true freedom. Or we can live in bondage to material junk, we can choose to love the world, love material things and have hell as a reward!

You can choose to hug a tree, work until you cannot work anymore, save for a rainy day, work to pay life insurance, leave enough junk for your children to fight over. Supply them with all the material things you can and pray the fight for your junk doesn't start before you die, because it can.

Instead, recognize your true treasure is intimacy with Jesus and you share Jesus with your children and neighbors! Approach them with a pure heart. Instill in them your love of God and your freedom from sin! Instill in them the love and trust of the One who said 'I will never leave you or forsake you'. Knowing Jesus said:

Hebrews 13:5 I will never leave you nor forsake you

This is freedom from the bondage of fear and the fear of losing your junk. Spend time with your treasures, talk to Jesus and your children, your neighbors and your loved ones and instill in them the love of Jesus. It might seem awkward at first but be truthful, tell them and show them how important they are to you. Read about the life of Jesus and share his love. Share the life of Jesus! Be the life of Jesus and love like Jesus loved unconditionally. That is true freedom and when you get to the end of your life you will not need a will or lawyers because the inheritance you give your children is already in their heart.

I know for sure eternity is a long time. We can give so much of our life to acquiring earthly material, to being successful, to learning how to play the game here on earth and to acquiring college degrees, and in doing so forgetting to prepare for life eternal. We will impress everyone here with our knowledge and our junk except the one who really cares, JESUS, and our loved ones. Remember happiness is the counterfeit of JOY. If what you are seeking only brings momentary happiness, it is not JOY. Bring

Glory to God by choosing Him over the junk of the world is freedom and joyfulness. Choose God not junk! Why would I want to watch a movie or work for more junk when I could spend time talking to my best friend Jesus and my loved ones?

I know my mom and dad are in Heaven and that brings me great Joy. I know I am having the time of my life right now every day because I don't look to my circumstances to bring me happiness. I look to the true love of God and in doing so, I know the joyfulness and freedom of a life without junk can bring. I know for a fact that God loves me. I am in true freedom from the world because I am secure in the love of Jesus. I do not need any material things and my life is full of Joy because material things no longer hold me in bondage. I don't wake up worrying about payments, insurance, bills, degrees or wanting of anything. I wake up and ask God, "What are we going to do today?" My life is surrendered to God and I know God will do great things through me today. Jesus is the truth that sets us free from the bondage of material JUNK.

Life is simple, it is childlike faith. Seek God with all your heart and you will find the love of your life waiting to spend time with you! Just talk to Jesus like He is your best friend, because He is!!! Jesus told me the way to have a great relationship is to listen. That's right, just listen. Jesus said:

John 10:27-28 My sheep hear My voice, and I know them, and they follow Me. And I give them eternal life, and they shall never perish; neither shall anyone snatch them out of My hand.

Yes, read and study the life of Jesus but most of all seek that personal relationship. Jesus said 'my sheep know My voice'. How will you know His voice if we are too busy to listen? How will we follow Him if we don't know Him? Jesus said 'seek and you will find'! When you do, Jesus promises us eternal life!!

Matthew 7:7 Ask, and it will be given to you; seek, and you will find; knock, and it will be opened to you.

Ask God for a relationship and it shall be given to you. Seek the truth of God's Word and you will find. Knock on the narrow gate and Jesus will open it to you.

My brothers and sisters and all our loved ones here today, I ask for you all to seek a relationship with Jesus. In doing so you will have joy in your life, peace that surpasses all understanding in your heart, the cleansing of forgiveness which is freedom for everyone you know, and freedom form yourself. Knowing Jesus loves you will make you free from yourself. No one can hurt you when you live for others because what they do or don't do, what they say or don't say is not going to make or break your day because the truth is YOU KNOW Jesus loves you! Knowing Jesus loves you is the truth that sets you free! People cannot hurt me because I don't live for their approval but I already have the love of Jesus in my heart. I live to love others as Jesus loves them. I would like nothing more than to see all my loved ones know the truth that sets us free! I love Jesus but more important than that I know Jesus loves me!!! I AM FREE!!!

Jesus wants intimacy with you. Your relationship with him can grow. You can ask Him anything and you receive an answer. For example, one morning while having coffee with Jesus I asked Him, "Jesus, I always describe Jenny as precious. How do you describe her?" Immediately I heard the words *delightfully precious*. I rejoice knowing my Best Friend and Brother Jesus calls my wife "delightfully precious"! You too can have this intimacy with God! In fact the real reason God sent His Son was to restore the intimacy with us. Forgiving sin was a small part of why Jesus came.

Notice in John 10:27 it also says, "and I know them"

Jesus loves me and I know it! Jenny and I will see Jesus and Father God and mom and dad someday. Your relationship with God is not just you knowing God, but rather you know that God knows you.

You could know everything there is to know about President Obama. You could study his life, you could know what he had for breakfast today. And if you went to see him at the White House, they would not let you in to see him. All that knowledge would not gain you entrance to visit him. But if President Obama knows you,

you will get right in. It is not enough for you to know God. You must have intimacy with Him and to do that you must know His voice and he has to hear your voice so the two of you can become one.

Jesus rejoices over us with singing. Yes Jesus sings over us like a mother holding a little one in her arms or when parents rejoice seeing their children make good decisions.

Zephaniah 3:17 The Lord your God in your midst, the Mighty One, will save; He will rejoice over you with gladness, He will quiet you with His love, He will rejoice over you with singing."

Jesus will even reveal the song he sings over you if you ask and listen for his voice.

Life eternal is not having a passport to heaven. It is having a relationship with Jesus and Father God and the Holy Spirit NOW here on earth! Jesus didn't just come to forgive us our sins. I am not just a sinner saved by grace. I am a son of God, I can talk to my Father through Jesus 24/7 and I do. The Joy of the Lord is ours just for seeking a relationship with the one who has already laid down His life for us! Please don't read His Word to see if it is true in your life. Read His Word believing it is true in your life and it will become true in your life. The best things in life are free because Jesus paid the price for me!

Please spend time with your Best Friend, seek Him with your whole heart, mind and soul. Teach your children to do the same and you will never worry about death. In fact you will rejoice in it. Your inheritance is in your heart!

Mom and Dad are in heaven! THANK YOU JESUS!!!

Mom and Dad are in the comfort of Jesus! I know they know what it is to be free! I know Jesus is love and God the Father is love and the Holy Spirit is love. I know the comfort of Jenny's love (unconditional love) is the most in creditable love we can experience here on earth. I believe Jesus when He said you can accomplish in creditable things on earth but if they were done without love, you have not accomplished anything. When Jesus was talking about the commandments, Jesus said the greatest of these is love. Life is simple! Read the life of Jesus and live as Jesus lived. He is our example! I have never read in the Bible where Jesus said the words 'I love you', but I know He does by what He did. Love is not saying I love you. Love is being loved every day in every way! Love is being Jesus!

Matthew 5:43-48 "You have heard that it was said, 'You shall love your neighbor and hate your enemy.' But I say to you, love your enemies, bless those who curse you, do good to those who hate you, and pray for those who spitefully use you and persecute you, that you may be sons of your Father in heaven; for He makes His sun rise on the evil and on the good, and sends rain on the just and on the unjust. For if you love those who love you, what reward have you? Do not even the tax collectors do the same? And if you greet your brethren[c] only, what do you do more than others? Do not even the tax collectors do so? Therefore you shall be perfect, just as your Father in heaven is perfect.

Yes we can be perfect for Jesus said so. Just be the love of God here on earth and God will make you perfect in His love!

Remember the words of Peter:

1 Peter 1:3-7 Blessed be the God and Father of our Lord Jesus Christ, who according to His abundant mercy has begotten us again to a living hope through the resurrection of Jesus Christ from the dead, to an inheritance incorruptible and undefiled and that does not fade away, reserved in heaven for you, who are kept by the power of God through faith for salvation ready to be revealed in the last time. In this you greatly rejoice, though now for a little while, if need be, you have been grieved by various trials, that the genuineness of your faith, being much more precious than gold that perishes, though it is tested by fire, may be found to praise, honor, and glory at the revelation of Jesus Christ

Jenny and Jesus and I love you all forever!!

21775824R00170

Made in the USA
Middletown, DE
10 July 2015